From Conception to Two Years

Recognising the importance of 'the first one thousand days', from the begin   of a woman's pregnancy until her child's second birthday, this comprehensive guide ta es a fresh look at the role of the practitioner in supporting families and children from conception through to early infancy.

A period of dramatic physical, social and emotional change for both the parent and child, an infant's experiences during his or her first two years of life have a significant impact on later development. *From Conception to Two Years* brings together key research, theory and experiences from practice to further practitioners' knowledge and understanding of this critical period, and it informs professional approaches to providing care. Offering an explanation of key issues affecting the care of very young children, chapters feature reflective questions and promote discussion and further thinking on topics including:

- understanding and supporting parents and families during the transition to parenthood
- building a positive practitioner–parent relationship
- development, growth and care during the prenatal period
- approaches to care in the perinatal period
- attachment and the development of emotional connections
- ethical issues surrounding the care of infants
- creating playful care opportunities with infants and their families.

Giving Early Years practitioners and students the knowledge, skills and confidence they need to effectively support and care for children and their families from the very start, *From Conception to Two Years* is an essential guide for the provision of high quality infant care.

Amanda Norman is Senior Le   ester, UK.

From Conception to Two Years

Development, Policy and Practice

Amanda Norman

Routledge
Taylor & Francis Group

LONDON AND NEW YORK

First published 2019
by Routledge
2 Park Square, Milton Park, Abingdon, Oxon OX14 4RN

and by Routledge
52 Vanderbilt Avenue, New York, NY 10017

Routledge is an imprint of the Taylor & Francis Group, an informa business

British Library Cataloguing-in-Publication Data
A catalogue record for this book is available from the British Library

Library of Congress Cataloging-in-Publication Data
A catalog record has been requested for this book

ISBN: 978-1-138-29893-4 (hbk)
ISBN: 978-1-138-29894-1 (pbk)
ISBN: 978-1-315-09829-6 (ebk)

Typeset in Optima
by Apex CoVantage, LLC

This book is dedicated to Diana

Contents

Acknowledgements

As a therapeutic play specialist, I want to send thanks to my tutor Shalini.Lilley who challenged me to critically think about emotional care, theory and practice beyond an educational frame. This was extended further with support and gratitude to Jenny Byrne, my doctorate supervisor at Southampton University.

I would also like to extend my thanks to the management and practitioners at Tiny Tots Day Nursery for enabling me to continue sharing experiences with the infants and young children cared for.

As a Senior Lecturer at the University of Roehampton I was given the opportunity to lead and teach modules, focusing on children under three for several years, so extend thanks to the Early Years team and their inspirational work, relating theory to practice. I would also like to acknowledge and include students who studied the Top-up degree at the University of Winchester. Together we have shared anecdotal stories and issues about caring for infants in a variety of ways. Additionally, I am very fortunate to be given the opportunity of writing about infancy and with this I give thanks to my supporting colleagues who have continually provided encouragement at the University of Winchester.

Finally, I give thanks to my four children, my husband Phil and family who have shaped my thinking and encouraged me in the writing of the book. They have motivated me to continually reflect on how I am as a parent, practitioner and professional in contributing to the dialogue of caring for infants from conception within Early Childhood Education and Care (ECEC) contexts.

Introduction

This book seeks to illuminate, explore and bring critical attention to some key issues relating to the period between conception to two years. It includes the complexities of emotional relationships and care approaches between parents, practitioners and infants, attending early childhood educational and care (ECEC) settings. The overall intention of the book is the opportunity to submerge into the world of infants from conception, assimilating and appreciating the magnitude of this transitional period of life.

Why conception to two?

> Babies are a bit boring really. They are ok when they get older and can respond through language, having a joke. I think many people find babies don't do much.
>
> (Anon, 2018)

This view suggests infants are passive recipients within relationships, with little to offer. However as research has progressed and we now recognise and confirm development is influenced from conception by the environment and the infant perceived as dependent yet active learner. Communicating, imitating others and having a rudimentary sense of self, new-born infants continue to actively contribute to the parenting relationship. Through the consistent care received by the parents, a sense of self emerges. Brain development is also dependent on stable and secure relationships with parents or primary main carer. When care is sought beyond the parents, practitioners may also share this role (Trevarthen, 2005). In recent years the regular caring of infants and young children has been increasingly sought beyond the home. Many parents place their infants into ECEC settings as they return to work or opt to share their childcare. Subsequently many settings who traditionally would have cared and educated children beyond two years have opened their doors and expanded, providing 'baby rooms' and facilities to enable them to include the care of infants under two within their settings. These have grown substantially and in 2018 most group ECEC settings accommodate infants, with some being able to care for large groups of infants in their care. Parallel to this is the rise in understanding the inner world of infants and the potential concern in adverse childhood experiences and long-term health risks. The study of neuroscience and its connections to emotions has also become part of the discourses in caring for children within this age period. Therefore, there is rising recognition of the importance and value from conception to two and I believe the book is a timely addition. It centres on high quality intimate infant care, understanding and valuing emotional interactions of relationships between infants and practitioners.

The purpose of the book for practitioners

This book is primarily for supporting and promoting positive practices and well- being with parents and their infants. Drawing on a broad range of themes the book includes concepts discussed to navigate the reader toward specialist subjects. The aim is a greater appreciation of studies and discussions that celebrate this unique period as valuable in the present and future context of healthy growth and well -being. Within each chapter there are examples for practice and reflective questions to discuss and consider in relation to the topics outlined. I have widened the lens to include the value of working with infants as part of a family group and the significance of parent relationships. In discussing those practitioners working with infants, I consider *family practitioner* to be a relevant term used highlighting the role within a family dynamic. In defining family practitioner, the term bridges the triad relationship of practitioner, parents and infant. At the end of each chapter I have included narratives of practitioners to illustrate their thinking on the topic discussed.

Multiple perspectives

This book aims to provide detail to warrant reflection and a spark for wanting to know more about emotional relationships. Therefore, I have created a story line around attachment and firmly believe attachment and close relationships are valuable in connecting care. I have chosen to focus on parental and practitioners' contributions in enhancing an emotional frame of understanding. From this perspective I have wanted to illuminate the parent's viewpoint and how a relationship approach with practitioners can enhance and reduce issues between them, when their infants are looked after in ECEC settings. I have chosen to focus on how developmental approaches are perceived and considered within emotions, language and physicality. I have drawn on key theories including Bowlby, Bakhtin and Gerber and complemented them with contemporary practice and discourses around the role of the key person approach, professional love, emotional labour and care pedagogies. I have also included the way regular care practices can become special and an enriching experience rather than a mundane routine of care.

The political landscape

This book has been constructed in a way that it is not intended to espouse a political agenda but a wish to understand theories underlying connected care and its practice in real world situations. The landscape of the earliest years has gained increasing recognition to the importance of the first two years of age and its effects on later life from an individualistic and societal perspective. Pre-natal factors through to infancy that affect development and growth include maternal health, diet and lifestyle choices. Less optimum conditions can therefore increase the likelihood of poor health outcomes and it is from this position that legislation has been included to critically engage in understanding how parents and infants are supported during this period. Broadly outlined are three themes: maternity care, health and wellbeing and relational pedagogies of care:

Maternity care: This will include the wider professional roles that have involvement in the transition to parenthood. The choices parents make and the care they desire and receive will also be included.

Health and wellbeing: This will include how optimum health and well-being is aspired to from conception to infancy and the current political climate in relation to specialised support in the community.

Relational pedagogies of care: A critical approach to the ethics of care and the current position of early year's practitioners will be included in the specific roles and expectations of settings. The focus will be on the connected care in practice rather than within a specific curriculum framework. A key implication of this pedagogy is also the necessity that practitioners remain reflective and critically engaged with their pedagogy and its potential for long-lasting impact (Papatheodorou and Moyles, 2009). Taggart (2011) argues that as a caring profession there needs to be much more transparency with practitioners critically understanding their emotional work, advocating care as central to their practice.

Boxed texts and images

Each chapter contains a boxed text with practitioner viewpoint and questions for discussion. The 'practitioner's perspective' is written from an autobiographical position of almost thirty years working in early years. During these years I have encountered and shared many anecdotal stories, experiences and reflections with practitioners. These have been intertwined into the practitioner perspectives as examples of practice, interwoven with my own fictional and anecdotal contributions. Each 'question for discussion' is intended to encourage discourses between practitioner and those studying this age range. These intended to provide a process of discussion and develop reflection with further thinking about specific topics and issues. The images are included as a visual point of reference to the topic I am discussing, and I believe helpful in reflecting further. I have used images known and personal to me, as an auto/biographical researcher in education. The individuals within the images may not be persons directly affected by the topic itself.

The chapters

The chapters will be framed around a care lens focus with topics connecting each chapter. The first chapter, on family centred care, will include an understanding of parents and families in the transition to parenthood and their adjustment to family life, in all its blended form. Relationships rather than partnerships will be the focus, between parents and practitioners. Practical ways to enhance these relationships will be included. The prenatal care chapter will include details of the transition to pregnancy and focus on the value of understanding the development and growth within a nature nurture frame in supporting the prenatal period. Understanding the complexities as a practitioner within this period will also be included. Perinatal care, the period at birth and beyond, otherwise known as the fourth trimester, or arguably defined as quadmester, will be discussed in the following chapter. It will focus on the value of understanding the development and growth of the new-born infant and the role as practitioner in supporting this trimester. A further chapter will focus on how developmental care is perceived and the predominant discourse around development and measuring development during this period. Emotional connections, as a chapter will then discuss the emotional connections. Attachment and practices in supporting emotions will be included. This will be further explored in the practitioner role as a professional carer and the ethics surrounding care, love and intimate relationships with infants and their families. Connecting with care will further consider attachment, but this time the chapter will include an application to practice in early childhood and care (ECEC) settings. This will be enhanced with the chapter on playful care, the connection to play and care with a focus of open-ended play, treasure baskets and musicality in various forms. The final chapter will include some topics from the previous chapters within a reflective perspective and promote the reader to think about the process of reflection as a subjective experience in further thinking alongside how reflection has been used as an objective approach in measuring professional success. A concluding note of the chapters will include areas of moving forward with recommendations for practice working and caring for infants in ECEC settings.

Glossary

- Infants: This has been used consistently rather than 'baby' as a generic term used with under two years, with a focus on the first eighteen months.
- New-born infants: Birth to one month.
- Babies: Specifically, those infants under one where clarity is needed beyond the term infancy. If a study has used the term baby then where appropriate this will remain.
- Care: Providing attention and attending to the needs of health and development through a connected approach.
- Carer: The term given when discussing both parent, primary adult carers of infants and practitioner as a shared voice.
- Early Childhood Education and Care (ECEC): Educational and care arrangements in a variety of forms for children from birth to compulsory schooling, regardless of the type of setting, funding, opening hours, or programme content.
- ECEC settings: Predominantly focused on day care nurseries, childminders contexts unless specified otherwise.
- Practitioners: A holistic term for those individuals employed and /or studying conception to two, with a practical element. Used in examples of application to practice.
- Family practitioners: A term used for those working in ECEC settings with infants to highlight their status and relation to parents and families.

The words defined above are not aimed to confuse but to give consistency to the following discussion.

▨ Bibliography

Appleby, K. and Andrews, M. (2011) Reflective practice is the key to quality improvement. In Reed, M. and Canning, N. (2009) *Reflective Practice in the Early Years*. London: Sage.

Brock, A. (2014) *The Early Years Reflective Practice Handbook*. London: David Fulton.

Dahlberg, G., Moss, P. and Pence, A. (2013). *Beyond Quality in Early Childhood Education and Care. Languages of Evaluation*. London: Falmer Press.

Karemaker et al. (2011) cited in Payler, J. and Georgeson, J. (2014) *Early Years Foundations: Critical Issues*. Milton Keynes: OUP Education.

Papatheodorou, T. and Moyles, J. (2009) *Learning Together in the Early Years. Exploring Relational Pedagogy*. Oxon: Routledge.

Taggart, G. (2011) 'Don't we care? the ethics and emotional labour of early years professionalism'. *Early Years: An International Journal of Research and Development*. 31(1): 85–95.

Trevarthen, C. (1979). Communication and cooperation in early infancy. A description of primary intersubjectivity. In Bullowa, M. (ed.) *Before Speech: The Beginning of Human Communication*. London: Cambridge University Press, pp. 321–347.

Trevarthen C. (2005) 'First things first: Infants make good use of the sympathetic rhythm of imitation, without reason of language'. *Journal of Child Psychotherapy* 31: 91–113. DOI: 10.1080/00754170500079651

1 Reflective practice in early care

Introduction and context

In recent years study programmes and employment policies have increasingly included reflection as a way for early years practitioners to develop their pedagogical experiences and evaluate their role and practice (Brooker, 2016). Practitioners are also regularly requested to complete reflective logs as part of assessment and professional purposes, specifically as a way of supporting annual appraisals in early childhood education and care (ECEC) settings. Whilst it is agreed that reflective practice is essential to professional development there has been a growing awareness of imposing and measuring reflective responses as a tool to determine professional effectiveness. Reflective practice is in danger of becoming a reductionist checklist or a confessional application, satisfying management agendas of job approval and promotion. This chapter supports reflection as being central to personal and social development, suggesting that successful models and approaches focus on the process rather than the sole outcome. This chapter illuminates the journeys taken as a practitioner and I have included my own journey of understanding multiple perspectives and theory working in a nursery setting as a way of illustrating the successes and challenges of reflecting critically rather than simply recalling events. I have also included practical approaches that could be used with the aim of informing the process of reflection in both moving forward between theory and practice.

Learning about reflection

Reflecting on practice is not considered a new concept and has been taught as stand-alone units and embedded within early years courses for several years, particularly with the implementation of foundation degrees and professional enquiry-based learning courses (Moon, 2013). Whilst this was welcomed, there is ongoing dialogue to the way reflective practice should be taught and assessed that enables students and trainees to engage with the learning process and also achieve a measured grade. Additionally, many areas of work now require a reflective approach within the work cycle, through regular reviews or appraisal. Typically, this means taking personal responsibility for:

- Continuing professional development
- Evaluating personal experience, strengths, qualities and skills as part of a role
- Identifying ways personal strengths can be used within a professional area
- Identifying training, practice or informal learning in supporting personal limitations and areas that could be improved
- A way of taking responsibility for behaviour and making useful contributions

(Reed and Walker, 2014)

Facing my fears: reflecting on internal and external perceived barriers

Reflective thinking: a process

As early years practitioners we are continually thinking about creating exciting learning potentials for the infants we work with. Everyday experiences beyond work, such as observing lighting and fabrics used in shopfront displays can provoke thinking about how they could be adapted and weaved into early years practice with the infants we care for. This type of thinking becomes habitual, and automatic in our everyday lives. This 'way of being' and reflecting, forms our professional identity. Through questioning our actions to why we think about our practice beyond and within, the merging of the two in our work setting enables a *professional artistry* to be developed as described by Schon (1983, 1987).

Practitioner's perspective

As a practitioner I have visualised reflective thinking in different ways and one example was a rotational washing line, with the lines at different heights but in a circular and continuous spiral. I then hang my washing from these lines, my perspectives, concepts, practices. The smaller sheets then represent the connecting, overlapping and parallel thoughts spinning and changing with studies and readings encountered. It is from this metaphorical representation that I can hang and visualise ideas and thoughts as they rotate. I also get frustrated with the rotational pull of the sheets and at other times rejoice at the clarity that occurs when contradictory thinking and abstract theories come together and make sense in practice. Whilst this is not the most sophisticated analogy it does illustrate how my professional and personal life merges together in my thinking. It provides a visual image of thinking about the past from different lenses rather than a superficial recall of past events with little thought of the how and why. Understanding and articulating the rationale supports our thinking and understanding as a professional.

Skills such as reasoning and observation enable practitioners to ensure their work is responsible and ethical. It promotes practitioners to make individual choices based on moral judgements, beyond the externally imposed. Reflection therefore can be described as a social experience between people toward a journey of developing the self and promoting individual agency. In recognising the voices from an ethical viewpoint and the development of the self is to consider the individual as an active, intentional agent, which can engage with and influence the world. An individual therefore has the capability of possessing reflexive self-awareness and conceiving alternative ways intrinsic to their own experiences.

Developing reflective thinking: a personal and social experience

Donaldson's (1986) theory, modes of mind, argued that we potentially develop the capacity for reflective thought from infancy. Initially the first mode is *Point*, being the here and now experience observed in young children. *Line* then begins to develop during the first year and infants begin to afford the capacity to become aware. As they grow older they begin to recall their recent past and anticipate future events as well as predicted possibilities in its simplest form. The *Construct Mode* then develops in later childhood and this is the capacity to construct concepts which are independent of specific instances and involves emotions, filtering what matters, and actions associated. The *Transcendent* then leads to complete abstract thinking and emotional forms, a mode many adults continuously develop and struggle with in their reflective thinking. Self-awareness and meaningfulness are therefore valued as aspirational in its achievement, developing a consciousness and understanding of the self in others, intersubjectivity. Brock (2015) agreed reflective practice is a state of mind, an attitude and approach beyond curriculum planners and critical incidents. It is a pedagogical approach with stories communicated and shared between individuals. Even if the ideas shared do not result in a desired outcome, reactions still occur and aid further reflection.

Gibbs (1998) included an emotional aspect contributing to how reflection occurs in the process:

- What were the thoughts and feelings of the event reflecting on?
- What were the positive and negative about the event or experience
- What sense could be made of the situation?
- Could something been done differently and if so what would this be?

If the experience of an event can be understood in the social context it occurs, then the possibility to develop future practice is possible (Hickson, 2011). Similarly, in recognising emotional learning with reflective practice, thinking about the individual process is enhanced. Subjective feelings are associated with the events and this culminates in reflecting on the way outcomes were experienced and differing possible outcomes. Therefore, the value is not simply on experiences gained but the process of reflecting on the experiences, making connections and changing future practice from the process of reflection (Schön, 1995). Larrivee (2000) agreed that reflection is much

Linking theory to practice: infants observing each other through a sensory experience. Would the removal of the bright coloured rug enhance the focused experience of the moving images in the water mat and support further movement?

more about the development of personal awareness through subjective interpretations and beliefs of event and situations rather than an objective procedure. For Brock (2015) it is these core values that shape and develop professional practice.

Reflection is, therefore:

- A way of theorising on our actions
- Develops confidence
- Develops an active agent in the daily routine of care
- Supports an agency of change
- Increase recognition and knowledge that empowers and improves quality
- Enables our vulnerability to be discussed and shared with colleagues
- Challenges and develops our own pedagogical thinking
- An advocate for children in activity evaluating multiple perspectives and development.

Reflective practice/practitioner is an increasingly familiar term when working in a caring profession, especially when it is an expected approach to practice and linked to quality improvement.

Reflect in action

Schön (1987) suggested professionals could 'reflect in action'. Reflecting in action requires practitioners to think spontaneously and work instinctively by drawing on similar experiences to solve problems or make necessary decisions. Schon suggested reflection in action was prompted by unforeseen situations in daily routines, both positive and negative. It helps to reframe, or look differently at knowledge in action, leading to greater understanding or maybe change.

• Knowledge in action – more conscious of this underlying knowledge
• Initiative knowledge TO conscious awareness
• Links between theory and practice.

Question for discussion

Select a recent surprise, a situation that you have had in your work that has caused you to consider or reflect on your routine practice. Note down what knowledge in-action was challenged by this surprise situation and the understanding gained from your reflection. Has practice been modified as a result?

A pragmatic approach to reflection

Reflective practice can be considered as an objective way of looking within ourselves and reviewing our past, present and potential future. Whilst we can articulate cognitive and intellectualise the process about learning, there is also a need to consider how the world is experienced as an individual and continual self-editing is influenced by those around us in our everyday interactions. In completing an analysis on personal strengths, weaknesses, opportunities and threats (SWOT) can be indicated and evaluated. This a technique often used by organisations to take a position statement of how the team or setting are functioning. It is a technique widely used in reflecting the self, providing the initial steps to begin thinking about the self in relation to internal and external factors as well as the influence of others in the process (Thompson and Pascal, 2012).

Recording reflections: initiating the physical organisation of reflecting

The collation of reflective logs can be recorded in journals, portfolios, proformas and e-portfolios, provide a helpful tracking tool to re-visit. Evidence based practice, bridges the gap between theory and practice. Being actively engaged in practice, making meaningful changes enables critical and considered multiple perspectives when making informed decisions (Hanson and Appleby, 2015, cited in Reed and Walker, 2014).

Questions for discussion

What could be included in a reflective journal or diary?

General information:

> Context, details, activities, outcomes if appropriate. Factual and objective, information
> Observations of an individual infant or groups.
> Reflections – your thoughts and feelings on what happened to cover the period you are recording

Interpretation:

> Theory – linking your notes and thoughts to support your knowledge and understanding Use this opportunity to find out more about the situation.
> Questions – ask yourself or others relevant questions. You may or may not get answers. You may find problems are solved and insights are gained

Evaluation:

> Identify the success of the happenings and identify any developments. This is the analysis of the effectiveness of the happenings. How has this experience improved my own practice?

◼ An experiential approach to reflection

Dewey (1910) advocated reflection as an experiential learning process. He believed individuals needed to actively develop the skills of thinking and reflecting if purposeful action was to occur. This could also be described as creative reflective practice; an understanding of an individual role and the impact they have on the context in which they work, and everyone involved. This reflective approach includes working and learning in collaboration with others. Dewey (1910: 34) determined that there are three natural resources in the creation of a reflective thinker: these being, curiosity, suggestion and depth. He argued that curiosity is the 'most significant and vital', and that we possess this from a young age. Rather than learning from experience he argued individuals learn from reflecting on their experience. If reflections do not occur there is a possibility of ongoing practices being based on predominately prejudice, outdated and uninformed ethically biased thinking. Fawbert (2003) discussed Dewey's work in contrasting routine action with reflective action. Routine day to day action was perceived as relatively static and thus unresponsive to changing priorities and circumstances. Whereas reflective action involved a willingness to engage in constant self-appraisal and development. Dewey felt the importance in any experience lay in the relationships and connections within the experience.

Practitioner's perspective

When I was practising in an ECEC setting in a 'infant room' for infants under two, I took satisfaction in being a competent reflective practitioner. It wasn't until I changed employment, within a different nursery setting, that I discovered other perspectives and definitions of reflective practice. I realised that previously I had been merely going through the imposed sessional routines of the setting, with a plenary at the end. This was what I had thought reflection involved. Whilst there was nothing wrong with this approach, I soon discovered I was drawing on limited experiences to inform my evaluations and not moving forward in my thinking or the play. This knowledge was from my own experience of observing and previous experiences of worked well and what to avoid, within the policy expectations of the setting environment (predominantly Ofsted). What I had not considered was other perspectives who were central to the impact of my actions – the infants and the colleagues I worked with. In my cycle of the session I had forgotten about the 'why' of what I was doing and the theory underpinning my practice.

A social discourse approach to reflection

A Bakhtinian approach to teaching focuses on the processes of discourses and from this we can infer reflection being part of a social dialogic process. Bakhtin's theories of dialogism to language is the notion of multiple voices of those in continual engagement with an individual during their everyday life, and these are drawn from the past, present and imagined future (White, 2016). Each dialogic event is therefore characterised by the polyphonic chorus of external voices, each voice competing and wanting to be heard. This is central to the thinking of reflection and he believes it is these voices that shape individual experiences and ethical values in given situations. The relevant focus to practitioners here is also about thinking and processing shared dialogue rather than the often-heard voice of authority being predominant. In a dialogic environment teaching and learning is exploratory, and the aim is about thinking and reflecting on each other voices, with opinions valued even if they contradict individual views. Bakhtin's theory of dialogism suggested that an individual's speech is shaped in continuous interaction with others' and utterances are developed through the experience of assimilating others' words. He argued that all utterances are filled with other individual's words encountered, which are processed, assimilated and reshaped to make sense in messages conveyed. Producing unique utterances involves ventriloquation, a term that Wertsch (1991: 59) defines as 'the process whereby one voice speaks through another voice'. In other words, individuals combine a variety of voices they have encountered throughout their lifetimes to produce unique utterances. Bakhtin differentiated between 'authoritative discourse' and 'internally persuasive discourse' (1981: 342). The authoritative discourse can be understood in many relationships and in this context senior management and practitioners in ECEC settings. As a practitioner, experiencing the assimilation of a senior authoritative voice, their words as a compact and indivisible mass, is either affirmed or rejected. In many settings appraisals and supervision is initiated by a senior member in meeting with practitioners to discuss and reflect on their practice. Traditionally this has been organised by the senior member entering the meeting with pre-determined points to be raised, the agenda set by the appraiser/supervisor with the appraisee/supervisee responding within the frame. Bakhtin proposed a positive experience would be to create an opportunity for authentic and organic dialogue allowing the practitioner to process and share their everyday experiences and interactions rather than feel they should be responding to an authoritative voice. Although this seems reasonable and is encouraged in many settings the internally persuasive discourse, including the practitioners, as receivers, to reflect on their own voice. Simultaneously the external voices listened and assimilated from those in authority can still remain challenging in terms of being heard. For Bakhtin the internally persuasive discourse results from an ongoing struggle of these two forms of assimilation, the authoritative external fixed discourse with the individual flexible discourse. Therefore, by recognising the way we perceive authoritarian voices, opportunities to reflect and engage in positive and flexible ways between senior members and practitioners in differing situations. This culminates in an ongoing creative reflective process that can be applied to new situations and re-shaping the way, in this example, dialogue is created about staff satisfaction in ECEC settings. This process theorises the way practitioners reflect on their experiences and process it. Listening to their own voice alongside others, including those in authority. In processing the two together they have the capacity to think beyond the expected course of action and question the why and what ifs much more, sharing their thoughts as, or with senior colleagues. Inherent in Bakhtin's (1986) concept of dialogism is therefore the idea all individual expression is ultimately the product of various voices including and beyond authoritative voices, linked to one another through the socially constituted fabric of language. In sharing their reflective thinking individuals speak back to their community of peers through re-externalized modes of discourse. The process of active reflection being as valuable as the reflection itself.

Questions for discussion

As part of a supervision meeting between the senior practitioner and manager, the manager wanted to discuss how the four colleagues were working together in the infant room. There had previously been conversations about managing behaviour and responding to crying with the infants who ranged from six to four-teen months. It seemed some practitioners were struggling with the noise level and becoming stressed themselves, leaving the senior practitioner to deal with the crying and behaviour by herself. The manager wanted to discuss group care and self-soothing but also support the senior practitioner in her role in leading practice. The senior practitioner was aware of the managers thoughts but did not want to advocate self-soothing as she believed they needed to be cuddled and responded to immediately where possible. She wanted to advocate individualised care within the group setting and encourage the practitioners to respond to the crying positively rather than getting stressed with the noise level.

Reflecting on Bakhtin's theories of dialogism to language what do you think is going on?

What are the voices telling the senior practitioner?

How could this scenario be shared and reflected on to create positive outcomes?

What creative processes could be discussed to support the infants in their care?

A reflective activist approach to reflection

To be a reflective activist is to have a critical consciousness of the world whereby individuals' question, examine and challenge different positions including their own; this involves 'active engagement in continual review and repositioning of assumptions, values and practice' (Hanson, 2012: 144). It includes thinking about the wider socio-cultural landscape and how it influences the current context practitioners' work in. In being a reflective activist, practitioners also consider how theory directly informs practice as a bridge to creating new meanings and consequently exploring different possibilities and solutions.

The value of process: personalised reflections applying Brookfield's lens to practice

Brookfield provided a way of critically reflecting in teaching which continues to be relevant in an early year's contexts, caring for infants. He applied four lenses of critical reflection as a way of illuminating different aspects to teaching and one that can be also applied to early years practice, mirroring the lenses to this text in terms of infant development, theory and practice. Using Brookfield's lens, I have illustrated the way practice and reflection came together and the rationale to why I think they are valuable in application to critical reflection.

Questions for discussion

Read the reflective lens approach illustrated and then map your own reflective journey, using Brookfield's lens. Did you find the experience deepened your reflective thinking?

The infant (student) perspective

To organise the environment, practices and support the development we need to try and find out what is going on within the infant and their perspectives to the care and education they experience. The student lens in early years is therefore in trying to understand how the infant learns and feels in given situations. For Brookfield it is recognising those remarks and actions we as practitioners and teachers think of as insignificant are payed back but interpreted quite differently by the student.

In working with infants, I recognised this in thinking about the ethics of care and how we use our expressions and gestures alongside verbal communication in supporting the infant. How we project our own feelings and actions in the infant room, such as laughing or being unresponsive can be interpreted by the infants as a significant signal to how they are feeling valued. It is therefore the lens that considers the power relationship and the power of the role that is given. If we assume as I purport that infants are creative autonomous agents then they have the capacity to be critical of their care either responding verbally of physically in signalling they want to be noticed, cuddled, talked to and handled in a certain way. Whilst many practitioners state they welcome criticism from the children in their care in differing forms there are few that honestly receive it positively and in the case of the infant, the activities, the environment or behaviour the fault for them not fully reaching their potential is generally considered to be in the infant rather than the practitioner's actions. The lens of the infant's eyes can reveal how practice is viewed from differing perspectives and reinforces how differing approaches should be, not just with for example, play activities but how those play activities should be approached by yourself with differing infants. I think in working with the youngest infants it is about reflecting on the power position and how we work ethically. By recognising our authority in the relationship and what we project in supporting infants throughout the day potentially provides the capacity to reflect and interact together in everyday routines such as nappy changing feeding and sleep times rather than reverting to an instructional approach. It is the balance between leading and caring.

The co-practitioners (colleagues) perspective

In some ways this encompasses positive team work and how as work colleagues we can support each other. This lens is about creating critical friends with work colleagues and sharing advice. Wenger's (2000) concepts of building communities of practice is about creating an open and honest space to share troubles and successes and for him it is therefore about listening and not just agreeing and praising each other, but also being honest and expressing stresses and anxieties too. Sharing insights into a given situation enables colleagues to appreciate that dilemmas are not unique and by offering multiple perspectives and viewpoints cannot just solve problems but re-examine them in differing ways.

The autobiographical (personal) perspective

In early years this is a valuable reflective lens in listening to the voices of practitioners working in early childhood education and care. For those working with infants the stories told can often hold more value and insight to the theory surrounding them. It is the personal telling of a story that can be identified with and in some cases shape and justify the work of practitioners. In many ways our own pedagogies are embroiled into how we practice. Our own personal experiences of learning, our own values and upbringing all play a significant role in how we deliver practice in the present context. How we view our own childhood and school experience with authority figures also impacts to how we react. Another layer to the relationship between infant, parents and practitioner is the emotional engagement. It is the balance and understanding of developing close relationships with infants, parents and those in paid caring roles simultaneously. This can be challenging when the practitioner's relationships are transitory and focused in the first few years of an infant life prior to schooling, together with the external expectations of professional work beyond the emotional relationships. For myself I remember spending time with an infant who needed constant reassurance that her mother was returning to get her. The infant was about fourteen months and was aware of a change in care and surroundings. In a bid to support her I had to make decisions not just with her care but the others I was also caring for, so they did not become frightened and upset by the sporadic and frightened crying. I had to decide if the lunch time transition should be changed to accommodate her when she would not eat, in the initial phase. I needed to consider if I should go and have a lunch break, knowing the separation would be really challenging for her. I had to reassure colleagues that together we could support each other although at the time she would not leave my side and I had additional responsibilities to carry out as part of my job. I wanted to be there to receive the infant at 8.00 am and then feedback to the parent at 6.00 pm, so we could develop a triad relationship rather than trying to replace the parent role, although I was only expected and paid to work seven hours. Whist this was and continues to be a familiar scenario of settling some children by reflecting on the process I began to critique my own position in the relationship and how I could move forward positively. I reflected on theory in framing my approach, but I was equally drawn to thinking of those subjective stories of past experiences that I recalled as a way of supporting the infant practitioner relationship during the day. Remembering personal and shared experiences and events provide another lens as way of how I perceive my role. How I embark on the relationship, the time frame I set myself and flexibility within a given day. Developing positive and open relationships between practitioner's mirrors not just the ethos of the setting but also supports my own pedagogical thinking. This includes tensions and stressful situations to be resolved in harmony rather than the imposed upon strategies that can be alienating and abstract to the daily experiences that occur in some early years' settings.

The theoretical perspective

The final lens of critical reflection is theory and in early years there are numerous journals, texts, specialists and advisory magazines to draw on. However, for many in practice, whilst classical theorists are known, there often remains a distance between what is carried out in practice to seeking theoretical advice from academic journal articles. Journal articles have an academic tone and many practitioners would seldom go to them unless they had a particular enquiry or the time to read them. Nevertheless, theory is presented in many forms, not just within academic articles. Reading topic related magazines and texts, alongside articles presented in a practice-friendly way provides valuable and exciting opportunities to engage with theory. In my own personal journey initially engaging with readings I was drawn to Rogers (1980) and the way he discussed relationships in a person-centred way. At the time I was working with vulnerable families and had been met with aggressive behaviour. I was feeling in part vulnerable but mostly inadequate in why I thought I could help in the relationships, having concerns I was expected to counsel or provide answers. It was through reading his work and applying some simple strategies I could listen to parent's complex situations from an educational and caring perspective. As I went into different roles going from a diagnostic way of thinking, to observing and interpreting, moving forward and valuing the art of listening. Person centred thinking is about allowing the space for people to find themselves rather than telling them the way to go. As a teacher of adults on a training course it sparked an approach that gave autonomy, recognising the potential in others rather than imposing a model to conform to. By engaging in varied job roles with colleagues, parents and infants I have managed to apply Rogers work to my relationships. In developing congruence, true to myself and accepting of my thoughts and feelings I have been able to share these authentically. In accepting others, I have developed a positive regard and caring approach in the form of a non-possessive love. I have also been able to empathise within my work and strive to provide genuine understanding. These three areas are what Rogers beliefs essential to moving forward and for me was the theoretical underpinning of an approach I could relate to but had previously unknown about. Subsequently this led me to develop my thinking about humanistic psychology and the subjective self. I not only developed my practice within a Froebelian philosophy, which places play central to learning, regarding the inner capacity of the infant and the value of the adult relationships. My work was skewed again when I embarked on a play therapy course. Whilst I was fairly confident in my work as practitioner of young children I had not appreciated how I was portrayed by the children in the relationship. By refocusing on myself within a therapeutic relationship I found the theoretical frame critiques and modified how I approached children in their play. I learnt to listen and slow down metaphorically and literally following the guiding principles of a person centre approach. Critical reflection is therefore evident when contemplating a theoretical lens. It enables both the opportunity to reflect on theory itself and what resonates with one's own pedagogy alongside how theory is approached in relation to contemporary practice.

Family practitioner summary

Sometimes new practitioners worry that they are not good enough. This may lead them to worrying about being critical of their practice. As a lead practitioner I try to show them that it is ok to feel apprehensive and reflections help them stand back and evaluate the whole situation, not just their own perspective.

It is not the end of the world if your practice is not perfect. Reflections show that you are continually improving and recognising that mistakes are simply areas that can be used for future learning and improving practice. Taking the time to reflect is helpful to highlighting the positive and challenges of our work.

Focused points

- Consider ways reflection could be included into practice using Brookfield's lenses
- Bridge the theory and practice of reflection
- Consider whether reflection should be a formal or organic process.

Concluding thoughts

This chapter considered the way reflection has become a way to externally measure performance and identify promotion. It has included the challenges of this perspective and the way reflection remains a superficial tick box process rather than authentically developing the skill of self-reflection. It has included a range of approaches and models as examples. The chapter promotes the idea that initially reflection is a learnt process but then can develop into a much more organic process of self-development beyond a goal orientated focus.

Bibliography

Appleby, K. and Andrews, M. (2012) Reflective practice is the key to quality improvement. In Reed, M. and Canning, N. (eds), *Implementing Quality Improvement and Change in the Early Years*. London: Sage.

Argyris, C. (1995) 'Action science and organizational learning'. *Journal of Managerial Psychology* 10(6): 20–26.

Bakhtin, M. (1981) *The Dialogic Imagination*. Austin, TX: University of Texas Press.

Bradbury, H., Frost, N., Kilminster, S. and Zukas, M. (eds) (2010) *Beyond Reflective Practice. New Approaches to Professional Lifelong Learning*. Abingdon: Routledge.

Brock, A. (2015) What is Reflection and Reflective Practice? In Brock, A. (ed.) *The Early Years Reflective Practice Handbook*. Oxon: Routledge, pp. 7–21.

Brooker, L. (2016) 'Childminders, parents and policy: Testing the Triangle of care'. *Journal of Early Childhood Research* 14(1): 69–83.

Brookfield, S. (2017) *Becoming a Critically Reflective Teacher*. San Francisco, CA: Jossey-Bass.

Dewey, J. (1910) *How We Think*. Boston, MA, New York and Chicago, IL: D.C. Heath & Co.

Donaldson, M. (1986) *Children's Minds*. London: Harper Collins.

Fawbert, F. (2003) *Teaching in Post Compulsory Education*. London. Continuum.

Gibbs, G. (1998) *Learning by Doing: A Guide to Teaching and Learning Methods*. Oxford: Further Education Unit.

Hanson, K. (2012) 'How Can I Support Early Childhood Studies Undergraduate Students to Develop Reflective Dispositions?' Ed.D. Thesis, Exeter University, available online at http://hdl.handle.net/10036/3866.

Hickson, H. (2011) 'Critical reflection: reflecting on learning to be reflective'. *Reflective Practice* 12(6): 829–839. DOI: 10.1080/14623943.2011.616687

Larrivee, B. (2000) 'Transforming Teaching Practice: becoming the critically reflective teacher.' *Learning, Literacy and Culture* 1(3): 293–306.

Moon, H. (2013) *Cherish the First Six Weeks*. UK: Three Rivers Press.

Moyles, J. (2010) (ed.) *Thinking About Play: Developing a Reflective Approach*. Open University Press: Maidenhead.

Pollard, A. (2005) *Readings for Reflective Teaching*. London: Continuum.

Reed, M. and Walker, R. (2014) *A Critical Companion to Early Childhood*. London: Sage.

Rogers, C. (1980) *A Way of Being*. London: Routledge.

Schön, D. (1983). *The Reflective Practitioner*. London: Ashgate.

Schön, D. (1987) *Educating the Reflective Practitioner*. San Francisco: Jossey Bass.

Schön, D. (1994). Teaching artistry through reflection-in-action. In Tsoukas, H. *New Thinking in Organizational Behaviour*. Oxford: Butterworth-Heinemann, pp. 235–249.

Todorov, T. (1984) *Mikhail Bakhtin: The Dialogic Principle*. Minneapolis, MN: University of Minnesota Press.

Thompson, N. and Pascal, J. (2012) 'Developing critically reflective practice'. *Reflective Practice: International and Multidisciplinary Perspectives* 13(2): 311–325.

Wenger, E. (2000) *Communities of Practice: Learning, Meaning and Identity*. Cambridge: Cambridge University Press.

Wertsch, J. (1991). *Voices of the Mind*. Cambridge, MA: Harvard University. Press.

White, E. (2016) *Introducing Dialogic Pedagogy: Provocations for the Early Years*. London: Routledge.

White, J. and Peters, A. (2011) *Bakhtinian Pedagogy: Opportunities and Challenges for Research, Policy and Practice in Education Across the Globe*. London: Peter Lang.

2   Family centred care

Introduction and context

This chapter begins with an overview of family composition and the complexities of generational family life. It will include the transition in becoming a parent and the styles of parenting with the arrival of the infant. The practitioner meets and engages with parents prior and after birth and the latter will introduce some applications to practice in supporting a parent practitioner relationship. This will be navigated using a person-centred approach and the ways person centred planning could be used to enhance relationships between practitioners and parents in ECEC settings. The term parent is including in its broadest sense and includes primary home carers, mother and father, rather than exclusively the biological mother unless specifically stated.

Developing a relationship between parent and practitioner

The relationship between practitioners and parents has a significant impact on infant development (Desforges and Abouchaar, 2003; Melhuish et al., 2008) and parents are viewed by the practitioner as the first primary adults the infant depends on for support in their holistic development. They are the first point of reference when it comes to infant's socially interacting with the world, communicating from conception. Practitioners meet parents in a variety of contexts, during and after pregnancy, perhaps in a health clinic, in a support group or a social service setting. Practitioners may also meet parents when they begin deciding on infant care arrangements within

ECEC settings, prior to birth. Therefore, collaboration can occur in a variety of ways in different contexts. What remains constant, however is the importance of the value placed on the relationship between practitioners and parents (Gully, 2014). When it is effective and meaningful to both parties' collaboration develops and mutual respect is achieved, recognising the contribution each key agent makes towards their infants' development (Baum and McMurray-Schwarz, 2004).

What a family is, what a family does

Infants create integrative and disruptive factors in family life and in their emotional healthy growth promote family units. The integrative factors from the infant's perspective include a degree of reliability and availability to which parents respond, in the capacity to identify with them (Winnicott, 1957, cited in Winnicott, 1992). This is also determined in the way parents were responded to in their own upbringing and this transcends into their potential capacities of parenting, strengthened and developed by the expectations of their infants (Sinclair, 2018). Therefore, in subtle and overt ways infants produce a family around them alongside the parents own knowledge about expectation and fulfilment of the parenting role (Davis and Wallbridge, 2004: 133).

Practitioner's perspective

As a childminder I have met several mums in the final phase of their adoption. They sometimes have very set ideas about the type of care they would like, the hours they will work and the concern of not being a stay at home mum, particularly spending a long time going through the adoption procedure. A professional couple in their late thirties came to me after adopting their son. They already had a daughter and the son was her biological brother. They had initially used a nanny with their daughter, but were looking for something a little different, having ideas about what they wanted. I made it clear that their initial requests may change and their ideas of what they want may differ when their son settled. As expected when they returned they changed their work pattern and hadn't appreciated the challenges of two children. Their family life functioned very differently to when they had just one and there was a lot of emotions and mixed feelings about working and staying at home. As time went on it was evident that their children although both under three years were producing the family around them as much as the parents in their expectations and fulfilment. It was a very positive experience and the open communication enabled emotions and practical requests to be worked through together.

Aspirations: family composition in England

In England the cultural context of the late twentieth century was a relatively stable uniformity of life, evolved around visible rites of passage, a cycle of school, marriage, work, retirement. These predominant life aims were generational patterns and provided a moral compass that individuals progressed towards, often adopting a religious framework of life. However, as the political and economic climate has shifted, alongside the accelerated use of technology, the navigation of life courses, including marriage and employment have been met with uncertainty and challenged (Sinclair, 2018). Employment has become less predictable and with more consumer freedom and geographical movement family life has mirrored the change. As one of the oldest and significant social constitutions around the world, families continue to exist but as a social construct evolve and adapt to society values and changes of the time lived. As a group of varying aged individuals, comprising of close relationships related in some form, they are conceived as the foundation of society and nurturing young infants and children, build strength resilience and moral values for future generations. The overall aim for family life adult members is to provide love and stability that enables the younger members (children) to grow and lead fulfilling lives.

Family aspirations: citizens in contemporary England

- Provide material, physical an emotional support so potentials are fulfilled
- Support self-worth and nurture and develop the capacity for self-worth in society
- Enhance intergenerational support between families
- Create communities that are positive and therefore thriving
- Develop and engage in services to support good family outcomes economically
- Be a part of the society being lived in.

(Desforges and Abouchaar, 2003).

Families are variable, complex and dynamic and whilst individuals generally continue to seek a partner similar to their own background values and beliefs family structures have changed with time. Traditional patriarchal relationships in the family group are challenged, with increased acceptance of gender equality and resisting the conformity of previous generational norms. Rites of passages are less fixed and with a reduction in religious moral codes and exposure to individuals challenging stereotypes, separation, divorce, surrogacy, adoption and same sex parents has become progressively accepted as possible trajectories to family living. Whilst it is appreciated that family pluralism is not a new phenomenon the growing tolerance and acceptance for all family types has increased over the past few decades and blended families, the re-forming existing family groups and creating new ones now defines family beyond a heterosexual couple with two children (Palmer, 2010).

Questions for discussion

Compare your parents with your own marital status. How have things changed?

Have you mirrored your parents' rites of passages?

If you are not married do you consider this a natural progression within in a relationship and are your reasons social, personal or religious?

Do you see marital status as time bound?

What do you think marital status could add to a relationship?

What are the links between marital status and family life, personally, socially and culturally?

Whilst family composition circumstances and functionality matter in identifying roles, it is the emphasis on healthy strong relationships within a family context. This is measured by the values of the given society and communities in of which they live. Therefore, support in maternal circumstances emotional wellbeing and physical health is necessary at a local and national level. The more citizens who are physically and mentally healthy, well educated, empathic and social contributing to the costs of society the better the society will flourish. However, there is a rise in the proportion of mentally vulnerable individuals, unstable relationships and financial constraints leading many into poverty, relying on the state for economic and social support. With greater understanding of what contributes to an improving society come greater responsibility, greater flexibility and understanding of how to help families achieve positive outcomes (Leach, 2018). Current Government rhetoric encourages women within the first year of giving birth to return to employment or certainly plan to return to return. Pugh (2010) argues parenting and families' relationships are well known to be established in the home context, but this is juxtaposed with the Government proposal that the only route to alleviating poverty conditions resulting in poor health outcomes is through employment. This leaves parents (mothers predominately) with feelings of concern not only about their own feelings of returning to work and balancing family life but also making decisions to who is going to care for their infants and what type of care they were seeking.

Questions for discussion

What does a family community comprise of?

How have family communities differed from the past to the present?

What defines a good infanthood?

What is the definition of a good infanthood?

Transition to parenthood

Whilst we accept the physical and emotional changes in women in their transition to motherhood, either biologically or other-wise, we cannot preclude the father's

A father's perspective

experience. Father's too experience an emotional transitional change. They may reflect on their own relationship with their parents with the feelings of their own anxiety, concern and sometimes ambivalence about pregnancy. Fathers similar to mothers may have feelings of being overwhelmed and stressed both financially and emotionally. They may have mixed feelings about their partner's physically changing body and feel insufficient and inadequate themselves. Stress and resentment between both partners may also occur with practical tasks around work and home having to be redistributed and giving up individual time they previously had (Craig, 2017).

Listening to a father's perspective

When my wife got pregnant it was assumed I would continue working and she would give up her job for a year and then return part-time if she wanted to. She was working as a manager at an insurance company and had been there several years. However, when we went finally sat down and thought how we would manage things it became evident that my job was more flexible being a taxi driver so I would cut my hours rather than her. This meant that I would be doing most of the childcare. I was really keen to do it and didn't really worry about it until my wife became poorly during the end of her pregnancy and then I began to feel very stressed and worried about stuff. . . . I ended up feeling it was all about the mother and shut out. As a couple we had made joint decisions, but this didn't feel accepted by outside professionals or even friends. I wonder if I should be the one to continue working now . . . even paternity leave of two weeks is rubbish, when do I get a chance to spend time at home with my new family?

During the time from before conception financial care and social decisions need to be discussed and in part finalised during the forthcoming months about who will be the main carer and how employment will impact on the care of the infant. Ordinary maternity leave is the first twenty-six weeks, with additional maternity leave lasting twenty-six weeks, pay being variable depending on employment contracts. Leave from work begins the day after the birth if the baby is early or begins if absence of work is due to a pregnancy related illness in the four weeks (www.gov.uk/maternity-pay-leave). Paid maternity and paternity leave is crucial whereby parents financially feel they can afford to care for their infants and emotionally manage and internalise their transition to parenthood, in a time frame that establishes nurturing relationships and bonds, attachments both beneficial to the parents and their infants (Gerhardt,

2003). Similarly, Berger and Waldfogel (2005) concluded paid leave is associated with better maternal and infant health, lower maternal depression, lower infant mortality, breastfeeding for longer periods and general positive well-being.

Listening to a mother's perspective on informal care support

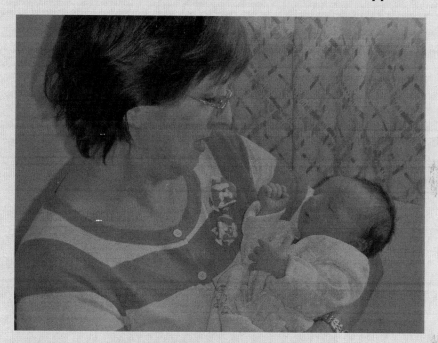

Grandparent and infant (day 3) communicating

The unsung heroes – the rise in grandparent care

When I fell pregnant I always knew I would go back to work as I enjoyed my job and the money would come in handy. My sister had been using a nursery nearby and it made sense for my baby to join her cousins once I had finished my maternity leave. I requested to have a day less, so I was working three days which I felt was a good balance. What I had not anticipated was to be expecting twins. Whilst the pregnancy had its own issues I gave birth at 37 weeks to identical healthy girls. I had spoken again to the nursery once I knew about my options and would get some money taken off but not very much (10% reduction for the second infant) and would need to complete some other forms to get tax relief. As the weeks went by I was getting more anxious about my plans. In the end my mother said she would help. When I had the twins I had no idea how tired I would be and as my return to work was approaching I turned to my mum for support. She was the person who looked after the children for three days until they were over one year and then continued to take them to a childcare setting one day a week when they were a year and half. She would continue taking them and collecting them. She would still see them at the weekend and was basically their main carer, alongside myself. Although my work was ok and I enjoyed it, and of course the money helped I could not help but feel a sense of loss at leaving my two exhausting bundles of joy. If I had not had a grandparent nearby I would not have been able to pay the bills and childcare was just too expensive with two the same age. I know people say I would have managed but we did the figures and I could not see a way out. I needed emotional support too and having someone close just meant I could talk to someone close. Someone said family members should help together but my poor mum was in her late fifties caring for twins just to help me and my husband in the earliest days! My health visitor said I was very lucky as many do not have a family member to help.

Grandparent care: tuning in with grandparent

Grandparents continue to contribute to the workforce longer and with more attention to healthy active lifestyles a significant number are sharing the care of their grandchildren in preference to solely using services beyond the home. Poehlmann (2003) state that many infants, whose parents both work, are looked after at least part of the time by relatives, usually grandparents. Currently grandparents are generally unable to claim any funding or financial support. Therefore, in many cases arrangements are based on goodwill and the flexibility of the grandparent's time and personal circumstances during the week. For many parents this arrangement may also be preferable where costs using ECEC settings are high until their infant is of an age they could claim support and funding for a place. However, whilst childcare cost was one aspect highlighted in the rationale of using grandparents it was not the only reason. Trust and love were included into the rationale and motivation for choosing grandparents. Slightly higher levels of vocabulary alongside positive association between socio-emotional development were also evident with infants looked after by their grandparents. However, the study does highlight those from more disadvantaged backgrounds continued to predominately benefit from more formal childcare (Poehlmann, 2003). They also concluded that whilst grandparent care did not improve school preparation they were not disadvantaged either. The idea of infants raised in a village takes the pressure of one parent and acknowledges the value of close carers beyond the immediate parents. Bronfenbrenner's (1979) ecological model reminds us that the infant can be viewed within the model of a system within a system. It is a reminder that humans are social beings and do not develop in isolation. The model emphasises the complexities of everyday life and five systems that guide human development, behaviour and interaction. Therefore, in planning for a family geographical location, mobility, family support and facilities in the area can decide the type of care beyond the home that is available. The selections of care are also chosen in preference to the one that is closest to personal values and beliefs of parents. The transition in becoming parents therefore includes big life decisions about how care will be sought and maintained, either with the aim of changing a current situation or keeping it similar as far as able to. Pooley and Qureshi (2016) evaluated parenthood between generations and found generational family members who generations were constant or physically present most influential. They also found in many cases the older generation were more influential in their feedback about parenting than advice received from professionals or the state. New forms of care such as safety or post-partum care were most positively received by parents whose older family members and close friends legitimised them. Therefore, they concluded parents cannot be viewed and discussed as isolated experts in their role but as part of an understanding of life long generational relationships. In nurturing the complex, historical forms parents and grandparents contribute to wider society policy makers can effectively work to support the welfare and care of families.

Good enough parenting?

Prior to conception parents begin to visualise and appreciate their transitioning role. Winnicott (1992) describes the infant as part of the mother and parents were not expected to become experts from the start. Good enough parenting was in defence of the ordinary mother and father against what Winnicott saw as the growing threat of intrusion into the family from professional expertise. He wanted to offset the dangers of idealisation of the perfect mother, focusing instead on the nurturing environment provided by the parents for the infant. Winnicott, therefore, suggests that initially the new-born is attended to by the parents as way to adapting to satisfy their infant's needs. For him, emotional growth involved the parents to initially adapting entirely to the infant, losing sleep and taking the lead from their needs expressed. As the infant grows he sees the gentle emerging allowance of some small amounts acts of frustrations from the infant to occur as a way for the infant to gain a sense of the external world separate from them. In this way separateness naturally evolves and the parents assume their role in meeting shifting demands and needs of their infant (Celebi, 2017).

Styles of parenting approaches vary depending on their upbringing, temperament, the support around them and their environment more generally. Studies have found the following forms of parenting approaches also include what they have observed by other parents, known and unfamiliar alongside what they have read and been advised by professionals and parenting books. Baumrind (1971) categorised styles of parenting and whilst this is argued to be generalised and parenting a mixture of styles, knowledge of a predominant approach is helpful in reflecting whether they contradict, or support practitioners own parenting experiences and care pedagogies.

Authoritarian parenting is where the parents establish the rules and expect family members to follow them without exception. Rules and boundaries are strict and there is little scope for flexibility of spontaneity. Punishment may be used instead of consequences and there is little room for negotiation. Whist this is not a parenting style advocated and is restricting it does resemble some parenting approaching advised by popular parenting gurus. For some 'parents to be' there is a high level of anxiety during pregnancy and certainly the infants first two years are not without challenges. Strict bedtime routines are sought very early, even before three months of age with the need for parental sleep. Feeding approaches, a source of frustration and worry can result in associated behavioural issues that anger and frustrate the parents. Breastfeeding has also been argued as a misguided and misinformed approach. Many mothers have resorted to formula feeds without being given comprehensive advice around breast feeding. Advertisements continue to promote strict four hourly regimes perpetuating and supporting some popular parenting guides without scientific or research background (Brown, 2016). As the infant develops and grows toward independence so too does the establishment of boundaries and guidance received by parents in regulating emotionally charged behaviour for infants before they are one years. In a bid to try and regain control in the household the parents often lean toward this type of parenting, particularly if they lack support about their concerns.

Authoritative parenting also has rules and boundaries and allowance of exceptions to the rules are given. There is flexibility in this parenting approach and whist limits are set the parent can appreciate and understand their infants' perspective and emotions. Infants are rewarded and through positivity the parenting style is relaxed, fun whist maintaining routines and advocating the code and morals of how they would like their infants to be, reflecting the society they live in.

Indulgent parenting and permissive parenting can be culturally led or result from the historical backdrop to the story of how the parents became parents. For some parents undergoing fertility treatments for a number of years and then successfully gaining an infant, indulgent parenting may be something they relish and feel honoured to do. Indulgent parenting is relative but there is an agreed balance that if the indulgent parenting inhibits the healthy development of both the infant and the parent then perhaps it needs attention. Similarly, permissive parenting does not offer much discipline and there tends to be leniency in behaviour and outbursts. Consequences may not be apparent, and rules and boundaries are lacking. This can cause uncertainty and anxiety in young infants. Routines changing may be difficult in predicting what is to occur next and seek parents to guide them (www.verywellfamily.com).

Neglectful parenting may tend to be uninvolved and often do not meet their infant's basic needs. This type of parenting may have begun prior to birth with the parent not self-managing their own health through differing reasons. If the pregnancy was unwanted or unexpected the parents may feel unprepared and challenged in appreciating how life changing an infant is going to be. Lack of education or inexperience of infant development may result in neglectful parenting. Attention and nurturing can be compromised and those parents with fragile mental health may lack or be troubled by their own parenting skills or repeating questioned negative behaviour from their own infanthood.

On many occasions, parents do not fit into a singular category and throughout pregnancy and beyond will probably experience each one at differing times, contexts and under different conditions. Communicating with parents regarding their approaches can enable parents to reflect on their own practice and upbringing, and where necessary make changes. Research highlights the importance of differentiating support for parents and support for parenting. Support for parents is essential to build self-esteem and resilience in parents to set the base for a change in parenting. Through the positive interaction cycle the parent initiates positive interactions with the infant, and the infant responds positively developing a sense of self-worth, self-esteem and self-efficacy. Through positive reciprocal relationships, infants learn to control their emotions, soothe themselves and relate to others.

Rather than considering the parenting styles above, Gopnik (2016) argues the word parenting became a familiar term in the 1970s, rising in popularity as traditional sources of wisdom about infant-rearing as previously embedded sources of support such as large extended families fell away. Gopnik argues that the message of this massive modern industry is misguided. It assumes that the 'right' parenting techniques or expertise will shape an infant into a successful adult. Shaping a product is the method of a carpenter and in referring to parenting very little empirical evidence supports this approach. Gopnik concludes it is the 'small variations' in what parents do that 'have reliable and predictable long-term effects on who those infants and young children become' (Gopnik, 2016: 23). For her raising and caring for infants is like tending a garden: it involves digging and wallowing to create a safe, nurturing space in which innovation, adaptability and resilience can thrive. Her approach focuses on helping infants to find their own way, even if it contradicts the parent's aspirations of them. Therefore, in Gopnik's not-parenting approach, genetic variation contributes to the wide range of infant's temperaments and abilities – some infants and young children are risk-takers, others timid, some are highly focused or natural hunters. She describes a wide range of experiments showing that infants and young children learn less through 'conscious and deliberate teaching' than through watching, listening and imitating.

Questions for discussion

Gopnik's (2017) 'carpenter' is the parent who has a preconceived idea of how the infant should turn out to be in adult life. It is according to a set of rules; if they are followed, it will be fit for purpose. The carpenter parent will raise the infant 'by the book', ignoring individuality and denying the opportunity for any experimentation in their practice, preferring to teach skills.

The 'gardener', by contrast, nurtures the infant similar to a plant in a rich, varied environment, allowing for personal growth. Some infants and young children, like dandelions, are tough and will thrive almost anywhere. Others, like orchids, need exclusive conditions. Every infant however requires 'a protected early period' when 'its needs are met in a reliable, stable and unconditional way', with 'space for mess, variability, and exploration'.

What do you consider to be the types of parents who you meet in early years and do what do they expect predominately from you when considering the two types of parents?

A professional relationship

Infants learn how to do things through their experiences with other people, not through words or instructions. They learn how to cope with small amounts of stress by having the experience of someone emotionally and physically available with them in sharing and overcoming anxious feelings. During infancy, the stress responses are not yet fully functional and therefore they get easily stressed, particularly when situations become or are perceived unsafe. This includes being separated from their familiar carer. Infants remain dependent on protective and calm adults during stressful situations, in the process of learning how to calm themselves and self soothe.

As an example of transition, take the case of Alfie. In the morning Alfie would cling to his dad, hiding his face and resisting the inevitable transition to nursery as they approached the door. He was met by a smiling practitioner who greeted them both warmly, as she said hello. She didn't reach out and take Alfie but rather stroked his arm and spoke softly. Dad would bend down, and the practitioner mirrored the action so Alfie had both his father and key person, the practitioner either side. He was hesitant but accepting of where he would spend the day and looked around familiarising himself with the room. This was the second nursery Alfie had attended in recent months. The first nursery was nearer to the family home and was primarily chosen because of its location. Alfie's mother had taken him, but he would not leave her, screaming and clutching tightly to her, sobbing as she attempted to peel him off. The practitioner there had advised to allow them to take him through to the adjoining room to minimise the stressful separation. This had become problematic and the decision by the parents was to move Alfie to another setting. The separation had been so traumatic for Alfie's mother that she was unable to take him to nursery, although would pick him up daily.

This is a familiar scenario to both practitioners and parents in their organisation of managing and becoming accustomed to childcare. Parents, particularly first-time mothers and fathers, in the transition to parenthood may not have fully considered childcare options. In resolving employment issues, they may not have prioritised out of home care, leaving where to place their infant to the last minute, having to accept or compromise on the differentiated ECEC settings offered to them.

Traditionally many parents, mothers predominately would have stayed at home with their infants and accepted this was part of having children. However, for many parents today there is a sense and increasing expectation to place their infant in some form of day care when maternity leave has been completed and return to employment in some capacity. Demographic trends in contemporary societies mean that ECEC services for infants after grandparents are the most popular form of childcare. Social, economic and labour market dynamics across much of England have seen participation rates of under – two years olds in ECEC settings rise with a 'shared care' approach between home and group being a regular occurrence (Dalli, 2006). Childminders and nurseries opening hours can be as early as 6am and as late as 8pm, with many caring for infants in groups, from three months old. Palmer (2010) polarises early years childcare: from the point of view of the infant, or the convenience of adults. In her view, the needs of the infant must be of primary concern and argues that in many ECEC nursery settings staff absences and high turnovers undermine the consistent and stable base advocated by professionals. She argues that the reality of what childcare can offer in terms of love and stable care is therefore challenging and if alternatives should be sought. However, Page (2017) recognises the reality that both parents are in employment for a variety of reasons and infants are increasingly attending ECEC settings frequently and for long hours prior to two years of age. The discourse she therefore argues should be focused on the type of relationships offered and the most suited environment to the family and infant, rather than whether they should attend settings beyond the home.

Parents and practitioner relationships

In Parents, Early Years and Learning Project (PEAL) (2008) the following were considered essential for relationships to prosper in a variety of ECEC contexts:

- Strong relationships (time needs to be given to staff to enable relationships to develop)
- Parents' interest and involvement in education (but this might need imaginative ways of involving parents and families)
- Active involvement in family, setting and community life (www.peal.org.uk)
- Recognition, praise and feeling valued (practitioners need to acknowledge, value and support parents' role in early learning and development).

(www.ncb.org.uk)

Generally, we assume parents take the lead from their local midwife GP and health visitor, nursery nurse assigned to the clinic. However, parents, whilst continuing to receive advice from these professionals, alongside family members and friends, are also turning to practitioners as a way of making informed choices. A survey completed by practitioners with more than five years' experience working regularly with infants concluded their role was supporting, advising, and sign posting information and reassuring parents. They considered an open-door policy essential but also scheduled meetings and event days as points of contact. Practitioners confirmed they met pregnant women from a variety of circumstances, some requiring regular home visits to develop the relationship. Special days were also set up for extended family members such as grandparents to visit and volunteering was also a way for parents to come and meet practitioners (Norman, 2018).

Kambouri-Danos (2017) found 40% of the practitioners thought the focal way of involving parents in the infant's learning experiences was to have parents' meetings or face-to-face chats, although only twenty six percent of the parents agreed. Practitioners also perceived activity and charity events as positive ways to involve parents in their infant's learning experiences and empower parent-practitioner partnerships, but the sampled parents did not feel the same. However, both practitioners and parents believed lack of physical time was the main barrier to empowering practitioner-parent partnerships. Parents also acknowledged their own lack of time or availability during the settings' opening hours rather than the practitioners' lack of time was influential.

For successful parent practitioner relationships, there is a need for settings:

- To acknowledge and actively address the barriers to collaboration, such as the changing demands on family life and the increase in demands upon practitioners
- To strengthen enablers to collaboration, such as the use of a range of methods to facilitate communications.

(Kambouri-Danos, 2017)

Listening to practitioners: reflections on their relationships with parents

In considering parent's relationships, a group of practitioners from various work backgrounds reflected on meeting parents for the first time and sharing the care role with myself. A pedagogy of care became apparent and was defined not only by what practitioners do in their role but what they think about their role, reflecting on their values and beliefs about what they want from the partnership with parents. These are some examples I have created to mirror their thinking;

- I would hope I was available to build bonds with the parents I meet, reassuring them and supporting them
- Not only advise but someone they can talk to, listening to them and letting them know there is never a stupid question to ask

- I found that the relationship grows further as the parents open up to me about their new pregnancy. I would also be helping the older sibling come to terms with another infant in the family.
- Supporting the family, including dads and grandparents
- Being adaptable, good communication, disseminating information and signposting information rather than relying on what I did when I was pregnant
- Support with concerns and responding sensitively to care questions without being opinionated

A pedagogy of care was therefore developed whereby:

- The infant's holistic needs were taken into consideration
- The parent's needs were taken into consideration, rather than the professional versus parent position
- Commitment and dedication in their roles with an authentic appreciation of the significance to development and care of infants was evident. Karemaker et al. (2011, cited in Payler and Georgeson, 2014) found that staff length of service was associated with higher quality provision for infants and young children (from birth to 30 months) in relation to listening and talking.
- Complex tasks were received and unpicked with high level of problem-solving situations received positively
- Practitioners became thoughtful agents in reflecting on their experiences, tensions and celebrations of their role.

(Appleby and Andrews, 2011)

For many practitioners developing an open dialogue and sharing information with parents about their infant requires a personal and sensitive relationship which can also be challenging and complex. Some questions raised by parents may require medical or health knowledge. Practitioners sharing their own family anecdotal experiences can equally be reassuring but also contradictory to current guidelines and contradict advice sought in settings. Whilst the relationship is certainly not a counselling relationship I believe a humanistic approach could be implemented. It could provide a positive way of engaging in dialogue without the relationship becoming too advisory and widening the professional parent gap. A person-centred approach has been used in many contexts, including education and person-centred planning as an ethical approach has been successful in working with vulnerable clients. In focusing on the voice of the parents, the infant and person-centred ways of working social justice and rights form part of a wider social movement. The guiding principles of person-centred planning is that:

- Parents are listened to and their views and feeling are considered
- Parents have the right to be consulted about their services they receive
- Parents are valued partners who play an important role in making things better
- To develop autonomy and empower parents
- Develop a person-centred culture, and how this is reflected in policies, attitudes and practices.

Person centred approach to developing parent relationships

Person centred approach is a humanistic way of working and looks at the intrinsic motivations of the individual. As practitioners, the following are the three core elements that navigate the parent relationship:

- Understanding – of a given situation and mindset
- Congruence – being open and honest in communication
- Empathy – not getting embroiled in emotions but appreciating situations and the emotions attached to them.

(Rogers, 1980)

Person centred approaches are about discovering and acting on what is important to a person, in this case, the parent and what is important for them. It is about finding the balance through a process of continual listening and learning about the parent's capacities and choices and if necessary signposting resources and services necessary. Listening with intention as well as attention is important in creating a supportive relationship. It also gives voice to the parent, so they do not feel ignored or silenced. Sharing power enables parents to work together and make choices rather than the practitioner's role being that of primarily informing. Rather in this approach it is about responsive action and deciding what is the practitioner's professional responsibility and together how the parents and practitioners can find solutions together. This is endorsed by the Children and Families Act (2014) which advocated supporting and involving families in decisions making and providing information to aid decisions in ensuring and supporting the best possible outcomes of their infants.

Person centred planning emphasises the importance of learning form observation and the intrinsic motivation. This can be applied at differing levels to both parents and practitioners in their roles. Tensions can exist to hide personal thinking when an individual is unsure or lacks confidence. Boundaries and tensions should be openly discussed and worked through together a sense of identity and purpose can be achieved (Lave and Wenger, 1991) Through self-reflecting and making sense of each other as a collective the following can be applied and shared:

- Description/what happened
- What were my feelings?
- What was good/bad about the experience?
- What did I learn from the experience
- What could I have done differently?
- If it happens again what could I do?

Personal construct theory is a way of understanding the ideas which shape each person's individual lens of the world. As predictions are made in understanding external events interpretations are made. As a practitioner, trying to understand some ones view of the world helps to understand their perspectives and listen meaningfully.

Planning together

Arnstein's (1969) and later Hart's (2008) introduction of a ladder in thinking about participation of parents helps think about where practitioners believe they should be involved in the planning and meeting that regular occurs. There can be an overlap in the following a ladder and at times context and situations may determine the rung of the ladder. However, in visualising it as a ladder the steps allow practitioners to observe the present and next steps with parents.

Planner
Partner
Participant
Consulted
Represented
Considered
Informed
Absent

Absent is when the parent or family unit is physically absent, but they are talked about as a case or an issue

Informed is when information is given, either small snippets of information's such as weaning, sleep patterns. This can be done through writing, leaflets, letters or face to face

Considered is referred to when judgments are made about a given situation. The consideration should be a genuine perspective of the parents although this can be tentative and subject to change. Again, the parent may not be available or unwilling to give their own thoughts

Represented could range from shared paper work where the parent may not physically be available to speak about things but be heard. Infant daily home records are good for this as they provide a tool that parents could write any changes or developments regarding care of their infant they want shared. If both parents cannot attend initial meetings, then perhaps the father has a list of questions that can be read by the other parent.

Consulted is when meetings together are held and there is an opportunity for the parents to speak and respond to decisions about care and development.

Participant is an approach whereby the parents can bring their own questions and ask. In consideration of the study where stay and play are deemed a positive opportunity to be involved then the parent can begin to exert influence and share in the decision making. They may even include their own upbringing and how their attachment issues have influenced their relationships as adults.

Partner is when the parent and practitioner together decide when they meet what they will discuss together. The process is two way and there will be opportunities for both to share thoughts. While we define the relationship as a partnership the equal collaboration is not always evident and yet one hoped to achieve.

Planner is when the parent feels comfortable in giving feedback about differing scenarios. They include what went well and what did not work for them. they may even be involved in the overall care of a setting and influence practitioners to change routines or practices.

Practitioner's perspective

A practical example

Many practitioners had used story sacs to extend learning and enhance communication opportunities. A parent who had recently moved brought in a sack one day with a few items she had got from home. The infant was approximately one years and was feeling quite emotional at transitional times. The event sack – moving home was given to the infant and was a resource for her to share her experiences of moving through objects. The parents had previously tried stories and teddies and this had not quite worked. However, she found by collating the infant's favourite things alongside photographs, pictures and associated objects the individual was expressing her thoughts about the move more clearly. The parents feedback enabled practitioner to reflect on their own practice and introduce resources that were more personable to the infants in their care.

Family practitioner summary

Remember your work is about the whole family and that your relationship with a infant is always more productive if you have a positive relationship with them. Listen to the parent without judgment. You may even not personally agree with them, but you did need to be professional in your approach as practitioner.

Focused Points

- Understanding parent relationships and approaches to supporting relationships
- Recognising families are diverse and supporting them
- Providing practical guidance to families

Concluding thoughts

This chapter looked at the way families come together and support individuals in their transition to parenthood. It includes generational influences and the perceptions about families today. It focuses on the challenges in the transition to parenthood and the ways practitioners can support them. It focuses on a person-centred approach in creating a relationship that suits both practitioner and parents in their roles. The term *partnership* is a challenging one with connotations that both practitioner and parent are from the same perspective. I prefer *relationship* which implies an active connection that has potential to flourish, pending both the practitioners' and parents' willingness to engage together.

Bibliography

Appleby, K. and Andrews, M. (2011) Reflective practice is the key to quality improvement. In Reed, M. and Canning, N. *Reflective Practice in the Early Years*. London: Sage.

Arnstein, R. (1969) 'A Ladder of Citizen Participation'. *Journal of the American Institute of Planner* (35)421: 6–22.

Baum, A. and McMurray-Schwarz, P. (2004) 'Preservice teachers' beliefs about family involvement: Implications for teacher education'. *Early Infanthood Education Journal* 32(1): 57–61.

Baumrind, D. (1971) 'Current patterns of parental authority'. *Developmental Psychology Monographs* 4(1).

Berger, L. and Waldfogel, J. (2005) 'Maternity Leave, early maternal employment and child health and development in the US'. *Economic Journal* 115(501).

Bowlby, J. (1993) *A Secure Base: Clinical Applications of Attachment Theory*. London: Routledge.

Bronfenbrenner, U. (1979) *The Ecology of Human Development*. Cambridge: Harvard University Press.

Brown, A. (2016) *Breastfeeding Uncovered: Who really decides how we feed our babies?* London: Pinter and Martin.

Celebi, M. (2017) *Weaving the Cradle*. London: Kingsley.

Coles, P. (2015) *The Shadow of the Second Mother*. London: Routledge.

Craig, C. (2017) *Hiding in Plain Sight*. Paisley: CCWB Press.

Dahlberg, G. and Moss, P. (2013) *Ethics and Politics in Early Infanthood: Languages of Evaluation Education*. London: Routledge Falmer.

Dalli, C. (2006) 'Re-visioning love and care in early infanthood: constructing the future of our profession'. *First Years New Zealand Journal of Infant and Toddler Education* 8(1): 5–11.

Davis, M. and Wallbridge, D. (2004) *Boundary and Space: An Introduction to the work of D. Winnicott*. London. Penguin.

Desforges C, Abouchaar A. (2003) 'The Impact of Parental Involvement, Parental Support and Family Education on Pupil Achievements and Adjustment: A Literature Review'. RR433. London: DfES.

Gallagher, T. and Arnold, C. (2018) *Working with Children Aged 0–3 and their Families. A Pen Green Approach*. London: Routledge.

Gerhardt, S. (2003) Available online at www.ecswe.net/wp-content/uploads/2011/01/QOC2-Chapter3-Why-Love-Matters-How-Affection-Shapes-a-Babys-Brain-by-Sue-Gerhardt.pdf

Gerdhardt, S. (2014) *Why Love Matters*. London: Routledge.

Goldschmied, E. and Jackson, S. (2004) (2nd ed) *People Under Three, Young Children in Day Care*. London: Routledge.

Gopnik, A. (2016) Available online at www.nature.com/articles/536027a

Gopnik, A. (2017) *The Gardener and the Carpenter: What the New Science of Infant Development Tells Us About the Relationship Between Parents and Children*. England: Vintage.

Gully, T. (2014) *The Critical Years: Early Development from Conception to Five*. Northwich: Critical Publishing.

Hart, R. (2008) Stepping Back from 'The Ladder': Reflections on a Model of Participatory Work with Infants. In Reid, A., Jensen, B., Nikel, J. and Simovska, V. (eds) *Participation and Learning*. Springer. Available online at https://link.springer.com/article/10.1007/s00148-003-0159-9

Jackson, S. and Forbes, R. (2014) *People Under Three, Young Infants in Day Care*. London: Routledge.

Kambouri-Danos, M. (2015) 'Investigating Early Years Teachers' Understanding and Response to Children's Preconceptions'. *European Early Infanthood Education Research Journal* 25(3). DOI: 10.1080/1350293X.2014.970857.

Lave, J. and Wenger, E. (1991) *Situated Learning: Legitimate Peripheral Participation*. Cambridge: Cambridge University Press.

Leach, P. (2018) *Transforming Infant Well-Being. Research, Policy and Practice for the First 1001 Critical Days*. Routledge: London.

McCormack, B. and McCance, T. (2010) *Person Centred Nursing*. West Sussex: Wiley Blackwell.

Melhuish, E., Mai, B., Phan, M., Sylva, K., Sammons, P., Siraj-Blatchford, I. and Taggart, B. (2008) 'Effects of the home learning environment and preschool centre experience upon literacy and numeracy development in early primary school'. *Journal of Social Issues* 64(1): 95–114.

Norman, A. (2018) Practitioners perceptions of parent's partnerships. Bournemouth Early Years Setting. Conference Paper unpublished.

Page, J. (2017) 'Reframing infant-toddler pedagogy through a lens of professional love: Exploring narratives of professional practice in early infanthood settings in England'. *Contemporary Issues in Early Years* 18(4). Available online at www.journals.sagepub.com/doi/abs/10.1177/1463949117742780

Page, J. (2011) 'Do Mothers Want Professional Carers to Love Their Babies?' *Journal of Early Infanthood Research* 1(14): 1–14. DOI:10.1177/1476718X11407980.

Page, J. (2013) 'Will the "Good" [Working] Mother Please Stand Up? Professional and Maternal Concerns about Education, Care and Love.' *Gender and Education*. DOI:10.1080/0954025 3.2013.797069.

Palmer, S. (2010) *Toxic Infanthood: How the Modern World Is Damaging Our Children and What We Can Do*. London: Orion.

Palmer, S. (2017) Available online at www.telegraph.co.uk/health-fitness/body/much-young-nursery-stressing-infant

Parents, Early Years and Learning (PEAL) (2006) Available online at www.ncb.org.uk/sites/default/files/uploads/documents/Early_years_docs/Activities_bookletV3_LoRes.pdf

Parents, Early Years and Learning (PEAL) (2008) Available online at www.ncb.org.uk/what-we-do/our-priorities/early-years/projects-programmes/parents-early-years-learning

Payler, J. and Georgeson, J. (2014) *Early Years Foundations: Critical Issues*. Milton Keynes: OUP Education.

Poehlmann, J. (2003) 'An attachment perspective on grandparents raising their very young grandchildren: Implications for intervention and research'. *Infant Mental Health Journal*. Available online at www.onlinelibrary.wiley.com/doi/abs/10.1002/imhj.10047

Pooley, K. and Qureshi, B. (2016) *Parenthood Between Generations: Does the State Alter What It Means to be a Parent?* Oxford: Oxford University Press.

Pugh, G. (2010) *Contemporary Issues in the Early Years*. London: Sage.

Rogers, C. (1980) *A Way of Being*. London: Routledge

Rogers, C. (2007) 'Experiencing an 'inclusive' education: parents and their children with 'special educational needs'. *British Journal of Sociology of Education* 28(1): 55–68.

Schön, D. (1983) *The Reflective Practitioner.* USA: Basic Books.

Sinclair, A. (2018) *Right from the Start.* Paisley: CCWB Press.

Stern, D. (1997) *The Birth of a Mother.* New York: Perseus Books Group.

Stern, D. (1998) *The Motherhood Constellation.* London: Karnac Books.

Winnicott, D. (1992) *Babies and Their Mothers.* Boston. Da Capo Press.

3 Prenatal care

Introduction and context

This chapter will outline physical growth and development during the neonate period. Genetics and the environment will be discussed alongside key issues around conception. The chapter's aim is to enable practitioners in ECEC settings to appreciate not just growth and development but also some of the circumstances parents may encounter and how it could affect their developing infant. This includes practitioner's own capacities for reflection empathising, communicating and understanding their role and experiences as front-line professionals in caring for parents and infants prenatally.

In developing this chapter, I have included prenatal areas I consider worthy for practitioners to have knowledge of when working with parents. Whilst I am not suggesting practitioners replace midwives, social workers, health visitors or clinicians, they are nevertheless the professionals regularly being asked questions and relied on for support, more often prior to birth, regarding fertility, health and social issues. This chapter therefore hopes to aid and introduce some of the key areas of prenatal care in promoting positive outcomes for the infant.

Questions for discussion

Growth is the process of growing, increasing in size and strength. Development is the significant change, event or occurrence, beginning simply to more complex attributes.

When does life begin:

- Birth of infant?
- Last three months of pregnancy?
- Conception?
- Birth of infants' parents?
- Before that?
- When does development of an infant begin?

Lifestyle change

From a health and psychological perspective, the optimum recommended time to begin planning for an infant is up to six months prior to conception. Whilst this can be argued to be a mythical time frame, the rationale is so individuals can reflect and make changes to their diet habits, weight fluctuations and overdue health checks. The focus is to begin building up the nutritional reserves and eliminating existing toxins such as alcohol and smoking from the body's systems. Whilst this is primarily aimed at females in preparing for pregnancy, conception includes fathers too, and therefore they should also address dietary and lifestyle choices to ensure the sperm is of quality. As soon as the mother conceives, nutrients are taken from her and support the development of her infant. Folic acid intake prior to conception has been recommended for several years and this has been found to reduce neural tube defects.

During pregnancy, the advice and support of health professionals is aimed at outlining optimum health for both infant and parent. The National Institute for Health and Care Excellence (NICE) advises that ideally before the ten-week gestation period, the initial visit to a health professional should address eating habits and levels of physical activity. Advice concerning moderate-intensity physical activity should therefore be given alongside the importance of avoiding an excessively sedentary lifestyle. Physical activity in pregnancy reduces the risk of excessive weight gain and adverse conditions including gestational diabetes, pre-eclampsia, pre-term birth, varicose veins and deep vein thrombosis (Royal College of Obstetricians and Gynaecologists, 2006). There is also some evidence correlating to physical activity during pregnancy with shorter labours and fewer delivery complications. A study in the United States showed that pregnant women who exercised in water had lower heart rates and blood pressure than women who did alternative exercises. The infants also benefited by having lower foetal heart rates after water exercises than when the same exercises were done on land (Freedman, 2002, cited in Bernard et al., 2007). NICE guidelines also include the value of dietary advice. In 2010, the Royal College of Midwives (RCM) conducted a survey, with parenting website 'Netmums' canvassing over 6,000 women about the advice they received concerning weight, diet and physical activity during pregnancy. The results concluded that the advice received could be better alongside more information and time from the midwife than they were currently receiving (Netmums, 2010). Whilst this is a little dated it highlights the mother's voice in wanting to receive information and support during pregnancy and pregnancy related concerns. This continues to be sought beyond the health professionals and therefore increasing the need for connected care information with early years practitioners and specialist professionals.

Conception and pregnancy in context

The conception and pregnancy experience are influenced by expectations the parents learned through their own upbringing. Factors such as parents' age, health, marital status, social status, cultural expectations and employment circumstances are influential within the parent's community and social 'norms'. In contemporary England, the dominant identification of the growing foetus is as a passive organism rather than a miniature human as historically perceived. This has implications for health behaviour and decisions made by the parents and the associated factors that influence their choices during pregnancy. In England contemporary home visiting programmes are underpinned by Bronfenbrenner's Ecological Theory (1979), emphasising the importance of the inter-relationship between the individual and the wider systems within which they are located including neighbourhood, society and culture. The focus of such programmes is supporting parents through pregnancy to develop strategies to prevent or address problems that can occur within each of these systems. Within the home visiting programmes there is a strong focus development underpinned by attachment theory in terms of promoting one-to-one interaction and supporting the development of secure attachment. For early years practitioners, home visits have been encouraged for number of years, alongside specialist professionals. Whilst the focus of the visit may be specific to the profession in most cases it is underpinned by the encouragement to build positive relationships and support healthy development of both parent and infant. Care approaches are also shared and visiting the family home enables both entering each other's communities, different to their own. Knowledge of development and care provides an opportunity for a dialogue to begin.

Foetal development

The forty weeks gestation period of growth and development during which the fertilized ovum becomes an infant is calculated from the date of the beginning of the woman's last menstrual period. The time of fertilization is measured approximately fourteen days after the beginning of the last menstrual period. The average pregnancy lasts 280 days when calculated from gestational age and 266 days from the time of fertilization. Conventionally, the gestation period is organized by trimesters of about three months each. These weeks are subdivided into trimesters, with the first trimester being the time when much development occurs, and potential complications presented. The first trimester is divided again, by embryologists as the germinal stage, the embryonic stage and the foetal stage (www.nature.com/stemcells).

Stages of development

The earliest sequences of development

- 12 weeks: the sex of the infant is visible. Toes and fingers visible and eyelids and lips formed

- 16 weeks: Limbs strengthening and movements are felt by the mother. Eyes are formed, bones are beginning to develop, ears fully formed.

- 20 weeks: visually the infant looks like a miniature self. The hair is growing, limbs strengthening. Fingers and thumbs may be sucked

- 24 weeks: the infant is now capable of breathing if born at this stage, although survival rates remain low. The infant can taste and be aware of sounds but cannot see. Eyes are formed but remain closed.

- 28 weeks: the nervous system can now function. Infants remain thin but with support could survive outside of the womb with support of warmth, extra oxygen and drugs to aid lungs interconnections between nerve cells (neurons) developed, weight is added, general finishing of body systems takes place.

- 40 weeks: at this stage infants are gaining muscle strength, fat and systems are in place.

(Adapted from www.nature.com)

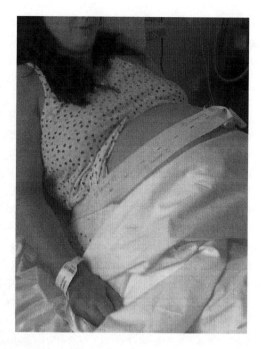

Monitoring the neonatal heart beat in preparation for birth

Nature nurture: genetic understanding

Whilst I have not included the factual detail of the female reproduction system and biological pregnancy growth I have included an introduction to the genetics to illustrate how biological differences can be environmentally influenced. Doubilet and Benson (2008) detail the visual and descriptions of the developing infant prenatally, including the growth of the mother and the associated conditions and genetic influence. So how can genes be influenced?

The sperm brings the genetic material from the male and the female egg contains the genetic endowment, combining to form the twenty-three pairs that will be the part of each cell in the new born infant. Each infant has a unique blueprint and have an inherited genotype of their own, hence why they are unique in personality. The genotype is the specific set of instructions contained in the genes. Body build, temperaments, hair colour, some aspects intelligence and potential learning dispositions. In twenty-two of the pairs the chromosomes look alike but in the remaining pair the sex chromosomes are different and usually referred to as the X and Y chromosomes.

A female has XX chromosomes and a male has and X and Y chromosome. Therefore, if the sperm carries an X chromosome the infant will have an XX pattern, a girl. If X then it will be XY, a boy. Identical twins are genetically the same – a single fertilized egg divided in half and each half becoming an individual. They are a good example of the interaction between inheritance and the environment and unique brain development. All of the differences between identical twins – for example, personality, tastes and aptitude – are predominantly due to differences in their experiences and the environment. Fraternal twins are when more than one egg has been produced and each fertilised by a different sperm. These twins are genetically unique and no more alike than siblings. The chromosomes in a pair carry the same genes in the same places. But there are different versions of the same gene. Different versions of the same gene are called alleles. For example, the gene for eye colour has an allele for blue eye colour and an allele for brown. For any gene, a person may have the same two alleles, or two different ones (www.nhs.uk/conditions/genetics). In genetic disorders such as cystic fibrosis (CF) caused by a recessive allele, two copies of the faulty allele inherited by mother and father are born with CF. If one copy is inherited then there is a possibility of being a carrier, symptoms associated with CF will not be evident. Whilst this a very simplistic description of CF it highlights the complexities associated with individual genetic differences and the changes when couples' genetics 'meet'. Couples, as individuals and together, with a known genetic condition will be supported and referred to a specialist for genetic counselling prior to conception or during stages of pregnancy. In some cases, family history is unknown, so pregnancy-related decisions made regarding the health of the mother and the infant can be challenging. For many practitioners, listening and supporting parental decisions without judgement is necessary, and whilst they may be referred to specialists many practitioners remain the familiar profession parents talk to (www.cff.org.co.uk). In creating optimum conditions for the developing infant to thrive, mothers can be supported in making healthy choices and expressing concerns without judgment or blame. Whilst the genotype carries the genes and blueprint of the growing infant, from conception the uterine environment will also affect the developing foetus. The quality of this environment has a profound effect on the wiring of the infant's brain and life in the uterine highlights the interplay of nature and nurture. The type of person that the infant becomes in terms of his or her capacity for relationships, feelings and beliefs about themselves, and their sense of who they are as a person, is not just shaped by healthy behaviours but also the earliest interactions with primary caregivers, influencing which genes are expressed. This process is known as 'epigenetics' and involves genes being 'turned on or off' because of chemical changes. These do not alter the structure of the gene, but influence whether the DNA becomes active (www.beginbeforebirth). Healthy choices such as diet and exercise, stress and caring interactions both before and after birth are significant because the of the way the environment influencing nature and long-term developmental trajectory of an infant.

> As early as the first trimester, the foetus will jump if touched by an amnio-centesis needle, turn away from the light of a doctor's foetal stethoscope (Goodlin and Schmidt, 1972) and foetal heart rates increase when pregnant mothers smoke cigarettes. . . . Already we see nature-nurture interaction; the foetus is its own being but also is being socialised. It learns to recognise sounds that it later prefers after birth, while culturally influenced tastes are also picked up, so that for example if the mother eats garlic during pregnancy, the new-born will show less aversion to it.
>
> (Music, 2016: 14)

Biologically the umbilical cord connects the circulatory system to the placenta and acts as a type of filter supplying the foetus with the nutrients from the mother's blood and taking waste back, so the mother can eliminate it. The filter is essential as it provides a way of reducing the intake of toxins to the infant. However, there are some viruses too large and pass through, reducing the nutrients to the embryo, attacking the placenta. Previously many professionals believed the foetus was protected and most of substances could not pass through and most harmful substances were filtered but today medical evidence suggests otherwise. There have been know causes and effects and high correlations of drugs such as alcohol, diet and stress in the development of the embryo, foetus and infant during the three trimesters (Macintyre, 2012: Carter, 2000).

The substances that cause effect are known as 'teratogens'. A teratogen is any exposure that can potentially and actually cause harm to an unborn or breastfeeding infant. Teratogens can be alcohol, prescription/non-prescription medications, illegal drugs, vaccines, illnesses, environmental exposures, occupational exposures, or maternal autoimmune disorders. The following are teratogens that can cause harm to differing degrees:

- Prescription drugs
- Substances – heroin, cocaine
- Social Drugs – alcohol, cocaine, smoking
- Disease – Rubella, Herpes Simplex, Varicella (Chicken Pox)
- Radiation – X-rays
- Maternal – Diabetes
- Poverty – environmental, poor housing, poor nutrition, stress
- Pollution – noise, atmosphere.

Some teratogens will increase this risk, but it is dependent upon the type and amount of the exposure as well as the timing in the pregnancy. Below are some examples of the effects of teratogens:

Cigarette smoking: Depending how much a parent smokes will determine the increased the risk of miscarriage, stillbirth, low birth weight, premature birth, Sudden Infant Death Syndrome (SIDS), possible increase in developmental delays.

Antibiotics: Most antibiotics are safe to take during your pregnancy, but there are some exceptions. If this medication is used in the third trimester, there can be decreased foetal bone growth. This type of antibiotic also should not be used while breastfeeding.

Antidepressants: Antidepressants intake can possibly include mild to moderate but temporary withdrawal symptoms at birth or premature delivery. However, the benefits to the mother using antidepressants may outweigh the risks to the infant.

Cocaine: Using cocaine during pregnancy can increase the risk not only of miscarriage but can also lead to premature detachment of the placenta, a low-birth-weight infant, brain damage, small head, limb abnormalities, gastro-urinary abnormalities, heart defects, and infant withdrawal (www.ttis.unt.edu).

Alcohol: The ethanol (alcohol) in pregnancy readily crosses the placenta and peak foetal blood levels to that of the mother. The elimination capacity of the foetus is low in early pregnancy and therefore the ethanol remains trapped in the amniotic fluid leading to reabsorption and exposure time affecting development (Nava-Ocampo et al., 2004). A range of effects occur, and significant prenatal alcohol exposure can lead to foetal alcohol spectrum. Alcohol can act as a teratogen beyond the first three months of pregnancy in varying forms. However, for many women pregnancies in the first three months is often unknown and messages around alcohol intake remain inconsistent. This vague approach contributes to the continuation of teratogen use and further education required (NHS, 2018).

Screening tests: ultrasounds and blood tests

During pregnancy interventions two or more ultrasounds to monitor growth and development is undertaken with information printed, mapping progress and any potential concerns the primary care team may have. The details are factual, and copies are given to parents. The questions associated with this may be challenging if presented to a practitioner for advice concerning the numbers and detail of the information given. Practitioners are encouraged to liaise with the midwife but everyday advice around smoking, diet, healthy eating and general support with parents is encouraged and welcomed in promoting a healthy and informed pregnancy.

The information a parent receives will include details of the growth during the gestational period:

- Maternal age, weight, height, BMI, smoker

Details about the foetus during the gestational period:

- Gestational Age in number of weeks and days
- Fetal heart action present
- Crown to rump length
- Nuchal translucency
- Fetal anatomy: skull/brain, heart, spine, abdomen, bladder, hands, feet.

In later months further details will include:

- Head circumference, femur length, cord: vessels
- Presentation (position of foetus), amniotic fluid, placenta.
- Estimated risk of chromosomal abnormalities
- Diagnosis: this will be recorded as low/high risk with further action identified where relevant.

Screening test are both routinely given to all pregnant women to ascertain whether they or their infant has any problems whilst some are given to at risk groups. If a test is given and a risk for a condition is identified then a diagnostic test will follow to see if the condition is present or not. Blood tests can test for genetic inherited conditions, nuchal scans can identify excess nuchal fluid to determine the greater risk of down syndrome and anomaly scans at eighteen to twenty weeks can check growth and development. Testing is not compulsory and many parents may decide not to be screened for a variety of reasons. Additionally, screening results may not be conclusive and conditions are missed or masked by other health issues (Doubilet and Benson, 2008; Davis, 2005).

Miscarriage

There are several types of miscarriage in the first trimester, with the threatened miscarriage being bleeding during the first months of pregnancy. In many cases, the pregnancy will continue if the cervix remains closed. An inevitable miscarriage involves considerable bleeding and the cervix opening up. Sometimes no heart beat has been identified but a sac is present and in the early stages of pregnancy the possibilities could be abnormal chromosomes, infection or an underlying medical abnormality of the uterus or cervix. In reoccurring miscarriages there may be significant reasons but many women do eventually try again and have successful pregnancies.

The foetal stage, the remainder of the seven months, is a time when the systems and structures, significantly the nervous system, is growing, refining and strengthening. After twenty weeks, a still birth is diagnosed rather than a miscarriage. Labour generally proceeds immediately and is allowed to occur naturally. Still births are often unexpected, resulting in great stress and anguish to parents, the memory returning in future pregnancies. The reasons, whilst not determined, can range from those living in impoverished circumstances, from abnormalities to the infant, higher risks if obese or at advanced age and women with no previous pregnancies (Macintyre, 2012). The complex development is why the medical profession classify twenty-eight weeks and after as the time frame in which infants develop and grow with minimal difficulties. Prior to this the nervous system and organs are less viable and associated difficulties can cause lifelong problem although with increasing sophisticated technology foetus are surviving from twenty-four weeks.

Questions for discussion

A record-breaking infant girl who was born at just twenty-one weeks and five days has spent Easter at home with her delighted parents after spending five months in neonatal care. Little Frieda was born on 7 November 2010, at Fulda Children's Hospital in Germany. She weighed just 1lb and measured 11 inches. Sadly, her twin brother Kilian died six weeks after birth due to heart and intestinal problems. Yvonne started to suffer from complications when she was just fifteen weeks pregnant. She was rushed to hospital at twenty weeks and two days after a doctor told her she was on the verge of going into labour during a routine check-up. Medics managed to delay the birth for a further 10 days, before placing the tiny brother and sister in intensive care. Yvonne said: 'Professor Repp us that his team would do everything for our children, but he could not promise anything.' Kilian died in December while Frieda's life hung by a thread before she eventually pulled through. 'Frieda was kept in a completely sterile environment, with her breathing assisted and fed through her navel,' Dr Repp told the *Bild* newspaper. He added that the medical staff at the hospital in Fulda were experienced at treating unusually premature infants.

(www.dailymail.co.uk/health/article-1380282/Earliest-surviving-premature-infant-goes-home-parents.html#ixzz55fG8lfN8)

The legal limit to terminate a pregnancy in England is currently during the first twenty-four weeks.

Can we and should we be discussing pro-choice and safe legal terminations with the increased survival rate for infants as separate areas for debate?

As a practitioner, professional and personal thoughts are often challenging – reflect on personal cultural and social frameworks and how these may be confirmed or tested when talking to parents.

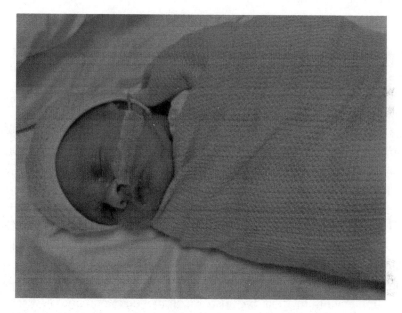

New-born infants may need care from prenatal conditions that have developed

Mental health

Oxytocin is considered the hormone of 'love and bonding' and pregnant women who had higher levels of oxytocin during pregnancy (from the first trimester) showed higher levels of bonding behaviour with their infant after birth (Feldman et al., 2007). However, pregnancy can also cause anxiety and stress and for many mothers and fathers and this can become overwhelming, reducing oxytocin dramatically. Levels of stress in pregnant women and chemical imbalances have been equally significant and shown to be associated with low birth weight and reduced gestational age (Rice et al., 2010). Whilst stress is arguably a subjective experience and the full mechanisms not fully understood, pathways have been identified. The best known is cortisol and serotonin exposure, prenatally. These influence the brain development and neuro cognitive functioning. From the extreme cases of domestic violence through to all incidences of violence and varying abuse can cause some pregnant women to develop negative representations of her developing an infant (DoH, 2009). Direct physical outcomes can result in miscarriage, low birth weight, placental abruption and pre-term delivery. Unplanned pregnancies or undesired pregnancies can also cause further stress and anxiety (Orr et al., 2008). This poses a need for increased prenatal care and support. Desired pregnancy can be sought via infertility treatment and this can have an impact on the parent's mental health beyond the success of the outcome.

Influences of development during the neonatal period

Insufficient 'healthy' diet in the last three months of pregnancy can potentially increase a poor immune system in the young infant and after birth more susceptible to infections and illnesses. Diabetes and pregnancy is generally Type Two where the body becomes resistant to insulin so that it cannot use it efficiently and is sometimes affected by pregnancy hormones. Urine is tested for glucose as there is an increased risk of miscarriage, pre-eclampsia and infection. Management of diet is therefore attended to and increased monitoring of growth and structural abnormalities monitored (www.patient.info/health/diet-and-lifestyle-during-pregnancy). The current advice in England is women should gain 25–35lb and in the first month only gain around 5lb. The weight gain in the last six months is the support of the growing foetus. Specific supplements to diets are also recommended for optimal development including calcium intake for bones and teeth, zinc, known to support development, reducing skin conditions such as eczema and associated specific learning difficulties. Folic acid is also recommended as a supplement in reducing neural tube defect during the early months.

The age of the mother

Today many women delay pregnancy for a variety of reasons and from a development perspective this can have implications.

Practitioner's perspective

Sally was thirty-three years old when she discovered she had blocked fallopian tubes and additional complications though referrals to specialists after trying for two years unsuccessfully to get pregnant. She was advised to have In vitro fertilisation (IVF). This a process whereby medication was received to stimulate the ovaries and to produce more eggs. She was to inject herself with drugs and be closely monitored for a month. Then when the time came she went under sedation to have her eggs removed by ultra sound. These were then mixed with her partners sperm and wait to see how many would fertilize. She was fortunate to have six fertilize initially although only four continued over the next day to divide further. Two were implanted through a simple procedure of injecting back into Sally and she had the option to freeze the other two if she wanted to have any further children. Pessaries were continued to be used daily to support the hormone balance and after a few weeks Sally found out she was pregnant, one of the embryos had implanted and grown. This was Sally's second round of treatment.

Sally shared her story with a childminder when she was seeking support two years later. She continued to be emotional effected by the conception procedure and was anxious she was doing the right thing, almost compulsively. Whilst the child minder wasn't a counsellor and did not pretend to be one, she listened and created an emotionally holding environment for Sally to grow in confidence, share her experiences and manage her feelings towards separating form her infant (Bion, 1992).

Infertility treatment

Infertility is medically defined as the inability to create a viable embryo after a minimum of one year of intercourse without contraception (Clark, 2009), and is often considered the period when referred to a specialist. Both men and women may be independently infertile with a small percentage being infertile together (Clark, 2009). Social support, specifically a positive marital relationship, modifies the psychological distress both during treatment and following failure of infertility treatment (Gibson and Myers, 2002, cited in Kopala, 2003).

Male infertility

- Low sperm count
- Physical defect affecting transport of sperm
- Genetic disorder
- Exposure to work environment substances
- Alcohol, caffeine and drug intake
- Advancing age.

Female infertility

- Vaginal structural problems
- Abnormal absence of ovulation
- Blocked or scarred fallopian tubes
- Uterine lining unfavourable to implantation
- Obesity
- Alcohol.

Fertility treatment is given medically with supporting education about changing lifestyle circumstances and choices to maximise success (Macintyre, 2012). Whilst fertility can affect any women and men irrespective of age the reduction of eggs reduces in time and therefor women are increasingly reducing their chances of pregnancy as they age.

Research has suggested the optimum age for child bearing is early twenties and pregnant women over thirty-five can have potentially increased complications during pregnancy, including miscarriage even if prenatal care is good. However, as we know many women are delaying pregnancy and poor prenatal care remains the predominant reason for complications than the age of the mother. However, some genetic compositions change with time and influence the embryo such as Down's syndrome. This is often, although not always associated with older mothers because the likelihood of the infants receiving an extra chromosome increases with age. There remain prenatal tests for syndromes during the first trimester and the increased use of ultrasound has created a discourse regarding the ethical consideration of decision-making regarding pregnancy and quality of life. Contemporary thinking views infants with varying syndromes from a social rather than medical model. With the right support all individuals, irrespective of needs, can lead fulfilling and rewarding lives with support from agencies (mencap.org.uk) or (www.mencap/downsyndrome.org.uk). Therefore, receiving genetic knowledge during pregnancy does not imply or result in the termination of a pregnancy. Whilst advanced age may increase medical concerns, young mothers are not precluded from concern. Adolescents becoming pregnant may also be a cause for concern with the associated lifestyle choices and the mental state of becoming pregnant. Stress can develop into lasting mental health issues and can cause heath and psychological issues for the mother and her growing foetus. Whilst publicly funded family services exist and contraception is offered, sex education continues to be targeted and support to those who continue to find themselves pregnant (www.nhs.uk/conditions/pregnancy-and-infant/teenager-pregnant).

Within contemporary society, attention has been directed towards pregnant women in the prenatal period, as a vessel protecting the health of the foetus, arguably perceived as having more importance than the woman herself (Lupton, 2012). Appropriate mother health behaviours include a healthy weight, not smoking or drinking alcohol and avoiding foods associated with increased risks to the foetus is targeted and women are expected to modify behaviours their accordingly (HSCIC, 2012). However, these representations often fail to acknowledge the lived reality of life (Hanley, 2007), and, as Wenham (2015) argues, pregnancy, particularly for young parents residing in marginalised areas, and those on low income can be characterised by vulnerability, uncertainty and a 'fragile' self-identity. Healthy behaviours may be reinforced by family members and friends, who strengthen the discourses of inadequate mothering. Subsequently, rather than modifying behaviours, vulnerable mothers may continue behaviours with a sense of guilt or denial and furthermore stop attending appointments. A practitioner could be the vital link in regularly meeting mothers and supporting them in sharing their vulnerability and creating a dialogue about healthy behaviour and healthy choices. Practitioners, in their knowledge about healthy behaviours may encourage modifying habits and changes in a safe, encouraging and less authoritative way.

Questions for discussion

As a senior nursery nurse in a health centre one of my roles is to promote positive health and education. I have been assigned smoking as a topic to discuss with the parents. Currently there are a number of parents pregnant and with young children attending who have decided to take regular 'cigarette breaks' whilst at the toddler group. Rather than stopping their breaks I wanted to reflect how I could promote the message to reduce smoking and stop. I have decided to do a short questionnaire and talk to the ex-smokers and non-smokers to develop some ideas. I have had one mother approach me about referring her to a support group to stop too which I felt was a positive step and could model her behaviour and what she felt most helpful. Many stated stress was the reason for continuing to smoke.

What else could be done?

The delivery

In England there are a number of options available to the mother pending health factors and facilities. Hospital births remain common, particularly with first time mothers. However, within the ward differing forms of births may be available such as water births, supporting the pain during labour, private rooms that can be paid for if the parents feel they would like to be on their own. Home births are also an option, particularly for those considered straightforward pregnancies.

Whilst practitioners may not be directly involved in the birth process of the infant having knowledge about the birth can be very important in understanding the parent's behaviour and attitude towards their infant and themselves, the infant's possible temperament and the associated physical and mental health that can be evident up to the first two years. There are many 'stories' regarding the birth experience but essentially the experience is personally unique and whilst the procedure may follow a similar pattern the subjective experiences can range from self-empowering to helplessness. During a vaginal birth the contractions become more frequent and the infant begins to enter the birth canal. On occasion this is prolonged, and decisions are then made about inducing the infant, so medication is given to onset labour and throughout the time the infant and mother is monitored. The delivery is generally in three stages:

> *The first stage* is called the onset and is the time from the start of contractions until the cervix is dilated enough for the infant's head to pass through. This can be the longest stages lasting between twelve and nineteen hours and longer for a first infant.
>
> *The second stage* is the actual delivery of the infant, the stage when the mother can push to help her infant is born.
>
> *The third stage* is the delivery of the placenta or afterbirth and other materials from the uterus.

Assisted delivery is when forceps or ventouse instruments are used to aid the infant in being delivered. These can only be used in stage two of labour and if the infant needs to come out before then a caesarean section is advised. In both cases, the delivery can be traumatic for both the infant and mother and the infant may be showing signs of distress, so a paediatrician is in the room in case of resuscitation. A caesarean section may be elective, emergency or crash with the operation taking about an hour in total. The infant takes about ten minutes to be delivered from the first incision and the stitching of the mother normally takes a further forty minutes whilst the muscle fat and skin are stitched back together. The after care is the most significant aspect of a C-Section as the mother's body needs time to repair and approximately eight weeks to heal. If the operation was planned, (elective) there is some time to forward plan but for an emergency and crash the decision is made so as not to compromise the infants and mother's health significantly. For many families, the experience of labour, whilst exhausting, is a major life event with a positive outcome and sense of achievement. However, with medical interventions and less than optimum outcomes the experience can leave lifelong psychological scars long after the physical ones have faded. Many women find the experience disturbing and the lack of control can impinge on their bonding experience with their new-born. Today birth trauma and the experience of the birth process is more readily discussed as contributing to relationships, health concerns, additional needs than previously considered. The fourth trimester is discussed in the next chapter.

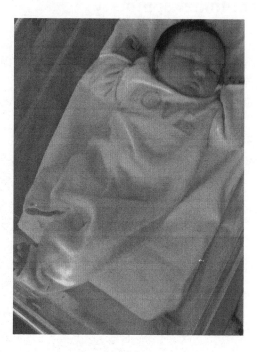

Birth

Practitioner's perspective

At three years of age a little girl in our care was diagnosed with mild cerebral palsy. She had weak muscle on her left side and walking, picking up objects was challenging. Had I known about the traumatic birth experience I may have been able to make some earlier connections. However, her mother did not acknowledge any delay and it took another year for her to open up about her experience of a healthy pregnancy but traumatic birth experience. I think she was still dealing with it.

On our course we study childbirth but as a practitioner it would be helpful to learn about pregnancy more and the birth experience. Knowing their story and understanding the birth experience helps to understand the parents' perspective and the reasons for their choices. Whilst we look after infants from a very young age we continue to be less open about certain areas related to pregnancy and birth. We aren't midwives but more open dialogues would be helpful in creating positive relationships.

Family practitioner summary

Understanding about pregnancy and pregnancy related conditions is really important to me as I work with infants who have additional needs. The understanding of pregnancy helps me appreciate the challenges and how important development from conception and no birth.

Focused Points

- Reflect on the changing female body in preparation to pregnancy
- The genetically determined features of growth and development
- The environmental factors that affect growth and development
- Parental perspectives during this period and support that practitioners could offer

Concluding thoughts

The psychological life begins well before the physical birth of the infant, with the foetus being an active being, responding to its environment and learning from it.

Therefore, the biological health of the mother and her capacity to process emotions can affect the developing foetus, with stress hormones and substances entering the placenta. This chapter is weighted towards the biological development of the unborn infant and how as practitioners we engage with this information. This chapter is not intended to provide midwifery or birth specialist knowledge but rather critically to engage with some key issues around parents' choices for their unborn infant, health choices they make and support that could be provided. In the next chapter, the care of the infant from conception will be discussed.

Bibliography

Bernard, A., Carbonelle, S., Dumont, X. and Nickmilder, M. (2007) 'Infant swimming practice, pulmonary epithelium integrity and the risk of allergic and respiratory disease later in life'. *Paediatrics* 119(6): 1095–1103.

Bion, W. (1992) *Experiences in Groups.* London: Routledge.

Bremner, G. and Fogel, A. (2009) *Infant Development.* Oxford: Blackwell Publishing.

Bronfenbrenner, U. (1979) *The Ecology of Human Development.* Cambridge, MA: Harvard University Press.

Brown, A. (2016) *Breastfeeding Uncovered: Who Really Decides How We Feed Our Babies?* London: Pinter and Martin.

Buss, D. (2009) 'An evolutionary formulation of person–situation interactions'. *Journal of Research in Personality* 43(2): 241–242.

Carter, C. (2000) available online at https://onlinelibrary.wiley.com/doi/abs/10.1111/j.1469-8749.1974.tb03442.x

Carter, C., Pournajafi-Nuzarloo, H. and Kramer, K. (2007) 'Oxytocin: behavioural associations and potential as a salivary biomarker'. *Academic Science* 1098: 312–322.

Chamberlain, D. (2000) 'Prenatal body language: A new perspective on ourselves'. *International Journal of Perinatal Psychology and Medicine* 12(4): 551–555.

Clark, D. (2009) 'Should Anti-TNF- Therapy be Offered to Patients with Infertility and Recurrent Spontaneous Abortion?' *Critical Public Health* 22(3): 329–340. Available online at https://onlinelibrary.wiley.com/doi/abs/10.1111/j.1600-0897.2008.00680.x

Davis, K. (2005) *Practical Parenting. Your Pregnancy Week by Week.* London: Hamlyn Health.

DoH (2009) Available online at www.gov.uk/publication

Doubilet, P. and Benson, C. (2008) *Your Developing Baby.* New York: McGraw Hill.

Feldman, R., Weller, A., Zagoory-Sharon, O. and Levine, A. (2007). 'Evidence for a neuroendocrinological foundation of human affiliation: plasma oxytocin levels across pregnancy and the postpartum period predict mother-infant bonding'. *Psychological Science Journal* 18: 965–970.

Hanley, L. (2007) 'Estates: An intimate history, London'. In Hoddinott, G., Craig, P. and Britten, J. (2012) A serial qualitative interview study of infant feeding.

experiences: Idealism meets realism, *BMJ Open*, 2(2).

HSCIC (Health and Social Care Information Centre) (2012) Infant Feeding Survey (2010). Available online at http://doc.ukdataservice.ac.uk/doc/7281/mrdoc/pdf/7281_ifs-uk-2010_report. Pdf

Kopala, M. (2003) *Handbook of Counselling Women.* London: Sage.

Lupton, D. (2012) '"Precious cargo": Foetal subjects, risk and reproductive citizenship'. *Critical Public Health* 22(3): 329–340.

Macintyre, C. (2012) *Understanding Babies and Young Children from Conception to Three. A Guide for Students, Practitioners and Parents.* London: Routledge.

Mencap (2018) *Down's Syndrome.* Available online at www.mencap.org.uk

Moberg, K. (2003) *The Oxytocin Factor.* US: DaCapo Press.

Music, G. (2016) *Nurturing Natures: Attachment and Children's Emotional, Socio-cultural and Brain Development.* Hove and New York: Psychology Press.

National Childbirth Trust (2017) Good exercises and sports in pregnancy. Available online at www.nct.org.uk/pregnancy/good-exercises-sports-pregnancy

Nava-Ocampo, A., Velázquez-Armenta, Y., Brien, J. and Koren, G. (2004) 'Elimination kinetics of ethanol in pregnant women'. *Reprod Toxicol.* 18(4): 613–617. Available online at www.ncbi.nlm.nih.gov/pubmed/15135856

Netmums, (2010) A Growing Problem – Does weight matter in pregnancy? Available online at www.netmums.com/assets/images/2012/A_Growing_Problem_Nov2010.pdf

NHS (2018) Available online at www.nhs.uk/conditions/genetics/

Orr, S., James, S. and Reiter, J. (2008) Unintended Pregnancy and Prenatal Behaviors Among Urban, Black Women in Baltimore, Maryland: The Baltimore Preterm Birth Study. Available online at www.sciencedirect.com/science/article/pii/S1047279708000604

Rice, F, Harold, G., Boivin, J., Bree, M., Hay, D. and Thapar, A. (2010) 'The links between prenatal stress and offspring development and psychopathology: disentangling environmental and inherited influences'. *Psychol Med.* 40(2): 335–345. DOI:10.1017/S0033291709005911

Royal College of Obstetricians and Gynaecologists, 2006. Exercise in pregnancy. Available online at www.rcog.org.uk/en/guidelines-research-services/guidelines/exercise-in-pregnancy-statement-no.4/

Wenham, A. (2015) '"I know I'm a good mum – no one can tell me different" – Young experiences: Idealism meets realism, mothers negotiating a stigmatised identity through time, families, relationships and societies'. *Societies Journal* 5(1): 127–144.

4 Perinatal care

Introduction and context

On the arrival of an infant many parents get quizzed about their transition. For many new parents the main questions by friends and strangers were:

- What is the sex of your infant?
- How big are they and how much did she weigh?
- They look just like . . .
- Are they good, easy well behaved?
- Do they sleep ok?

(Brown, 2018)

This chapter will be framed around the period when the infant is born from the comfort of the womb to the transition and reality of the external world, during the first few weeks, more commonly known as the perinatal period. This includes the twentieth to twenty-eighth week of gestation ending around the sixth week after birth. The focus will be on the post delivery period though so will be considered as the *fourth trimester*. The chapter will include a healthcare lens of the infant and include ways the growth of the infant is measured alongside patterns of crying, sleeping and feeding during this period. The aim of the chapter is to consider the significance of this period and the health care associations and surveillance, so practitioners not only understand how growth and development is measured and attended to but also reflect on their role, whether working closely with parents, as joint carer or an advisory role. An understanding of how development and care is monitored can also aid practitioners in early childhood education and care settings to learn more about individual stories, creating not just a care pedagogy but also a relational pedagogical, drawing on past events to inform present. The perinatal period is often a time where parents receive advise and information whilst in the process of establishing relationships with their new-born infant. The care encircled around their development is discussed within this chapter to enable practitioners gain an understanding of the processes and the ways the connectedness between the parenting and new-born life is a continuation of life in-utero in the external world. By referring the period as the fourth trimester it is emphasising infants' continual dependence with their parents rather than birth being perceived as a transition of physical and emotional separation. Familiarity during this period enables practitioners an understanding of the infant within the family context. It also reveals patterns of behaviour associated with care needs during this stage. If meeting a parent and infant in ECEC settings when the infant is beyond six months an understanding of the in-between space that connects the past to present, the perinatal period to the current context practitioners can critically reflect on individualised family and infant behaviours and care pedagogies.

Measuring the healthy development of infants at birth

In England, new-born infants are observed at birth to ascertain their wellbeing and identify any immediate interventions necessary. Paediatricians use the Apgar scoring to observe competences. The Apgar score is determined by evaluating the new-born infant on five simple criteria on a scale from zero to two, then summing up the five values thus obtained (Apgar, 1953). The resulting Apgar score ranges from zero to ten. The five criteria are: Appearance, Pulse, Grimace, Activity, Respiration (APGAR). Infants are usually given a score and assessed again ten minutes later. This is helpful because if any birth trauma has occurred but then subsided it will be noted. Scores between seven and ten are considered satisfactory. If, for example the infant is continuing to grimace, and breathing is associated with a grunt, then the score would potentially be low. If this continues and the grunts do not subside interventions may take place, such as taking the infant to a neonatal intensive care unit (NICU) for monitoring and specialist breathing support. This does not necessarily mean there will be long term breathing problems, rather an initial and immediate care plan in ensuring the health of the infant is attended to following birth. Therefore, the assessments may indicate problems with more tests to find out if there is an underlying cause (Finster and Wood, 2005).

Neonatal screening

The following are normally carried soon after birth for all infants:

- Guthrie test: detects the rare inherited disorder of phenyltenioa which can cause health and learning issues

- Congenital dislocation of the hips: if perhaps a breech birth and large a infant may have dislocated their hip during birth and therefore the thigh bone is not placed in the socket, resulting in growth impairment if left untreated. to support with the use of brace to support the development of the hips

- The thyroid stimulating hormone test: if the thyroid gland is not working properly then growth and development may be impaired

- Further immunisations are then carried out as the infant grows and these are administered by the health visitor. Advice and support are given so the parents are informed and understand why they are administered.

(Dare and O'Donovan, 2009)

Practitioner's perspective

I am a Senior nursery nurse with a degree, working towards in a health surgery supporting health visitors. Yesterday I was weighing a new born infant and talking to a parent. She told me her cousin had a two-year-old and was not being immunised as the mum did not agree with them. She said her cousin had been hesitant at first but after the first set of immunisations felt her infant was very distressed and ill afterwards. I reassured her that the jabs were done as swiftly as possible to minimise distress and the health of the infant was in the best interest of everyone. I also encouraged her to read the literature and the effects. She said she had investigated giving combined immunisations separately, but they had to be paid for and was quite confusing to know what to do. Again, I advised her to talk to the health visitor. I didn't want to tell her what to do but knew I should encourage immunisations. I then wondered if she had a cousin or was asking for herself.

I decided to speak to the health visitor, for further support but it made me reflect on:

My own thoughts about interventions
My role as a health professional advising

As a practitioner I feel comfortable giving objective advice recommended but if I was a parent would this influence how I advocate practice and delivered health messages that contradicted parents' ideas?

The balance between understanding and judging parents of new-born infants and the choices they make when they themselves are perhaps feeling vulnerable and anxious.

Initial examination

Most of the post examination is to confirm what has already been noted or observed during the ultra sound scans prior to birth. However, on occasion an ultra sound may not have been carried out or omitted a minor medical condition. Depending the severity, the parents are prepared prior to birth and supported where necessary. On the arrival of the infant the paediatrician as part of her role carries out the following check of the infants that have been delivered under their care. The hearts and lungs are examined, and the head is measured. The head is also examined for their anterior fontanelle, a diamond shaped soft spot on their head, which closes with the skull at around twelve to eighteen months. There can be an infection or pressure around the brain If a bulge is observed on the fontanelle. The eyes are examined although tears do not appear until the third or fourth week and colour of eyes established by six weeks.

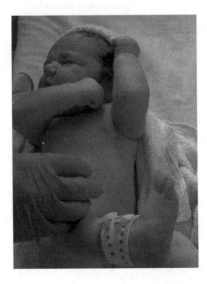

Observing and checking at birth

The position of the ears is observed and holes within the roof of the mouth for cleft palates or tongue ties. The umbilical cord is also observed and for the next few days to be checked again in case of infection as it withers away, leaving a scar, the naval. Genitalia is observed for abnormalities and the back is checked for spine development (Dare and O'Donovan, 2009).

Questions for discussion

During my thirty-week scan having twins it was noted that one of my girls had developed a lump in her kidney. They could not tell if it was next to it or on her kidney, but she still seemed to be passing urine normally. When she was delivered she was sent to NICU for a few days and then scanned again for her lump. They said it was a cyst and needed monitoring, but all looked ok. I am glad I had known about the cyst before giving birth as I felt a bit helpless as she was taken away for an afternoon to be scanned. A care plan and referral were already made, and I felt reassured she was being monitored and followed up rather than just left I now have to pass the information to anyone who looks after her and to alert me if they think she has a urine infection. The practitioners do not actually need to do anything just be aware.

As a practitioner where would you record this information?

How would you know when an infant has a urine infection, especially a non-verbal infant?

Do you think it was helpful for the mum to know prior to birth and how do you think she felt when her infant went into NICU at birth?

Appearance of the new-born infant

The infant will be wet from the amniotic fluid and bloodied from the birth canal. The head is large in proportion to the body and possibly a strange shape due to the way the delivery was carried out. Infants can look skinny and shrivelled or wrinkled and plump and is dependent on many things, genetic and environmental. The vernix from in-utero is still present on the skin and is found in the folds of the skin, as a creamy white substance. Lanugo, a downy hair is also present on infants. The new-born may have a full head of hair or no hair at all, again this can be determined by their genetic make-up.

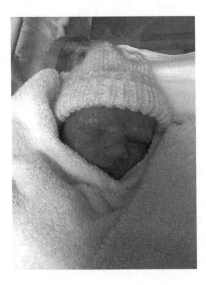

Vernix on the face: the creamy substance covering the infant is not washed immediately to discourage a sore face

Examination of the nervous system: reflexes

The infant's reflex response indicates the heath of the nervous system. They are visible in utero and postnatally and functional in early life. Stimulus reflexes are regulated from the sub cortex of the brain – the most primitive part Infants at birth have reflexes as their sole physical ability, supporting the infant's learning to perform specific functions and are involuntary. They die away completely or are modified into voluntary actions (grasping) as the infant grows and develops. Reflexes provide the child with their 'earliest vocabulary of movement' (Goddard Blythe, 2005). A reflex is 'an involuntary muscular response to a sensory experience'.

Tonic Neck Reflex: This is also called the fencing reflex, because of the position the infant assumes. When you lay your infant on her back and her head turns to one side she will extend her arm and leg on that side while the opposite arm and leg bend, assuming a 'fencing' position. This reflex is present only until about the fourth month.

Rooting Reflex: Infants turn their head toward anything that brushes their faces. This survival reflex helps them to find food such as a nipple. When an object is near a healthy infant's lips, the infant will begin sucking immediately. This reflex also helps the child get food. This reflex usually disappears by three weeks of age.

Gripping Reflex: Infants grasp anything that is placed in their palm and most can potentially support their entire weight in their grip.

Twins grasping each other's hands at three weeks old – reflexes can become intentional movements

Toe Curling Reflex: When the inner sole of a infant's foot is stroked, the infant will respond by curling toes. When the outer sole is stroked the infant will respond by spreading out their toes.

Stepping Reflex: When held upright with feet placed on a surface, will lift legs as if marching or stepping.

Sucking Reflex: The sucking reflex is initiated when something touches the roof of an infant's mouth. A premature infant may have delayed sucking reflux or just get tired of sucking prior to having enough milk. Aids such as feeding tubes or spoon feeds are given to infants requiring extra help such as twins, being born early.

Questions for discussion

Listening to a parent's perspective

I spent many days talking to the nursery nurse and midwife about feeding when my infant was born and given a feeding tube. We were encouraged to change the tube and insert the tube ourselves and feed the infants through the tube. I found this very stressful and could not bring myself to take the lead with it. In front of me was this tiny person and I was having to feed her in a very alien way. Some of the other mothers seemed very pragmatic about it but I really struggled. Together with the nurse I was able to hold my infant while she helped with the feeding. She was calm and encouraging and I felt I could be honest in telling her about my anxieties of not wanting to even try to do it. She didn't

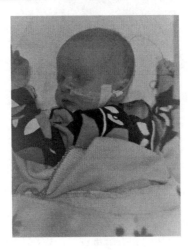

force me and was patient and kind listening to my worries. I was in the ward for a month and never did manage to do it!

How is this information helpful in your role as a practitioner in a care position?

What implications may this have on the mother and infant relationship in the forthcoming years?

Startle/Moro Reflex: Infants will respond to sudden sounds or movements by throwing their arms and legs out and throwing their heads back. Most infants will usually cry when startled and proceed to pull their limbs back into their bodies.

(MacGregor, 2008; Doubilet and Benson, 2008)

The presence of reflexes at birth is an indication of normal brain and nerve development, as the image shows with the twins modifying and disappearing as they develop. If reflexes are not present at birth or continue to be observed past the time they should disappear, brain or nerve damage is potentially indicated, and further screening, testing and observations carried out to determine the rationale.

Understanding the new-born infant: a caring approach

Infants although completely dependent on their carer are not helpless beings but active agents with many abilities and with a conscious approach to caring can be supported, not just in their overall wellbeing but in their emotional, physical and cognitive functioning. Gopnik (2016) argues that the search for the correct techniques in rearing and caring for an infant is pointless. She explained that the relationship is far more complex than a set of consciously manipulated variables as childcare experts insist. Secure attachment is the consistent and availability of carers. They are attuned to their infant's emotions at least some of the time and infant's ability to withstand the absence of the parent during small periods of time, increasing gradually as they grow (Brink, 2013). In providing a secure, consistent and stable environment an infant will gain independence and a sense of themselves in their surroundings. However, in today's fast paced and technological culture of work and leisure schedules the same strategies and approaches have been applied to childrearing. In a bid to find the formula with maximum results and further proof of success, publications of popular childrearing books have increased considerably, irrespective of their contradictory or complimentary approaches to academic and peer reviewed practice research. Harries and Brown (2017) studied 354 new mothers' use of infant training books and found the more parents read the more they displayed depressive symptoms and lower self-confidence. There was a space between the expectations and reality of caring for a new-born infant. Stalden (2018) concluded that parents reading and applying textbook childcare found caring for their new-born an apathetic and boring experience (www.naomistadlen.com/psychotherapy/). The focus on rules rather than getting to know their infant as an individual created a detachment from the care, resulting in a procedural and mechanical approach when meeting their infant's demands. As a tutor, I asked professional practitioners to evaluate mainstream parenting books available. In their evaluations they, too, felt many books were patronising, leading, idealistic and in the extreme de-humanised the infant, advising restriction and time bound affection when the parent demanded it rather than the infant. Whilst guidance and education are valuable and informative it should be balanced with developing a unique and personalised relationship between the infant and their parent, the primary carers.

The fourth trimester

In the first few weeks, known as the fourth trimester, there continues to be a focus around preparing for the next few months, whether it be childcare arrangements, organizing the household or trying to regain the life pre-infant. Whilst I am not advocating a technique-free approach, there needs to be more emphasis on the welcoming time in making connections and allowing the infant to lead the relationship and a continuation from life in the womb (Liedloff, 1986). In spending time nurturing the relationship, the rhythm of daily patterns tends to evolve and emphasise of a one size fit all is shifted to what works well in the current circumstances. Pikler's (1960) vision for a healthy infant was an active, competent and peaceful infant, who lives in peace with himself and his environment. Communicating with the parents she promoted infant development, based on parent's view of the child and her own observations, providing supportive guidance to parents about upbringing practices and how to create an optimal facilitating environment for their infant. The approach is based on a respectful relationship between an adult and infant, through tender care moments, a naturally paced motor development, free movement and uninterrupted play. Through intuitive parenting social interaction occurs from birth and contact as infants are fed and stroked so physical needs they are attending to close emotional engagement and creating a conversational setting through face to face contact.

Understanding the new-born: caring for individual differences

Infants do not arrive exactly on their due date and there is a window of time approximately between thirty-eight to forty-two weeks when the delivery date according to the health guidelines (Doubilet and Benson, 2008). However, for some infants they may be born before or after these weeks and these infants are increasingly vulnerable to heath and development risks:

- Pre-term: before 37 weeks.
- Post-term infant: after 42 weeks

A high proportion of mothers and fathers develop an attachment to the infant during the third trimester of pregnancy but when an infant is premature, the parents may not have had the same opportunity. Giving birth to an infant with a medical condition, having needs can disrupt the bonding experience. Medical interventions and challenges to everyday care can cause anxiety among parents and grieve for the infant they may have desired to the reality before them (Tassoni, 2016). Mortality rates be higher for an infant born with special needs ad this may inhibit some parents from risking attachment. Regularly visiting the infant in NICU is also influenced by the geographical distance and the number of other children in the home and can be challenging in building a bond (Latva et al., 2007). The challenges of bonding may have a larger long-term impact on the infant greater than that of their medical condition (Wigert et al., 2006). The studies, therefore, highlight the importance of enhancing positive relationships and physical touch between parents and their infants from the beginning, even in NICU environments, where traditionally care has been centred around a medical model.

Practitioner's perspective

Working in a small nursery I grew close to the families and their children. I remember one family where the mother had become pregnant and during a scan they had diagnosed a heart defect. A major operation was booked once the baby had been delivered and the prognosis was concerning. I spoke to the mother and father about this and they were glad to have been given the information and were still trying to be optimistic and visualise their baby. On arrival the parents were mentally and physically prepared, as best they could, for the medical interventions and separation of their daughter. As a practitioner I tried to remain open and available for them to chat to me. It was a challenging time and made me think about the value of bonding prior to birth, and the physical and mental bonding time of 'being in the moment' making the most of the present rather than in constant preparation of the future.

The value of touch

In 1948, Halliday (cited in Hayward, 2009) in made the link between mortality in infants and touch, noting how infants deprived of maternal bodily contact were more inclined to lose appetite and would waste away resulting in death. Subsequently, volunteers were encouraged to attend children's hospitals and provide fretful and vulnerable infants with regular caresses, handling and rocking them. This resulted were dramatic and led to a steady declined in mortality rates. The importance of touch goes further back in history and infant's death in foundling hospitals and institutions were almost 100%. The primary concern was the influence of professionals advocating a strict regime of not picking up the infant, feeding to the clock and focusing on physical health being. However, there remained a concern that whilst clinical sterilized environments were perceived as high-quality infant mortality remained high. By the mid-twentieth century it was apparent that infants in the poorest homes, with a 'good mother' despite the lack of hygiene physical conditions had a good chance of flourishing and developing. The warmth of the mothering approaches with their infants in being carried, cooed to and the sensory experience of the skin yielded positive results. Klaus, Kennell and Klaus (1995) considered the maternal sensitive period as the time shortly after birth as important for bonding to occur and this is not unique just to the mother but also to other family members too. Therefore, contemporary practices such as kangaroo care, the early touch practice named because it resembles how kangaroos care for their young (Christensson, 1998). The skin-to-skin contact with parent or sibling is as valuable as it ever was and contradicts the often hands-off approach that for so many years was advocated in a bid to ensure health care was optimum. We now know touch and handling is important even and especially when those infant's new-borns are attached to machinery and have tubes inserted for their physical survival. Kangaroo care comforts and soothes infants particularly preterm infants (Field, 2014). The infants are warm, they have regular heart rates, respiration. They sleep more deeply and cry less. For the carers the skin to skin encourages breast feeding and bonding with their new-born (DiMenna, 2006; Stern, 1997).

The value of touch

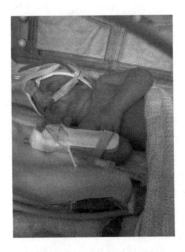

An infant in Neonatal Intensive care unit (NICU) can vary in size and age pending the health concern. Irrespectively the medical 'interventions' can suggest a hands-off approach in fear of causing more harm.

Practitioner's perspective

A mother's perspective in connecting practice

My son was in NICU for a few weeks as he was premature. When I saw him in the incubator I was quite frightened and thought if I cuddled him I may pull one of his tubes or knock something. With gentle reassurance by the practitioner I was able to sit carefully in a chair and hold him on me for a few hours. The nursery nurse practitioner on the ward gently unclipped the tubes and passed him to me. She responded to questions and helped but then moved away and allowed me the time to hold my son. I will never forget the feeling of happiness, watching him in my trembling hands. It definitely helped me bond with him and I felt more confident to care for him when we got home a few weeks later. The practitioners were supportive, and I was visited by nurses and those specialised in infant care about how things were going.

The use of skin-to-skin holding as a means to secure parents' attachment to their infant and support their child's rest and recovery in the neonatal intensive care unit, has therefore been recognized historically and supported by research. The importance of sleep to the infant's developmental outcome was recognized and the use of skin-to-skin holding as a means of increasing stable infant sleep and rest was implemented.

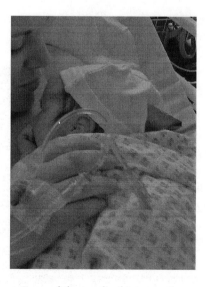

Beyond the medical intervention

Understanding maternal mental health

Pregnancy and the postnatal period have been defined as being key periods in terms of the opportunity that they provide to equalise the life-chances of all children. The vulnerable mother-to-be and the post-partum woman can impact on her capacity for parenting, with long-term consequences for their infant. This is due primarily to the fact that pregnancy and the postnatal period are sensitive developmental periods. These are biological time frames during which the impact of experiences on the brain of the foetus and infant are particularly strong, and when certain types of experience need to be present to ensure optimal development. The wellbeing of infants is often viewed within the context of family life although for a significant minority the family context is missing (Leach, 2018; NSPCC, 2013). For these vulnerable family's interventions and care interventions prior to birth, during and after are required, promoting quality of experience that can have a longer-term impact on mother child relationships. Birth traumatised mothers often feel rejecting of their infants and the relationship can be tense and struggle in their recovery (Music, 2016). Although a traumatic start can be overcome, and the infant mental state alleviated it there is no doubt that a good start provides the optimum conditions for a better emotional beginning with equal capacity to bond. When mothers feel emotionally safe and cared for risks are reduced in postnatal negative emotional states. On occasion physiological conditions may cause complications but generally if the psychological and social support is available then the biological complications are reduced, and preparation for birth is met so both parent and infant can experience the process as positively as possible. The release of oxytocin during labour enhances the bonding experience, immune responses and protects against physical pain (Moberg, 2003). In a successful birthing experience greater doses of oxytocin are produced when mothers feel supported and cared for (Music, 2016). It is a biologically "sensitive period" between mother and baby when they are both able to recognise and bond with each other (Klaus et al., 1989). Odent (2001) states this can be challenging in caesarean operations, when a woman's 'love hormones' are reduced resulting in a number of psychological consequences for mother and child. These may include lower childbirth satisfaction, more concern about the condition of the child and maternal depression. There is an expectation of happiness when a mother gives birth to her infant, with the father being as smitten with his new offspring. However, the reality is pregnancy and a new infant can bring excessive demands of both parents. It is a transition that can be emotionally challenging, requiring significant adjustment to lifestyles and relationships (Rees, 2017). Women may develop a mental illness during pregnancy or within the first year after giving birth. Examples of these illnesses include antenatal and postnatal depression, obsessive compulsive disorder, post-traumatic stress disorder (PTSD) and postpartum psychosis. Many studies have focused on the postnatal phase, however, mental health problems often arise during pregnancy. All these problems require attention, and these conditions often develop suddenly and range from mild to extremely severe, requiring different kinds of care or treatment, from medical intervention to support in minimising the dripping tap of emotional mishandling and neglect in caring for their infant (Bauer, 2014). As pregnancy progresses, women begin to develop what is described as 'maternal representations' of their unborn infant. This refers to the mental images or thoughts about her unborn infant and what they will be like. Parents with rich mental representations are more likely to have infants who are securely attached at twelve months, while mothers who have disengaged or distorted representations of their infants are more susceptible to having infants who are insecurely attached or disorganised. For many parents with mental health their own vulnerability and refusal to think about their infant may be rooted in internalised issues from their own childhood, known as 'unresolved parenting'. These parents may be less able to parent their infant when they are born because the infants crying and distress triggers their own stress and painful memories of vulnerability and dependence, so they are unable to respond sufficiently to their infant. These parents are often unable to mentalise about the distress of their infant and make inaccurate assumptions about the reasons for such behaviours unable to bond or relate to her developing infant (Barlow, cited in Leach 2018: 53). The concept of 'ghosts in the nursery' was introduced by Frailberg (1975) providing a psychoanalytic approach in problematic impaired infant-mother relationships. It examines the process of trauma and how it can be transferred across the generations and repeated by the parent with their own child. This is based on the idea that parents enact with their infant 'scenes from their own unremembered, but still painfully influential early experiences of helplessness and fear'. Frailberg argues that parents who couldn't remember their childhood emotional feelings in particular memories of their childhood abuse were more likely to repeat the abuse with their own children.

Whilst the relationship between parent and infant affected by mental health can set the trajectory for a child's later life and development, by focusing and targeting support on the ante and post-natal period there is still opportunities for transformation. Drawing on the well evidenced studies around brain development including the neuro plasticity of the brain, early intervention in supporting at risk parents as a preventative model in reducing and eliminating later adverse childhood experiences. The transition to parenthood offers both risk and hope in child development and if families are supported holistically from the outset from pregnancy greater impacts on the physical and mental health of infant's well-being can be achieved. Since 2009, the policy and guidance document for health commissioners has been the Healthy Child Programme. The programme focuses on pregnancy and the first five years, providing a schedule of the standard for evidence-based prevention and early intervention programme for children and families. The guide is for commissioning agents within the NHS service and the integrated children's services. The Healthy Child Programme – Pregnancy and the First Five Years of Life (2016) provides an evidence-based programme of interventions aimed at optimising foetal and infant wellbeing by supporting expectant parents:

- universal services (aimed at everyone)
- universal plus services (for targeted groups)
- partnership plus services (aimed at high risk groups) levels of interventions.

Prevention is therefore the focus rather than redeeming established problems often associated with mental health. The priority at this stage is therefore concerned with looking at the problems within the relationships formed and established from conception, rather than just the child at a later stage.

Questions for discussion

How could the early years (family practitioner) complement the midwife/health visitor?

Develop and evaluate strategies to facilitate good practice.

If primary care during pregnancy and in the first few weeks of life is the job of the midwife what do you think is the role of the early years' family practitioner and care professional during infancy and infanthood?

In what contexts would practitioners be employed?

Monitoring health: measuring charts

When an infant is born they receive a record developmental book where the height, length and head circumference are measured and recorded on a chart. The head is measured for any growth concerns and the length and weight not only highlight any immediate issues but also any significant drops or increases as the infant grows. There are separate charts for boys and girls, as growth rates differ slightly between genders. The lines on a growth chart are called 'centile' lines and show the range of normal weights and heights – the charts have nine centile lines: the 0.4th, 2nd, 9th, 25th, 50th, 75th, 91st, 98th and 99.6th centiles. As an example, if your child's weight is on the 25th centile, it means that compared to 100 children of the same age and sex in order of weights, your child would probably be number 25; 75 children would be heavier than your child, and 24 would be lighter. The weights and length/ height of most children will lie between the 2nd and 91st centiles. There is also allowance for premature infants and recently twin centile charts have been implemented to give a true reading rather than calculating from the actual birth date and the expected birth date. Recording on the centile charts enables the possibility for early intervention to be implemented where necessary (www.rcpch.ac.uk/resources/growth-charts). Caution is therefore taken in the readings because other factors such as illness and change in feeds may contribute to the fluctuations and plateau of growth. Feeding choices are shared between professionals and parents because formula fed infants tend to gain more weight than breasts fed infants. Sleep patterns during growth changes may alter and communicative crying may be a vocalisation of illness, hunger or attention. The plotting of growth on the centile chart is therefore encouraged every few weeks to allow for growth change and short-term issues. The centile charts focus on the sustained pattern of growth and if growth continues to be slow or drops for a prolonged time then additional monitoring is advice and possible action taken. Practitioners are often asked about feeding, sleep and crying by parents, generally about issues that have arisen.

Feeding

Infant feeding takes many forms and whist it appears the alternatives are breastfeeding or bottle feeding within these approaches many more individualised styles are adopted and specialist equipment used. Breastmilk can be given to the infant in a number of ways including exclusive breastfeeding, mixed breastfeeding and continued breastfeeding, after an infant has turned one years of age. Exclusive breastfeeding is when the infant receives human milk directly from the breast, and the infant is not introduced to any solid or other liquids for the first six months of their life (Labbok and Krasovec, 1990). Mixed breastfeeding is when the infant, from six months, receives human milk from a bottle as well as being introduced to solid and other liquids such as water. Mixed feeding is also carried out by parents and this generally follows a pattern of breastfeeding an infant and then topping up with formula feed in a bid to satisfy the infants hunger. Premature infants may also be given breastmilk from a spoon if they are unable to suck as required from breast feeding. In the United Kingdom (UK) an infant feeding survey is conducted every five years to estimate the duration of breast feeding and other practices mothers adopt; and in 2010 figures displayed 81% of women initially start breastfeeding immediately after birth, however this immediately drops to 69% in one week and at six weeks it becomes 55%; then within the next six months only 34% of mothers are continuing to breastfeed their child (IFF Research, 2010). What was once universal has now become a life choice, deciding the option to be more self-beneficial and supporting existing lifestyles. Additionally, despite breast-feeding being considered a natural act, it still requires many mothers to learn and understand how to feed their infant in a way that stimulates milk and the infant successfully latching onto their breast. In the process of doing this some mothers find the time and challenges too difficult, coupled with the 'Best is Breast' approach that adds to the guilt and inadequacy if not achieved immediately. As a result, formula feeding has become a culturally convenient viable and reliable option (NHS, 2014; Healthy Start, 2014). Contemporary literature suggests the decision to breast or formula feed is entwined with numerous factors, including consumer marketing of formulas, and rather than advocating best is best feeding promotion should be focusing on normalising breastfeeding in a culture climate where the choices of bottle feeding are favoured. This includes the discourses around the milk value itself, the successes of breastfeeding and the attitude and flexibility of feeding within communities. Rather than bottle versus breast the discourses should be on feeding approaches and how much support parents are offered to breastfeed. For practitioners, support is therefore central and spaces and attitudes towards parents wanting to continue to breastfeed whist their infants attend ECEC settings should be welcomed.

Questions for discussion

Feeding

Infant feeding preferences and the reasons for parental choice continue to be culturally embedded and generationally bound. Grant et al. (2017) have explored mothers and grandmothers Inter-generational Views and Experiences of Breastfeeding using visual artefacts and narrative. They concluded that culturally mothers felt they were under surveillance by the public and their decisions were challenged whether bottle or breastfed. The use of artefacts alongside narrative provides a useful way of exploring parent's perspective and one that could be extended to practitioners.

As a practitioner caring for infants in a professional capacity photograph one image that depicts infant feeding. Do not photograph an infant or anything that personalises an individual. Share with colleagues. Were their images of the feeding area, the equipment used, the cleaning equipment . . .?

Could you repeat this exercise with the parents, asking them to bring in an object (artefact) that depicts their feelings of feeding or a similar caregiving act? Could you get them to share this with parents or yourself as a way to open up verbal discussions about shared care and feeding options?

Discuss parental choices of feeding in group/out of home care.

Discuss challenges of feeding information given and whether it contradicts or corresponds with health messages.

(Mannay, 2016)

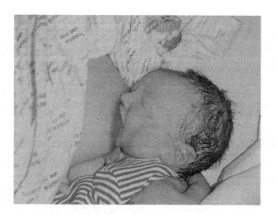 

Breastfeeding AND bottle feeding: support and sensitivity

Practitioner's perspective

I have been approached numerous times by a parent asking that her baby is given some rice to complement her milk at lunch. The baby is three months old. I explained the NHS guidelines of weaning at six months and she responded it was different in other countries and her own mother had suggested it. I provided her with relevant literature and support her in increasing feeding without introducing food and share her request with the health visitor. Formula or breast milk should only be given prior to six months and I have to ensure the message is clear even though it may contradict parents' choices and views on feeding.

Scenario 1: At nursery we now make up bottles of milk as needed and do not store anything. There are ready made cartons brought in by parents too. Bottle feeding has become very convenient and I wonder what impact this has on breast feeding choices, particular for working mothers . . . sometimes I smell the cartons and the milk does smell! It does not seem right to simply pour it in a bottle and give it to a new-born but is a convenient, popular and expensive way to feed, especially out and about.

Scenario 2: In our small nursery we had a mother who was keen to continue breastfeeding whist her seven-month daughter attended the setting twice a week. The mother worked nearby and would attend at lunch and provide us with expressed milk. We created a snug for her in the rest room with cushions. At first it felt a bit awkward a lunch time can be quite busy and chaotic, a mum coming in and wanting to breastfeed initially felt like this was adding to the hectic lunchtime period. However, after a couple of weeks it was as if she had always been there. Breastfeeding just became part of the day and as a result we have made posters and set up a small support group within the setting for prospective and current parents. We are hoping to attend training on breastfeeding too to support parents, an area not considered in our role before. It was great to observe to loving connections and I reflected how beneficial it was and easy, with a little bit of planning and thought. It actually made us aware of how we delivered lunch times and why it was chaotic, making changes there too . . . breastfeeding also made us think about other care practices such as sleep and routines before infants attend our setting.

Rest and sleep

In the first few weeks of external life, sleep is divided into active sleep and quiet sleep. In active sleep the infant is in active sleep phase with eye movements twitching. The infant is more likely to wake during this initial phase of sleep and REM (Rapid Eye Movement) indicates brain activity occurring during this phase. In quiet sleep the infant breathes rhythmically, and muscle movements are less frequent. At this stage, infant sleep is very unorganised and revolves around food, and meeting needs. It is a period of rapid growth and during this period the infant's stomachs is tiny. Therefore, feeding little and often is advocated although this involves sleep patterns not associated with adult sleep for longer periods. Feeding up infants has been considered a way of getting infants to sleep longer but the minutes of time saved does not justify the potential health of overfeeding at this early stage (Brown and Harries, 2015). Therefore, accepting that sleep occurs little and often during this transitional newborn period can reduce the stress of both parent and infant, aligning to the infant's sleep patterns rather than the parents. However, in re-creating the womb-like environment an infant will feel secure and safe but also begins to adjust to the external world, peaceful and calm during sleep times. The physical location of where the infant sleeps is dependent on culture and the parents' own upbringing. Co-sleeping or sleeping in a crib may be a parent's preference, pending their own lifestyles and experiences, although the infant remaining in the same room is recommended during the first few months. Mothers are in tune to their infants and the infant may find the transition from womb to cot challenging, so the closer and more convenient to demand feeding the more successful in developing a close bond at the infant's pace. The focus at this fourth trimester period is the recognition of infants short and frequent sleep patterns rather than the longer night sleeps patterns associated with an older infant. Therefore, this period is not about trying to promote a sleep pattern regime similar to an adult but rather to meet the needs of the infant and observe their cues in when they are in active or quiet sleep. Additionally, sleep patterns change at four months and again at six months, then at a year and again at three. Therefore, the necessity to get the correct regime is futile as sleep patterns are transitional until they are much older. Rather, parents need to alternate their own sleep patterns, so they manage day sleeps and night sleeps simultaneously to meet their needs of their infant, seeking time out from other carers and regulating themselves to shorter and more frequent sleeps. Whilst I recognise this is challenging and although I am not undermining the concern of sleep deprivation in adults and the need for sleep I do think night time can be reconceptualised as a time of connection with a natural pattern of sleep emerging.

- Infants sleep three to five hours in total and seventeen hours out of twenty-four
- By six months they sleep ten hours a night and, in the day, perhaps have about four hours
- By one year they may have a total of thirteen hours with one small nap
- Over six months, a sleep pattern may begin to occur, but strict regimes should be avoided and self-soothing should be carefully considered and carried out for short periods, not left for more than a few minutes at a time.

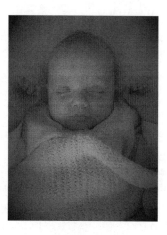

REM sleep

Practitioner's perspective

In our nursery, and previously at a childminders, parents have often asked for their infant to be kept awake for longer, so they sleep better at night time. We have tried to reassure them this is not the case and most infants under two years need a nap/rest and sleep for some part of the day. Depriving them of a sleep can be quite harmful and challenging. The infants that do not fall asleep often just fall asleep later in the day anyway and still become restless at night.

Self-soothing to sleep

Sleep routines have always been a concern for parents and carers. It is something parents have really struggled with, as they are often tired themselves. It can be challenging in group care too.

The main areas we try to share consistently with parents are:

Keep calm

Be consistent

Allow for wind down times

Transitional objects such as cloths and pacifiers are introduced at this stage and act as a comforter but nor replacement to a parent's physical touch in soothing an infant to sleep

Infants do not sleep like adults – so do not expect them to sleep the same

Night time does not always mean sleep time and napping is something parents may need to try

Infants grow all the time and sleep patterns change too. We try to advocate an enjoyable time with the infant where they can spend time with them rather than the stressful, crying scenarios often related to bed time

Infants shouldn't be left to cry continuously. Certainly, if an infant is stressed and left they will not sleep and we try to think how we would feel left alone. Most infants do eventually sleep, a calm atmosphere certainly helps . . . sharing adult responsibilities help – getting a night off can put things back into perspective.

Some generational advice has been that if parents do not get it right from the beginning then their infants will have asleep problems for the rest of their childhood. This is quite a negative and startling thing to be told as an exhausted parent. The majority of infants will not follow the same pattern as they grow, and a relaxed connected close night routine is more valuable to both parents and infant's emotional development than leaving an infant to cry for long pro-longed periods in a bid to get them to self soothe. Most children's sleep patterns shift considerably after three years and when they attend school, so a consistent routine is encouraged but not forced and negatively carried out (Gully, 2014).

Infant temperament from the beginning

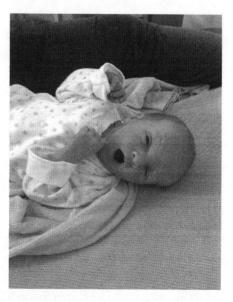

What is this infant communicating?

Communicative crying

Infant vocalisation comes in many forms and is pitched differently depending on their needs. Crying, particularly persistent crying, is a noise somehow divorced from the infant and to an adult ear is a noise that needs to be stopped by whatever means necessary. However, what is more beneficial is tuning into the cry and listening, attempting to decode the crying, finding out what they are trying to say. The amount of crying, a little like talking, is a subjective vocalisation. Some infants cry louder, or more frequently than others. Perhaps by reflecting on the crying, communication needs can be met. Generally, when needs are met the crying does subside and the infant is at peace for a short period, or until they need again. The reasons for communicative crying range from:

- Hunger
- Thirst
- Discomfort
- Loneliness and anxiety
- Too hot/cold
- Over stimulation
- Colds
- Allergies
- Pain.

For some parents the process of crying and meeting the infant's needs can be stressful and challenging, particularly when needs have been addressed and the crying continues. Infants 'feel' this anxiety and this can aggravate a stressful situation further. Parents resort to comparing their infants to other infants and can feel inadequate in their own role. So why do some infants cry more?

Returning to nature and nurture, infants are born with unique temperaments. The term temperament refers to aspects of the infant's personality that are regarded as being 'innate' or determined by genetics and biological factors rather than aspects of their personality that develop as a consequence of their interaction with the environment, or as a result of learning. Temperamental disposition such as for example, being 'introverted' or 'extraverted', are as such thought to be present at birth and to exist prior to other aspects of cognitive or social development.

Thomas and Chess (1977) identified three core temperaments in infants:

- Easy infants are very easy-going and develop regular eating and sleeping patterns with ease

- Difficult infants tend to be very emotional, irritable and fussy, and cry a lot. They also tend to have irregular eating and sleeping patterns.

- Slow-to-warm-up infants have a low activity level and tend to withdraw from new situations and people. They are slow to adapt to new experiences but accept them after repeated exposure.

Research suggests that temperament overall is stable over time, and that it can play a significant role in terms of influencing how the infant responds to his or her environment. What is particularly important is the degree of 'fit' between the infant's temperament and the environment into which they are born. For example, an infant who is 'difficult' and who is born to a first-time mother who is experiencing postnatal depression is at increased likelihood of poor outcomes because of the poor fit between his high level of need and his mother's inability to meet that need. However, an infant who is difficult temperamentally but who is born to a confident and experienced mother, may develop as well as an infant who has an easy temperament.

Understanding a child's temperament can help reframe how we interpret crying and emotional behaviour and the reasons for behaviours. Knowing the infants' temperament helps to support infants in ways that respect their individual differences, working with infants rather than try to change them.

Family practitioner summary

Today everyone is in a rush for the next stage. My children are all grown up and I really miss the time when they were so little. I continually tell the parents I work with to slow down and enjoy the moment, don't get too stressed about things. The first few weeks may seem endless when you are in it, but it is such a small window so enjoy it and ask for help. In my work as an early year's specialist, I support the parents WITH their infant.

Focused points

- Appreciating the fourth trimester
- Connecting the care to the new-born
- A responsive approach to the new-born infant
- Professional support

Concluding thoughts

This chapter focused on the time frame where many parents try to resume normality as quickly as possible. The aim of this chapter was to support practitioners in encouraging parents to reflect on this period as the fourth trimester and allow the infant to lead the care. In allowing parents to attend and respond to the infant outside of fixed routines there is the opportunity to get to know the infant as an individual and tune into their needs rather than follow an external force that is generalised to all infants. In pursuing a flexible and relaxed schedule, both day and night, a gradual routine will begin to evolve that both the parent and infant engage in.

Bibliography

Apgar, V. (1953). 'A proposal for a new method of evaluation of the new-born infant'. *Curriculum. Research. Aesthetic Analogue.* 32(4): 260–267. DOI:10.1213/00000539-195301000-00041. PMID 13083014.

Barston, S. (2012) *Bottled Up: How the Way we Feed Infants Has Come to Define Motherhood, and Why It Shouldn't.* London: University of California Press.

Battersby, S. (2009) Midwives and formula feeding: An evaluation of midwives' knowledge of formula feeding and their role in supporting mothers who formula feed their infants. Available online at www.hipp4hcps.co.uk/dynamic-content/media/documents/JFHCBattersby[1].pdf

Bauer, A. (2014) The costs of perinatal mental health problems. Personal social services research unit. Available online at http://eprints.lse.ac.uk/59885/1/__lse.ac.uk_storage_LIBRARY_Secondary_libfile_shared_repository_Content_Bauer%2C%20M_Bauer_Costs_perinatal_%20mental_2014_Bauer_Costs_perinatal_mental_2014_author.pdf

BBC (2014) Breastfeeding. Was there ever a golden age? Available online at www.bbc.co.uk/news/magazine-25629934

Belsky, J. and Rovine, M. (1988) 'Nonmaternal care in the first year of life and the security of infant attachment'. *Child Development* 59: 157–167.

Belsky, J., Burchinal, M., McCartney, K., Vandell, D., Clarke-Stewart, K. and Owen, M.T. (2007). 'Are There Long-Term Effects of Early Child Care?' *Child Development* 78(2): 681–701.

Brink, S. (2013) *The Fourth Trimester.* Berkeley: University of California Press.

Brown, A. (2018) 'Feeding Approaches'. Available online at www.youtube.com/playlist?list=PLoflLgxNjBdyr7i2Zx-ArwTEU2PwXWgf4

Brown, A. and Harries, V. (2015) 'Clinical Research Infant Sleep and Night Feeding Patterns During Later Infancy: Association with Breastfeeding Frequency, Daytime Complementary Food Intake, and Infant Weight'. *Breastfeeding Medicine* 10(5). DOI:10.1089/bfm.2014.0153

Carmichael, S., Shaw, L. and Gary, M. (2000) 'Maternal Life Event Stress and Congenital Anomalies'. *Epidemiology* 11(1): 30–35. Available online at https://journals.lww.com/epidem/Abstract/2000/01000/Maternal_Life_Event_Stress_and_Congenital.8.aspx

Christensson, K. (1998) 'Randomised study of skin to skin contact versus incubator care for rewarming low risk hypothermic neonates'. *Lancet* 352(115).

Dare, A. and O'Donovan, M. (2009) *A Practical Guide to Working with Babies* (4th Edition). Cheltenham: Nelson Thornes.

DeCasper, J. and Fifer, W. (1980) 'Of human bonding; new-borns prefer their mothers' voices'. *Science* 208(4448): 1174–1176.

Department of Health (2009) *Healthy Child Programme, Pregnancy and the First Five Years of Life.* London: DoH.

DiMenna, L. (2006) 'Consideration for implementation of a neonatal Kangaroo care protocol'. *Neonatal Network* 25(6): 405–412.

Doubilet, P. and Benson, C. (2008) *Your Developing Baby.* New York: McGraw Hill.

Eheart, B. and Martel, S. (1983) *The Fourth Trimester: On Becoming a Mother.* Connecticut: Appleton-Century-Crofts.

Field, T. (2014) *Touch.* US: MIT Press.

Finster, M. and Wood, M. (2005) 'The Apgar score has survived the test of time'. *Anaesthesiology* 102(4): 855–857. DOI:10.1097/00000542-200504000-00022. PMID 15791116.

Frailberg, S. (1975)' Ghosts in the Nursery. A Psychoanalytic Approach to the Problems of Impaired Infant-Mother Relationships'. *Journal of Child and Adolescent Psychiatry* 14(3): 387–342. Available online at www.jaacap.com/article/S0002-7138(09)61442-4/abstract

Gavitt, P. (2006) Breastfeeding and Wet-nursing. In Schaus, M. (ed.) *Women and Gender in Medieval Europe: An Encyclopaedia.* Oxon: Routledge.

Glover, V. and Barlow J. (2014) 'Psychological adversity in pregnancy: what works to improve outcomes?' *Journal of Children's Services* 9(2): 96–108.

Goddard Blythe, S. (2005) *The Well-Balanced Child: Movement and Early Learning (Early Years).* London: Hawthorn Press.

Gopnik, A. (2016) *The Gardener and the Carpenter: What the New Science of Child Development Tells Us About the Relationship Between Parents and Children.* London: Vintage.

Gopnik, A., Melzoff, A. and Kuhl P. (1999) *How Babies Think: The Science of Childhood.* London: Weidenfeld/Nicholson.

Grant, A., Mannay, D. and Marzella, R. (2017) '"People Try and Police your Behaviour". The impact of surveillance on mothers and grandmothers' perceptions and experiences of infant feeding'. *Families Relationships and Societies* 4: 1–17.

Gully, T. (2014) *The Critical Years: Early Development from Conception to Five.* Northwich: Critical Publishing.

Hayward, R. (2009) 'Enduring Emotions: James L. Halliday and the Invention of the Psychosocial'. *Isis Journal* 100(4): 827–838.

Harries, V. and Brown, A. (2017). 'The association between use of infant parenting books that promote strict routines, and maternal depression, self-efficacy, and parenting confidence'. *Early Child Development and Care* 1–12. Available online at http://onlinelibrary.wiley.com/doi/10.1002/imhj.20071/pdf

Healthy Start (2014) Safe Bottle Feeding. Available online at www.healthystart.nhs.uk

IFF Research (2010) Infant Feeding Survey. Available online at www.hscic.gov.uk/catalogue/PUB08694/ifs-uk-2010-sum.pdf

Johnston, C., Stevens, B., Pineli, J., Gibbins, S., Filion, F., Jack, A., Steele, S., Boyer, K. and Veilleux, A. (2003) 'Kangaroo care is effective in diminishing pain response in preterm neonates'. *Paediatric Adolescent Medicine* 157(11): 1084–1088.

Klaus, M. (1998) 'Perinatal care in the 21st century: Evidence that supports changing the management of mother and infant'. *Report for the National Breastfeeding Policy Conference*. Washington, DC.

Klaus, M. and Kennell, J. (1982) *Parent-Infant Bonding*. St. Louis: Mosby.

Klaus, M., Kennell, J. and Klaus, P. (1995) *Bonding: Building the Foundation of a Secure Attachment and Independence*. Reading, MA: Addison-Wesley.

Klaus, M., Kennell, J., Robertson, S. and Sosa, R. (1989) 'Effects of Social support during parturition on maternal and infant morbidity'. *British Medical Journal* 293: 585–587.

Labbok, M. and Krasovec, K. (1990) 'Toward Consistency in Breastfeeding Definitions'. *Studies in Family Planning* 21(4): 226–230. DOI:10.2307/1966617

Latva, R., Lehtonen, L., Salmelin, R. and Tamminen T. (2007) 'Visits by the family to the neonatal intensive care unit'. *Acta Paediatr.* 96(2): 215–220. Available online at www.ncbi.nlm.nih.gov/pubmed/17429908

Leach, P. (2018) *Transforming Infant Well-Being: Research Policy and Practice for the First 1001 Critical Days*. London: Routledge.

Liedloff, J. (1986) *The Continuum Concept*. London: Penguin Books.

MacGregor, J. (2008) *Introduction to the Anatomy and Physiology of Children: A Guide for Students of Nursing, Child Care and Health* (2nd Edition). London: Routledge.

Mannay, D. (2016) *Visual, Narrative and Creative Research Methods: Application, Reflection and Ethics*. Abingdon: Routledge.

Miller, L. and Cable, C. (1992) *Professionalism in the Early Years*. London: Hodder Education.

Moberg, K. (2003) *The Oxytocin Factor*. US: DaCapo Press.

Music, G. (2016) *Nurturing Natures: Attachment and Children's Emotional, Sociocultural and Brain Development*. Hove and New York: Psychology Press.

NSPCC (2013) Available online at www.nspcc.org.uk

Odent, M. (2001) *The Scientification of Love*. London: Free Association Books.

Pikler, E. (1960) Eight Guiding Principles. Available online at http://thepiklercollection.weebly.com/pikler-principles.html

Rees, J. (2017) Early Years Conference Presentation. Available online at www.youtube.com/watch?v=ipNDwddnAlw

Rice, F., Harold, G., Boivin, G., Van De Bree, J., Hay, M. and Thapar, D. (2010) 'The links between prenatal stress and offspring development and psychopathology: disentangling environmental and inherited influences'. *Psychology Medicine* 40(2): 335–345. Available online at www.ncbi.nlm.nih.gov/pmc/articles/PMC2830085/

Stern, D. (1995) *The Motherhood Constellation: A Unified View of Parent-Infant Therapy*. New York: Basic Books.

Stern, D. (2000) 'Putting time back into our considerations of infant experience: A microdiachronic view'. *Infant Mental Health Journal,* 21: 21–28.

Stern, D. (1997) *The Birth of a Mother*. New York: Perseus Books Group.

Stevens, E., Patrick, T. and Pickler, R. (2009) 'A History of Infant Feeding'. *The Journal of Perinatal Education* 18(2): 32–39. DOI:10.1624/1058123409X426314

Tassoni, P. (2016) *Supporting Children with Special Needs*. London: Hodder Education

Thomas, A. and Chess, S. (1977) *Temperament and Development*. Oxford: Brunner/Mazel.

Wigert, H., Johansson, R., Berg, M. and Hellström, A. (2006) 'Mothers' experiences of having their new-born child in a neonatal intensive care unit'. *Caring Science* 20(1): 35–41.

5 | Developmental care

Introduction and context

Descartes (1596–1650) believed the mind and the body were separate function-ing entities. The mind led, and then the body followed. Contemporary research now confirms that the mind, the body and its physical behaviours, responses and emotions, are interlinked and interdependent. The use of technology has provided a lens to understand learning and development in utero, particularly during the last three months of development.

> No neonatal pattern can be considered to originate at birth, as the foe-tus has already the full repertoire of movements which will be found in the neonate. The only difference lies in the quality of movement, most probably because of the increased influence of gravity after birth.
>
> (Piontelli, 1992: 30)

This repertoire includes:

> at ten weeks . . . hand and face contacts, stretches, yawns, jaw opening, and movements of the tongue can be observed. At twelve weeks both the hand and the mouth contact. Observations of sucking and swallowing as well as fine finger movements can visible on the ultrasound machine.
>
> (Piontelli, 1992: 30)

The foetus is therefore an exploring actively in the uterine environment with foe-tal movements strengthening neural pathways in the brain, helping to form the intricate landscape of pathways necessary for construction of the nervous system.

(continued)

(continued)

This chapter will explore holistic and sequential approaches used to measure development. In reflecting on infant development further I have included a developmental care lens, developmental being concerned with the development of something, in this discussion, care. Therefore, this chapter will, alongside growth and development, examine ways developmental care approaches has been used to understand infants and the way they respond to their environment and carers. I will use the term carer as a general term to imply both practitioner and parents when discussing developmental theory although will highlight practitioner within the examples. I have selectively included theorists, Stern and Bakhtin, to introduce alternative viewpoints about developmental care.

Questions for discussion

For many years the prenatal period was considered simply as a period of growth and maturation.

What are your thoughts about learning in utero?

So what is 'typical' development?

- Development is 'Cephalocaudal' – the change of spatial proportions over time during growth. For example, the change in head size relative to body size
- Development begins from the head to feet so structures near the head are more developed than those near the toes
- Development is progressive
- Organs are not presented as miniature version of their final form, but develop first characteristics which then continue to develop over a period
- Development is sequenced; the important organs' such as the heart and brain developing first.

(Hepper, 2002)

▨ Physical development from birth

Predictable changes in physical functioning occur from birth through uncoordinated and jerky actions to smooth and intentional co-ordinated movements. The infant explores and begins to learn about their physical environment. In using a sequential

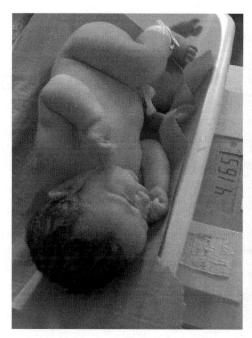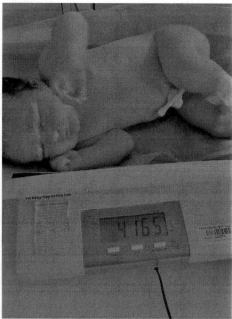

Weighing at birth

perspective theorist, such as Piaget (1950s), practitioners can identify the specifics of development and in focusing on the maturational process, begin to understand about the growth of the physical body and the progressive abilities of motor skills (Reed and Walker, 2015). Whilst Piaget did not claim that a stage was reached at a certain age, age was often included in the stages as an indication of the average time frame a child would reach.

> Sensorimotor Stage (Birth to two years): This is the time frame when the main accomplishment during this stage is object permanence – knowing that an object still exists, even if it is hidden and the exploration and understanding of physicality and cognition through sensory investigation.
>
> (Macleod-Brudenell, 2004)

Questions for discussion

Physical development often follows predictable sequential stages although this may differ within individuals:

* Head Control (difficult because the head is SO big in relation to the body) occurs around eight weeks

- Rolling occurs around three to four months, first side to back and then back to side
- Sitting develops around six months with head being help upright
- Anxiety (Separation; fear of depth is observed at around seven months)
- Crawling is developed approximately seven to eight months and can be carried out in a variety of ways such as seal, commando . . .
- Furniture standing and independent walking may be seen at around ten months.

(Macleod-Brudenell, 2004).

Does knowing about sequential development cause reassurance or anxiety among carers and parents?

How does this knowledge of development guide your caring approaching?

The vestibular system

Swinging back and forth

The sense of motion and position begins to develop prenatally through the mother's movement of swinging, rocking her body through everyday movements. Once the infant is born their physicality progresses over first two years to activities including sliding and climbing. These all enhance the development of the vestibular system and of balance. The vestibular system controls the experiences of balance and awareness of gravity, with the brain co-ordinating sensory information from the eyes, the muscles, the soles of the feet and the palms of the hands, adjusting the physical systems of muscular tone, heart rate and blood pressure accordingly. An infant exploring their own physicality and their own physicality in relation to that of others is central to the development of what is known as *proprioception*:

- Getting to know how our bodies work and gaining control of this
- Developing an understanding of where the body begins and where it ends
- Developing an awareness of how our bodies connect with what is 'on the outside' – other bodies, objects and the environment
- Stages of development: an evolutionary perspective on fast-forward.

There are therefore three key senses that are integrated when a baby learns to crawl:

- The vestibular (movement and position)
- The proprioceptive (the sense of inner self and awareness of body parts)
- The visual (being able to look into the distance as well as down at the hands).

(Laurel, 2009)

Movement and position

The integration of these senses is vital for development of balance as well as *perceptions of space and depth*. Perception is the sensory information and process of an immediate awareness of what is externally occurring (Phillips-Silver and Trainor, 2005).

Depth and sensory perception

At ten weeks of age, colour perception, with a preference to brightness or hues, is developing visually. Form perception is also increasing, and the infant begins discriminating between two- and three-dimensional objects. Depth perception also develops, illustrated by Gibson and Walk (1960) in their hypothesis that depth perception is inherent rather than a learned process. Thirty-six infants, between six and eight months of age, were placed on the shallow side of the visual cliff apparatus. The researchers found that twenty-seven of the infants crawled over to their mother on the 'deep' side without any problems. A few of the infants crawled but were extremely hesitant. Some infants refused to crawl because they were confused about the perceived drop between them and their mothers. Whilst this experiment uses a small sample and could be critiqued, it does for me highlight the connecting perceptions – auditory and visual – alongside infants' increased understanding about their environment. The infants knew the glass was solid by patting it, but the infants would not cross and vision was relied on to navigate movement and depth perception. In addition, their trust in the mothers on the other side was observed, weighing up the space between their mothers and themselves.

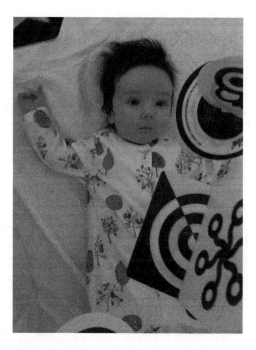

Visual perception: contrasting colours, black and white

In understanding perception, activities to support the infant can used more unobtrusively and ethically considering the infants feelings, reducing fear and unwanted confusion during the process. Observing infants playing with different types of mobile hangings at various lengths is a playful way of observing infants' growing capacity of interest and physicality and perception of their surrounding environment.

Practitioner's perspective

Development and monitoring of auditory perception

> Mother: When my son was born he failed his hearing test twice and on the third test I was referred to a specialist hospital. My son had a hearing test which scanned his brain and it took over a month to decide he had some hearing loss in his left ear. When he was tested his ears were so small he couldn't fit the apparatus in!
>
> It was quite stressful, but the lady was very calm, and I was able to hold my baby during the tests.

This was a conversation that a mother had with a practitioner during an initial visit to attend a childminder

Working together with the parent we shared practical activities to support development and encouraged sensory play. His mother was asking about speech development. As a result, we contacted a speech therapist to gain further advice, although he seemed to be vocalising as would be expected for his stage and development. Some of my role was continuing to support the mother through her monitoring check-ups and listen.

Hearing develops in utero and internal noises, such as the mother's heartbeat, as well external noises including human voices, music and most other sounds can be heard. After delivery, a new-born may have some temporary mucous and fluid inside the ear but they can hear sound from birth. In England all infants are tested at birth and if they 'fail' the test then a further test is carried out. Otoacoustic emissions are the basis of a simple, non-invasive, test for hearing defects in infants.

A wider lens on development

Many early years texts have explored child development within a maturational development theory (sequential approach) of areas – physical, intellectual, language, emotions and social development (PILES) or social, physical, communication and emotional development (SPICE) – as a way of understanding and measuring abilities. Through signposting and plotting milestones, parents and practitioners can check development at an anticipated rate. As a framework SPICE, like a jigsaw puzzle, has influential parts that are important to know as an introduction to development. However, it is also advantageous to think about the connections and holistic development alongside each area. In adopting a purely maturational, theoretical approach to development there is the assumption a controlled sequence of changes will inevitably occur. If this does not transpire within a time frame, concern and strategies to promote the sequence of change may be implemented. It is therefore helpful in making generalisations, but only provides part of the picture and for many individuals the influence of illness or other external inhibitors can interrupt the milestone approach (Music, 2016). Maturational development theory therefore acts as a specific source of knowledge guiding practices but in critically thinking about the developing infant we assume they are not yet developed and this may affect the way their emerging identity and learning is approached and evaluated. Repositioning developmentalism captures the tension practitioner's encounter in both supporting infants and parents from a development perspective alongside its application to practice (Yelland and Kilderry, 2005). Therefore, I propose to think about the infant, both from a sequential model and a holistic view point in a complementary frame, shaping how practice and support is enhanced. In balancing the present context and the infants' development stage nature and nurture are entwined.

The biopsychosocial approach to development: influencing practice

Increasingly an interdisciplinary model of development, referred to as the biopsychosocial model, is being considered in approaching both health and development. This includes biological development of the brain and genes, psychological areas including emotions and cognition and the social which encompasses perceptions of the self and the self in relation to social settings. There is growing interest to how these three domains interact with each other, particularly during the early years' life course. The biopsychosocial has been a useful model for child health when focusing on physical and mental health, providing an approach that looks at outcomes and designs of interventions (Frankel et al., 2009). The biopsychosocial model differs to the biomedical model, which attributes disease to only biological factors and considers other disciplines such as psychology and sociology not only in treating individuals but also in services and professional's responses to child health (Engel, 1977, cited in Frankel et al., 2009). The model is based in part on social cognitive theory and in a philosophical sense it states the workings of the body can affect the mind and the mind affect the body. This means there is a direct interaction between mind and body and indirect effects through immediate factors. In approaching development in this way, practitioners look at the individual infant development through a social and cultural lens, providing care and meeting needs.

Neuro biological approach to development

Neuro biological research has positioned child development at the heart of translational research integrating existing new knowledge from a range of present theory, providing new understanding and implications for practice to be considered. Translational research has provided evidence about the interaction between experience and the developing brain. The brain of an infant begins to grow early in pregnancy as it forms all the systems needed to connect to the nervous system. The brain appears as early as three weeks after conception and then develops rapidly. It is through stimulation primarily social and emotional that these areas are 'wire up'. It is the synapses that are crucial and make the connection between cells. It is the neurons where information is exchanged with many continuing to occur after birth. Brain development is discussed further in Chapter 6 but in reflecting about it within neuro-biological research and development it is important to recognise the shift in concep-tual thinking from nature versus nurture to nature *with* nurture, highlighting how the environment is centrally linked to the developing brain (Collins et al., 2011). As the two are interrelated, the care the infant receives connects the brain to the environ-ment (Gerhardt, 2014). Stimulation from the environment causes learning either by stabilizing existing networks in the brain or forging new ones. The ability to develop synapses is known as plasticity and whilst this can continue generally after three years it is at a much slower rate. However, rather than thinking about the infant's brain as having sensitive periods, Fox and Rutter (2010) prefer the metaphor of the growing brain to be a window of opportunity potential for learning and development with a remarkable capacity to change.

> [T]he kind of brain each baby develops is the brain that comes out of his or her particular experiences with people.
>
> This means it is built up through experience, probably for a good evolu-tionary reason: so that each new human can be moulded to the environmen-tal niche in which he finds himself. Precisely because we are so dependent as babies, and our brains are so 'plastic' (that is, easily changed), we can learn to fit in with whatever culture and circumstances we find ourselves in . . . our brains our socially programmed.
>
> (Gerhardt, 2014: 37–38)

The environment: social communication

Studies have evaluated that foetal heart rates slow down when hearing mothers voice and infants brain waves are different when hearing their mothers voice as opposed to another female voice even if the words are not clearly distinguishable. DeCasper and Spence (1984) measured the sucking mechanism of new-borns and concluded these rose and lowered on hearing their mother's voice as opposed to an unfamiliar woman. In being closer to their mothers, Filippetti et al. (2013) found new-borns preferred watching another new-born being stroked on the face if their face was being stroked the same way, integrating, understanding and making sense of the world around them (Music, 2016: 28). This can be diminished, however, in both foetuses and neo-nates of depressed mothers, who show inferior performance tests in face and speech discrimination tests. Therefore, experiences will influence the infant's potential to communicate (Field, 2010). Tronick et al. (2005) observed new-borns' facial expressions and behaviour when their mother showed emotion and then became facially still. Infants showed distress at the still face and sought a response from their mother. The re-connection was equally powerful to observe in the change to facial expressions and behaviour when the infant's responses were acknowledged. Further studies observing infant and mother where the mother had depression showed a marked difference to the infant seeking a response. The infant was observed to be passive and not seeking a response whilst the mother unemotionally talked and intermittently observed them. Whilst it could be argued that the infant's facial expressions are an interpretation of what they are internally thinking, these studies, in differing contexts, highlighted infant responses in various ways and the value of emotional connection between mother and infant, with an infant's sense of self in the relationship (Bremner and Fogel, 2009).

An emotional dialogue

In the home and early childhood education and care (ECEC) settings, the close relationship between carer (both parent and practitioner) and infant, experiencing the world physical and emotionally, is known as intersubjectivity. Intersubjectivity was first described as the secure meshing that occurs between caregiver and infant, with the caregiver allowing an infant to be introduced into their understandings of the society and culture they exist in (Anning and Edwards, 2006). It is considered as a meeting of minds when one person brings another into their culture. It demands considerable attention to the emotional state of the infant, and the carer needs to gradually tune into the infant's way of experiencing the world (Hopkins, 1988). Trevarthan (1993) considered infants are born with the readiness to know another human and engage with them. He evaluated interactions between carers as being mutual, with infants taking the lead within the interaction rather than simply responding to their carer's behaviour (cited in Meil and Dallos, 2005). Murray and Trevarthen (1986) described this mutual interaction between infant and carer as turn taking. Through turn taking the carer can adapt their interactive behaviour to the rhythms of their infant and encourage the infant to lead the interaction Degotardi and Davis, 2008). These early exchanges between infant and carer have been termed proto-conversations. As the term suggests, the patterns of turn taking include mutual attention, changes in movement, smiling and so on, and these early interactions have been regarded as embodying the fundamentals of the relationship and the communication between carer and infant (Meil and Dallos, 2005). As described in the studies observing mother's facial expressions infants will initially take the lead in the interaction but then if they consistently fail to receive a response from their carer will resign into silence (Murray and Andrews, 2005). This confirms that infants seek their carer's attention to interact with them and communicate (Brazelton, 1990; Davis and Wallbridge, 2012). Brazelton's (1990) concept of joint action regarded the behaviours of the partners as contingent and reciprocal, so rather than simply asking who started a sequence, or who controlled it the focus was on how each continually influenced the other. Braidley (1989) considered it was the quality of the relationship, not just quantity of arousal and stimulation, that was significant in enabling the infant to develop emotionally, and for attachment to occur (cited in Meill and Dallos, 2005). From birth, the infant is not only able to respond to its mother's voice, movements, gaze, smiles and so on, but is also able to actively influence her behaviour. Communication is, therefore, a collaborative interactive process. Interactions can fall into categories such as mutual gazing into each other's face and using gestures and interactions between carer and infant change over time and have the power to influence the relationship and gain a sense of self within the relationship (Fivas-Depeursinge, 1991, cited Meil and Dallos, 2005).

Developing a sense of self

The self refers to the child's sense of who they are as a person, and the foundations of the child's sense of self during the first four years of life. Stern (2006) identified four key stages of self-development:

Emergent self (0–2 months): At birth, the infant experiences the world as unrelated sensory stimuli, gradually learning to make connections using cues such as the emotional quality, and temporal and intensity patterns between stimuli. This process of integrating and organizing experience, called the emergent sense of self, continues until about two months.

Core self (2–6 months): At approximately two months, the infant's organization of sensory experience develops so they can sufficiently organize experience to have integrated episodic memories. This enables a higher level of sophistication in organizing future experiences. The infant can link objects with the environment and arrive at generalizations about what is expected in the future from their environment. In this process, the infant gains a sense of core self as an entity distinct from other objects in its environment. The infant also develops generalized representations of interactions with their primary caregiver during this time, a concept related to and informed by attachment theory. The infant learns about dependence and the types of affective and behavioural responses it can expect in specific situations.

Awareness of our bodies in relation to others

Subjective self (7–15 months): Around seven months, the child begins to be aware that their own thoughts and experiences are distinct from other people, and there is a gap between their subjective reality to others. With an attuned primary attachment figure, the infant becomes aware that this gap can be bridged through intersubjective experiences, such as sharing affect and focus of attention.

Verbal self (15 months upwards): At this stage the infant develops capacity for symbolic representation and language, becoming capable of creating complex abstract mental representations of experiences, and facilitating intersubjectivity. The focus is towards those things represented and communicated in language.

Developing a sense of self in the physical environment

In addition to developing a sense of self, infants are also developing a sense of agency. Agency refers to the infant's growing sense that they can influence their environment. For example, when an infant cries and a caregiver responds regularly the infant develops a sense that his needs will be met and that he is able to influence them being met. If, however, a caregiver responds erratically or not at all to an infant's cries, the infant begins to develop a sense that their needs will not be met and that they have no agency.

A sense of self in relation to others

Stages of developing agency

Fonagy and Target (2002) suggested the following stages of development of agency:

- Physical agency (0–6 months): During this phase of development infants are developing an awareness that actions produce changes in the physical environment.
- Social agency (3–9 months): During this phase infants are becoming aware that their actions produce behavioural and emotional responses in other people;
- Teleological agency (9–24 months): Infants become aware that their actions can achieve goals and develop a sense of purpose. Intention and action are not seen as separate at this stage.
- Intentional agency (2 years): By this age they are able to recognise that actions and intentions are separate, with actions being caused by prior intentions and mental states.
- Representational agency (3–4 years): Young children are now able to develop a sense of themselves with a mind, and other people as having minds.
- Autobiographical self: Children organise memories based on personal experiences and linked to earlier self-representations and awareness of personal history.

(Fonagy and Target, 2002)

For the infant to begin to develop these aspects of self and agency they need emotionally available interactive involvement from their primary caregivers.

Caregivers' interactions: mind mindedness

Carers, both parents and practitioners, in their own contexts have the capacity for maternal mind mindedness or reflective function (Meins et al., 2001; Slade, 2005). The concept of mind mindedness is the carer's ability or willingness to represent their likely thoughts and feelings. The outcomes of success are deemed to be related to the security of attachment and theory of mind. Appropriate mind related comments by carers include; 'Oh you want me to help you get the bricks' when the infant gestures to it, responding in a way that shows the infant they understand their requests. Reflective function refers to the carer's capacity to understand the infant's behaviour in terms of internal feeling states. Reflective function is linked to 'maternal parenting' behaviours such as flexibility and responsiveness, although this extends to all, including those beyond the home, who develop close relationships with the infant and create a safe base. The mid-range interaction of not being too intrusive or passive between infant and carer is important because it strikes a balance in an appropriate way and promotes later security in attachments. Practitioners in ECEC can draw on the understanding of mind mindedness and reflective function as a way of tuning in and connecting with infants, avoiding making assumptions and interacting on a superficial level. Mind mindedness has therefore been significantly related to practitioner sensitivity and stimulation levels (Degotardi, 2011). Taking time to reflect, the practitioner can be flexible and responsive in communication and listening to cues authentically to the infant in their care (www. aimh.org.uk/about.php) and respond to their development holistically.

Holistic development and systems theory: Brazelton

Approaching infant development from differing perspectives enables interactions within a family context to be included in the understanding of, and responses to, infant's needs. The touchpoint model for Brazelton posits that development proceeds through predictable time frames of temporary disorganisation while the reorganisation and emergence of new skills and capacities occur. Subsequently, temporary disruptions in sleep, feeding patterns and growing abilities in self-regulation and behavioural control are all examples of touchpoint periods within infant development. The responses of the infant to the touchpoint periods are increased crying, clinging and seeking of physical contact (Plooij, 2003). Strong relationships of a caring nature can therefore help prevent development barriers and guide the infant's development through these transitional, temporary crises. Viewing development within micro life events (the influence toward external influences) provides opportunities where understanding can be deepened, and relationships strengthened, offering support of the child's development with positivity and reassurance (Sparrow and Brazelton, 2006). The touchpoints can cause great anxiety in both the infant and carer. It can undermine the carer's own caregiving role during transient decline, resulting in self-blame and feelings of inadequacy, feeling disjointed from their infant's development. Understanding infant's behavioural responses to their environment and how they are embedded in their own development can provide a shift in thinking about development from, in part, a maturational view point. Whilst this could be argued to be a narrow vision, the important point for me is the response by the carers to these crises. In understanding behaviours and appreciating this observed emotional communication development, connectivity and tuning in can be directed towards the infant. In developing thinking about the behavioural emotional states of infants, we can appreciate that, on occasions, they may not mirror the carer's emotions towards them. The emotions of infants are often evaluated as a measurement of the success of the caring and if emotions do not always correspond this can influence the carer's responses to them. The knowledge of touch points recognises this is part of an infant's development and shouldn't undermine caring practices and the interaction in caring for infants.

Holistic development: language and Bakhtin

As an educator and teacher, Bakhtin's approach to language was shared with his colleague Voloshinov (1895–1936). It highlighted language as taking place in social contexts that are laden with meanings, further captured in the theory of dialogism. Though Bakhtin did not specifically focus on early years development, he did refer to the role of language in a young child's life and for me this connects to emotional communication and the way language is interpreted (White, 2015).

> From the lips of those close to him . . . they are the words that for the first time determine his personality from outside. The child begins to see himself through his mothers eyes and begins to speak about himself in his mothers emotional volitional tones.
>
> (Bakhtin cited in White, 2015: 49–50).

Language is the way an infant begins to view themselves and their personality. Language is therefore a life-long journey of ideological becoming rather than transmitting language as a purpose for learning codes. For Bakhtin what is learned is less to do with linguistic and cognitive functioning but more concerned with the development of the creative personality as an infant engages with a multifaceted and social world.

Practitioner using verbal and non-verbal language to encourage communication

Skaz

Communication and language include all the different ways an infant understands and communicates, only part of which is spoken language. Bakhtin refers to language in its holistic term, including the way it is used and conveyed to communicate. Bakhtin determined language was dialogised and imbedded in relationships with others rather than viewing of language as transmitted from expert to novice, as suggested by Vygotsky and Chomsky. Although they agreed language was social, both suggested the adult and infant had distinct roles. For Chomsky, the adult was the expert in exposing and extending language and the linguistic rules within it. He considered there was a critical period for language and for verbal language to be developed it had to be heard – this was known as the language acquisition devise (LAD) (Skidmore and Murakami, 2017).

Bakhtin stressed that language is not sequential and does not possess a universal hierarchal pattern, as suggested by Piaget. Rather 'skaz' (language) was a fluid narrative representing voices through discourses. Language for him contained both revealing and concealing meanings, presented in the self in many forms. Therefore, meaning is not fixed and exists within and between living spaces. The words spoken are therefore influenced by the values of those involved and the unspoken language, gestures, facial expressions, body language all play a role in social language (White, 2009).

Appreciating the value of communication in this way extends the possibility of language being more than a mode of receiving symbolic verbal codes. The infant is perceived as a dialogic partner rather than a novice in the communicative relationship. Moreover, Bakhtin provides an interpretation of language that invites consideration of a dialogue as a living event, fluid in its use of interactions. Practitioners are therefore involved in this conceptualisation, keeping the infant as the central source rather than leading the dialogue themselves. Developing the intersubjectivity of the relationships leads to a shared understanding and promotion of greater learning. A dialogical approach invites practitioners and parents, in their caring approaches, to lovingly linger with infants, to wholeheartedly engage and communicate and experience the in-between aspects of the event itself, the dialogic space (Vice, 1997).

Family practitioner summary

It is important to understand about development but not just about the areas taught on professional course. I would like to think about the holistic development and the influences that support development. As a practitioner I am seeing the overlap and links to all areas and how emotions seem to underpin it.

Focused points

- Development can be viewed holistically AND separately
- A theoretical perspective aids practitioner to understand the diversity and flexibility of development
- Connecting care as an emotional and communicative way to support development
- The encouragement of free movement on a baby's spirit, intelligence and physical being.
- The importance in the way an infant is physically and metaphorically held

Concluding thoughts

This chapter focused on development and the ways developmental care could be supported with infants. It draws on a connected care approach and how this can be enhanced in developing a sense of self. It then drew on the theory of connectivity and communication to underpin the above with examples of practice to extend thinking.

Bibliography

Anning, A. and Edwards, A. (2006) *Promoting Children's Learning from Birth to Five*. London: McGraw-Hill.

Bakhtin, M. (1981) *The Dialogic Imagination*. Austin: University of Texas.

Braidley, B. (1989) *Visions of Infancy*. Cambridge: Polity Press.

Brazelton, T. (1990) *The Earliest Relationship*. USA: Perseus Books.

Brazelton, T. and Sparrow, J. (2006). *Birth to Three: Your Child's Emotional and Behavioural Development*. Cambridge, MA: Da Capo Press.

Bremner, J. and Fogel, A. (2009) *Blackwell Handbook of Infant Development*. Oxford: Blackwell Publishing.

Bronfenbrenner, U. (1979) *The Ecology of Human Development: Experiments by Nature and Design*. Cambridge., MA: Harvard University Press.

Collins, W., Maccoby, E., Steinberg, L., Hetherington, E. and Bornstein, M. (2001) 'Toward nature with nurture'. *Am Psychol*. 56(2): 171–173. Available online at www.ncbi.nlm.nih.gov/pubmed/11279811

Dahlberg, G. (2001) Everything is a beginning, and everything is dangerous: some reflections of the Reggio Emilia experience. In Penn, P. (ed.) *Early Childhood Services: Theory, Policy and Practice*. Buckingham: Open University.

Davis, M. and Wallbridge, D. (2012) *Boundary and Space: An Introduction to the Work of Dr Winnicott*. London: Karnac Books.

DeCasper, A. and Spence, M. (1986) 'Prenatal maternal speech influences new-borns' perception of speech sounds'. *Infant Behavior and Development* 9(2): 133–150. DOI:10.1016/0163–6383(86)90025–1

Degotardi, S. (2011) Two Steps Back: Exploring Identity and Presence While Observing Infants in the Nursery. In Johansson, E. and White, E. (eds) *Educational Research with Our Youngest. International Perspectives on Early Childhood Education and Development*. 5. Dordrecht: Springer.

Degotardi, S. and Davis, B. (2008) 'Understanding infants: Characteristics of early childhood practitioners' interpretations of infants and their behaviours'. *Early Years* 28(3): 221–234.

Degotardi, S. and Pearson, E. (2008) 'Relationship theory in the nursery: Attachment and beyond'. *Contemporary Issues in Early Childhood* 10(2): 144–145.

Degotardi, S. and Pearson, E. (2010) Knowing me, knowing you: The relationship dynamics of infant play. In Ebbeck, M. and Waniganayake, M. (eds), *Play in Early Childhood Education: Learning in Diverse Contexts*. Melbourne: Oxford University Press.

Descartes, René (2004) [1637]. *A Discourse on Method: Meditations and Principles*. Translated by Veitch, John. London: Orion Publishing Group.

Field, F. (2010) *The Foundation Years: Preventing Poor Children Becoming Poor Adults. The Report of the Independent Review on Poverty and Life Chances*. London: Cabinet Office. Available online at www.frankfield.co.uk/review-on-poverty-and-life-chances

Filippetti, M., Johnson, M., Lloyd-Fox, S., Dragovic, D. and Farroni, T. (2013) 'Body Perception in New-borns'. *Current Biology*. 23(23)2413–2416.doi: 10.1016/j.cub.2013.10.017

Fivaz-Depeursinge, E. (1991). 'Documenting a time-bound, circular view of hierarchies: a microanalysis of parent-infant dyadic interaction'. *Family Process* 30(1): 101–120.

Fonagy, P. and Target, M. (2002) 'Early Intervention and the Development of Self-Regulation', *Psychoanalytic Inquiry* 22(3): 307–335. DOI:10.1080/07351692209348990.

Fox, N. and Rutter, M. (2010) 'Introduction to the Special Section on The Effects of Early Experience on Development'. *Child Development* 81(1): 23–27.

Frankel, R., Quill, T. and McDaniel, S. (2009) *The Biopsychosocial Approach: Past, Present, Future*. Rochester: University of Rochester Press.

Froebel, F. (1920) *Mother's Songs, Games, and Stories*. London: William Rice.

Gerhardt, S. (2014) *Why Love Matters. How Affection Shapes a Baby's Brain*. London: Routledge.

Gibson, J. (1966) *The Senses Considered as Perceptual Systems*. Boston: Houghton Mifflin.

Gibson and Walk (1960) Available online at www.kokdmir.info/courses/docs/.com

Gopnik, A., Melzoff, A. and Kuhl P. (2001) *How Babies Think: The Science of Childhood*. London: Weidenfeld/Nicholson.

Hepper, P. (2002). Prenatal development. In Slater A. and Lewis M. (eds) *Introduction to Infant Development*. Oxford: Oxford University Press.

Hobson, P. (2002) *The Cradle of Thought: Exploring the Origins of Thinking*. London: Macmillan.

Hopkins, J. (1988) 'Facilitating the development of intimacy between nurses and infants in day nurseries'. *Early Child Development and Care* 33: 99–111.

Laurel, T., Xiaoqing, G., Jing-jiang, L., Lehtovaaraa, K. and Harris, L. (2009) 'The primal role of the vestibular system in determining musical rhythm'. *Cortex* 45(1): 35–43.

Macleod-Brudenell, I. (2008) *Advanced Early Years Care and Education*. Oxford: Heinemann.

Meil, D. and Dallos, R. (2005) *Social Interaction and Personal Relationships*. Milton Keynes: OUP.

Meins, E., Fernyhough, C., Fradley, E. and Tuckey, M. (2001). 'Rethinking Maternal Sensitivity: Mothers' Comments on Infants' Mental Processes Predict Security of Attachment at 12 Months'. *Journal of Child Psychology and Psychiatry and Allied Disciplines* 42(5): 637–648. DOI:10.1017/S0021963001007302

Murray, L. and Andrews, L. (2005) *The Social Baby Richmond*. London: CP Publishing.

Murray, L. and Trevarthen, C. (1986) 'The Infants role in mother-infant communication'. *Journal of Child Language* 13(1): 15–29.

Music, G. (2016) *Nurturing Natures: Attachment and Children's Emotional, Socio cultural and Brain Development*. Hove and New York: Psychology Press.

Nash, J. (1997) 'Fertile minds'. *Time Magazine* 49(6): 50–58.

Nutbrown, C. and Page, J. (2008) *Working with Babies and Children from Birth to Three*. London: Sage.

Phillips-Silver, J. and Trainor, L. (2005) 'Feeling the Beat: Movement Influences Infant Rhythm Perception'. *Science* 308(5727): 1430. DOI:10.1126/science.1110922

Piontelli, A. (1992) *From Fetus to Child: An Observational and Psychoanalytic Study.* UK: Psychology Press.

Plooij, F. (2003) The trilogy of mind. In Heimann, M. (ed.) *Regression Periods in Human Infancy.* Mahwah, NJ: Erlbaum.

Reed, M. and Walker, R. (2015) *Early Childhood Studies: A Critical Reader.* London: Sage Publications.

Skidmore, D. and Murakami, K. (2017) *Dialogic Pedagogy: The Importance of Dialogue in Teaching and Learning.* New Perspectives on Language and Education. UK: Multilingual Matters.

Slade, A. (2005)' Parental reflective functioning: An introduction'. *Attachment & Human Development* 7(3): 269–281. DOI:10.1080/14616730500245906

Sparrow, J. and Brazelton, B. (2006) *Touchpoints. Birth to Three.* Boston: Da Capo Press.

Stern, D. (1985) *The Interpersonal World of the Infant.* New York: Basic Books.

Stern, D. (2006) *The Interpersonal World of the Infant: A View from Psychoanalysis and Developmental Psychology.* New York: Perseus Books; Karnac (Books) Ltd.

Tomasello, M. (1999) *The Cultural Origins of Human Cognition.* Cambridge, MA: Harvard University Press.

Tomasello, M., Kruger, A. and Ratner, H. (1993) 'Cultural learning'. *Behavioral and Brain Sciences* 16(3): 459–511.

Trevarthen, C. (1993) 'Predispositions to cultural learning in young infants'. *Behavioral and Brain Sciences* 16(3): 534–535.

Tronick, E., Messinger, D., Weinberg, M., Lester, M., LaGasse, L., Seifer, R. and Liu, J. (2005). 'Cocaine Exposure Is Associated with Subtle Compromises of Infants' and Mothers' Social-Emotional Behavior and Dyadic Features of Their Interaction in the Face-to-Face Still-Face Paradigm'. *Developmental Psychology* 41(5): 711–722. DOI:10.1037/0012-1649.41.5.711

Vice, S. (1997) *Introducing Bakhtin.* Manchester: Manchester University Press.

Vygotsky, L. (1987) *The Collected Works of L. S. Vygotsky, Volume 1: Problems of General Psychology, Including the Volume Thinking and Speech.* New York: Plenum.

Vygotsky, L. S. (2004) 'Imagination and creativity in childhood'. *Journal of Russian and East European Psychology* 42(1): 7–97.

White, E. J. (2009) 'Bakhtinian dialogism: a philosophical and methodological route to dialogue and difference?' *Annual Conference of the Philosophy of Education Society of Australasia.* Available online at www2.hawaii.edu/~pesaconf/zpdfs/16white.pdf

White, E. J. (2015) *Introducing Dialogic Pedagogy: Provocations for the Early Years.* London: Routledge.

Yelland, N. and Kilderry, A. (2005) Against the tide: new ways in early childhood education. In Yelland, N. (ed.) *Critical Issues in Early Childhood Education.* Maidenhead: Open University Press.

Emotional care connections

Introduction and context

> Teaching parents-to-be about bonding and attachment, and the importance of holding, talking and gazing at their child, cannot be underestimated. It is possibly the single most important role that a parent has in terms of the child's emotional development, yet most parents are completely unaware of how infants' brains develop or what they can do to give their infant the best start in life.
>
> (www.infants.uk.com/about-us-prenatal-classes/dreams/)

The rationale for this chapter was sparked, in part, from an all-party parliamentary group (APPG, a UK group composed of politicians from all political parties) that produced the *1001 Critical Days Manifesto* (www.1001criticaldays.co.uk). It highlighted the need for increased training and skills for those working with infants, so they are informed and understand child development, including the value of relationships and attachment. In contemporary research, many breakthroughs in science have contributed to understanding the relationship between the physical body and emotional experiences. This chapter aims to introduce the core topics of emotional relationships, a reflective approach and supportive practices.

Emotional relationships

In an ideal world, infants should be wanted, nurtured, loved, protected and valued by emotionally available and sensitively responsive parents. Such an environment allows the child to optimally, with emotional wellbeing, form and maintain relationships, a healthy brain and a richness of language to socially communicate. During the prenatal period, parents can be supported in understanding what to expect physically and emotionally. The symbiotic parent–infant relationship begins at conception, with the influences of nutrition, physical and emotional health impacting on development. Effective, timely, consistent and non-judgemental prenatal support means parents feel better prepared for their transition into parenthood and the arrival of their infant.

Questions for discussion

Pregnancy is a powerful emotional experience for the pregnancy women as well as her partner. What are the:

    Biological needs of the pregnant women?
    The psychological needs?
    The social needs?

Prior to six months of age, infants do not have a conscious awareness of processing their own complex emotional states but can experience internal states of comfort

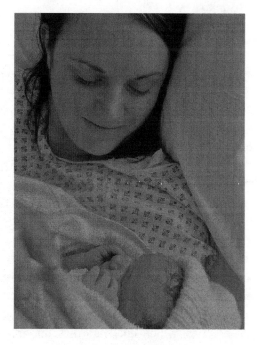

Close contact from birth

such as feeling sleepy, warm and physically comfortable and discomfort. They are therefore dependent on their caregivers to help them to develop self-awareness and regulate these feelings. Infants are also able to discriminate different emotional states in other people. Murray and Andrews (2005) describe stages of social relatedness in terms of the nature of the social relationship that is needed by the infants during their first two months.

- New-born, during the first month
  - Attraction to others, especially parents
  - Attraction to eyes, voice, maternal odour
  - Relatedness mainly through holding and touch.
- Two months
  - Core relatedness
  - Infants are highly motivated to respond socially; they sustain eye-contact, and show active social behaviours (e.g. smiles, vocalisations, gestures), and face-to-face interactions are close and emotionally expressive.

Therefore, as the brain grows it is being wired according to the emotional environment they experience (Conkbayir, 2017).

The flourishing brain

The brain is developed rapidly in utero and is affected by diet, exposure to stress, maternal health and lifestyle. As the brain develops, the foetus is able respond to familiar sounds and tune into their parent's voice (Kisilevsky et al., 2008). During the first trimester the neural tube begins to grow, leading to growth and change forming the forebrain, midbrain and hindbrain around foetal development of six or seven weeks. The primitive region of the brain is the first to form, and is known as the brain-stem, the survival aspect of life. It is vital because it controls the heart rate, breathing and the flight or fight mechanism. During the second trimester the brainstem further matures, and the cortex, neurons and synapses appear, visible in the foetus being able to make voluntary movements. The brain development is accelerated by this sensory input and the grooves and ridges on the brains surface, gyri and sulci, start to form, leading to the thickening of the cerebral cortex and myelination. Myelination is the fatty sheath coating of neurons, which enables quick information processing. The development of myelination contributes to higher order brain regions that control feelings, thought and memory. The key factor here is that, in facilitating myelination, the experiential input of regular positive experiences, stimulation of play and sensory development is essential (Conkbayir, 2018; www.zerotothree.org). This draws attention to the close link between brain development and the influence of varying external contexts to which it is exposed.

The emotional brain

The following is a summary of the emotional brain – the limbic system.

- The thalamus: This is located at the top of the brain stem. It takes in sensory information and then passes it to the cerebral cortex. It also regulates conscious sleep and controls the motor system, directing body movements and co-ordination
- The hippocampus: Controls the memory, learning and regulating emotions
- The amygdalae: These are two almond shaped structures situated close to the hippocampus. It decodes emotions, possible threats, preparing the body for emergency situations and storing fear memories
- The hypothalamus: This region of the brain controls chemical messengers. This includes temperature, hunger, thirst and sleep. It also controls the release of hormones
- The cingulate gyrus: This part of the brain regulates emotion and pain and identifies fear
- The basal ganglia: This region assists regulating automatic movement, focusing attention and connecting the cerebral cortex with the cerebellum.

(Blakemore and Frith, 2005; Conkbayir, 2017)

Practitioner's perspective

Reflections on learning about brain development

When I trained many years ago we were taught primarily about the SPICE (social, physical, intellectual, communication and emotional) of life as separate areas of development. For me the brain was about the physical growth and then after birth intellectual development. It was not until I went on a course about memory that I began to appreciate the complexity of the brain in processing information and how for some children this was very challenging. More recently I attended a conference about adverse childhood experiences and appreciated the close connection to emotions and the brain beginning prenatally. I reflected on the various traumas, both small and great which the infant may be exposed to and the lasting impact this may have.

I was always advised and taught a caring but hands-off approach, leaving the infant to settle themselves and not over stimulate them. For me, reading and developing my own thinking about brain development has unbalanced my inner core of care and emotional relationships. It has brought another layer of understanding and one which I feel needs to be cascading much more into early years practice. I feel that I need to re-learn my caring approaches and share my anxieties with colleagues in understanding behaviour and practices. Day to day we do not have opportunities to do this. I now know that the:

- Right hemisphere has growth spurt in first one and a half years and is dominant for the first three years
- Early attachment experiences may impact development of the right brain
- Healthy right brain activity supports mental health throughout our lifespan.

(Abbott and Burkitt, 2015)

Emotionally connecting at two days

The limbic system, the section of the brain registering and storing emotional information such as fear, anger and happiness, has a specialised system of neurons that support individuals to read the emotions in the faces of others. This system is called the Mirror Neuron System (MNS) and is one of the core neurological systems that helps understand the actions of others. It provides an understanding of how to read other individuals internal emotional states therefore developing a capacity for empathy (Abbott and Burkitt, 2015).

Positive experiences

The infant's brain continues to be 'wired' after birth and this occurs through connections made from neuron to neuron across the space between the neurons, known as synaptogenesis, which is when synapse networks are established. Eliot (2001) describes brain cells, or neurons, as transmitting information, responding to life experiences and continually remodelled to adapt to them. A neuron is comprised of

- a cell body
- axon
- dendrites.

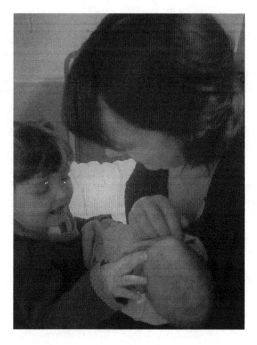

Born to be social

The neuron communicates through firing tiny chemical charges. The neuron has a nucleus, which accumulates small electrical inputs from the dendrites, connecting to countless other neurons. When the neuron cannot hold any more charge, an impulse is then fired down the single outgoing axon, which subsequently branches out to other dendrites that lead to other neurons. Neural networks are created by the reciprocal serve and return interactions between socially primed infant and carers (Johnson, 2001). An infant is born ready to relate to the social environment and has social competencies that support this from birth. Therefore, synapses are connected are either formed, strengthened or pruned (reduced and lost) in response to stimulation and early experiences of the external environment (Blakemore and Frith, 2005).

The experiential brain

Although emotional connectivity within the brain begins prenatally the maturation of the brains orbitofrontal regions predominately occurs postnatally. This area of development is positively or negatively shaped by early experiences. Experiences become incorporated into the developing synaptic connections of the infant's brain because of what is known as 'experience-expectant' and 'experience-dependent' mechanisms (Conkbayir, 2017).

> Experience-expectant development: Experience-expectant is the environmental input and the way the external experiences form a necessary aspect to organising the developing nervous system. The most important experience-expectant abilities are the sensory pathways of vision and hearing, social and emotional development, language and cognition. Experience-expectant development occurs within specific time frames and if insufficiently achieved then long-term development is potentially compromised.
>
> Experience-dependent development: Experience-dependent is the way individual experiences produce a unique wiring of their brain. Experience-dependent develops with the individual child adapting to specific features of the personalised environment they inhabit. Development and responding behaviour is not restricted to specific and sensitive time frames and this is its defining characteristic. It therefore highlights the brain's plasticity across the lifespan, which is what makes it possible to adapt behaviours, and learn new skills during the lifecycle rather than restricted to critical periods of time.

Socio-emotional development is both experience-expectant and experience-dependent. It is experience-expectant in that children need small and simple amounts of input to learn how to develop relationships. Infants cared for outside the home who are not given the opportunity to develop attachment relationships, may have their ability for such attachments compromised. Experience-dependent is therefore valuable because the type of early attachment made shapes infants future emotional relationships. These are influenced by both positive and negative experiences with individual care givers (Schore, 1994: Rosenzweig et al., 1972).

Polyvagal Theory

Polyvagal Theory (PVT), developed by Porges et al. (1994), emphasises the link between brain, heart and emotions. It is concerned with the brain and the nerves in processing emotions. Within the PVT the nerve connects the brain, facial muscles, heart and gut, managing the three general states in which humans exist:

- Social engagement
- Fight or flight
- Frozen.

If an infant feels they are at risk emotionally, physical changes will occur. There is increased heart rate, rapid breathing, increased sweat production and a slower working digestive system as blood supply is re-directed. Porges et al.'s (1994) insight enables an understanding of the function of the nervous system when trying to regulate emotions. When an infant feels safe and happy their physical systems – the heart, the social engagement system of face, eyes, mouth and middle ear and gut – work in harmony, resulting in positively learning and functioning. However, if they have or are experiencing adverse childhood experiences, then they will be operating in a consistently high alert mode, using too many fight or flight strategies. Their physical health is compromised in the present with subsequent health issues in later life, such as coronary heart disease, diabetes and cancers (Zeedyk, 2018). Similarly, the carers, both parents and practitioners working in early childhood and education and care (ECEC) settings, own emotional wellbeing and stress levels will impact on young infant stress levels, highlighting the emotional care connections between carer and infant.

Stress and emotional relationships

A stressful environment for a mother during pregnancy results in the production of the stress hormone cortisol. The hormone crosses the placental barrier and circulates round the foetal body, overwhelming its capacity to regulate its own stress response. Many of the effects of prenatal stress can be minimised and overcome by sensitive caregiving, especially during the first year. If the mother or other close consistent carer is well attuned to the infant and responsive to their needs, this can help enormously with future development. Everyday experiences therefore help shape an infant's brain from the experiences to the daily routines.

Evidence from brain development research suggests:

- Elevated stress hormones can be hazardous to the brain, dampening electrical activity
- Very young infants experience large cortisol (stress hormone) surges during aspects of daily care (undressing, bathing)
- Sensitive care buffers cortisol surge: sensitivity impacts on a child's development.

(Eliot, 1999)

Parents and practitioners who have responsibility for infants must understand the 'brain story' in developing their pedagogical choices of care within the environmental context. Responsive caring, in my view, acting on increased knowledge about the growing brain and emotions, can promote caregiving buffers against infant stress, wiring up the brain positively for learning and emotional literacy. Within the home this could be parents and, in ECEC contexts, the practitioner responsible in the care of the infant. Emotionally attuned interactions therefore help infants to learn about their motions and provide them with cues on how to moderate their own responses (Campos et al., 2004).

Questions for discussion

Brain development in practice: going for a walk

Zeedyk's study (2008) of forward facing buggies, concluded that the design of strollers shaped infants emotional and brain development. Having a buggy that faces away, especially during the first year, makes it more difficult to let parents know they need them, reduces communication and causes stress. The more time that infants have to spend in anxiety, the more their brain comes to expect anxiety, and thus goes on to actually create it. Blaiklock's study (2013) also investigated the frequency of parent-child interactions that occur when parents accompany young children in prams while moving between shops. They found minimal levels of interaction were observed between parents and children under two years when infants were transported in prams facing forward and could not see their parents, making interaction more difficult. Support for the value of being able to face towards parents was seen in the higher frequency of language interactions that occurred when young children were transported in supermarket trolleys although only a small frequency of parents had face fronted prams.

Therefore, sensitive care, in this example selecting buggies that face parents and carers faces, can reduce an anticipated stressful experience and buffer cortisol surge.

Infants don't need constant attention. They do, however, need enough attention. And they need it at crucial times. Infants especially need attention and comforting when they are feeling uncomfortable and at risk of being overwhelmed. It is in these moments that they most need reassurance, which comes through the responsiveness of someone they trust. It is through relationships that infants learn how to deal with their discomfort and anxiety (suzannezeedyk.co.uk).

What other everyday experiences could be potentially stressful for infants and how can they be minimised?

Attachment is therefore central to a sense of security, leading to social competence and resilience. It is essential for their survival that infants are in relationships that are reliable and sensitive to their needs. Winnicott (2012) concludes that when infants are responsive and expressive in their facial and body movements parents respond and give them the sensitive care that they need. By observing the subtle, shifting patterns of infant's facial and body movements, parents become aware of their infant's cues and provide further experiences to support them (Murray and Andrews, 2000; Gerhardt, 2014).

Questions for discussion

Critical periods or everyday interactions? Read the below extract and reflect on it. Do you agree with Stern?

Personalities are conceived as being shaped more by their everyday interactions with parents than by isolated dramatic events or major developmental stages, according to Stern (1990). In contrast to some of the more established sequential stages in behavioural science, Stern asserts there are no critical phases in a child's life, as Freud suggests within the oral and anal periods of psychoanalysis, but rather a long continuum of smaller but important moments. For him the infant discovers the first inkling of autonomy, from small acts of assertion. At four months of age the infants may avert their eyes; at about twelve months they have the physical ability to walk away and at eighteen months say, "No." All of these are considered acts of will – each infant behaviour is influenced by the natural development of the central nervous system. As this evolution continues, self-affirmation creates the sense in an infant's mind that they are an individual with a personalised will. However, it can also be skewed, by carers whose own needs thwart an infant's normal urge for independence, happening continually, quickly and in ways so small that it is unrealized. For example, the carer who always insists on meeting her infant's gaze or directing their behaviour even when the infant turns away is engaged in a subtle battle of wills. Another example is the carer who continually under matches her infant's level of excitable activity, will eventually learned to be passive, unable to provoke attention from their carer. However, the psychological imprints of these early encounters, Dr Stern believes, are not permanently set and can be overcome in later positive interactions. "Relationships throughout life continually reshape the inner working model of relationships and therefore an imbalance at one point can be corrected later. Therefore, for Stern there is no crucial period early in life but an on-going, life-long process, with multiple varied emotional connections.

Emotional care connections

Historically emotions have been considered a vague and elusive domain in development psychology. However, as Dunn (1994) states, this is a scene that has been changing, and science (neuroscience) specifically linking brain functioning to emotions has gained research momentum through the advancement and availability of technology in measuring brain function. Neuroscience supports emotional care connections, specifically the theory of attachment being an instinctive behaviour, with a biological function. Attachment is the emotional process deriving from instinctive behaviour and that a biological control system drives this behaviour. The strong affection infants feel for key carers in their lives leads to feelings of pleasure through their interaction and being comforted by their closeness during times of stress (Bowlby, 1997). Whilst I have included more detail of Bowlby's theory of attachment in Chapter 8 it is valuable to include its connection to biological function while understanding that attachment is a regulatory theory and can be defined as the interactive regulation of biological synchronicity between organs. Ainsworth and Bell (1978) concluded Bowlby wanted to update psychoanalytical theory and with the advances in biology provide an interdisciplinary perspective. These relationships are considered prototypes for later socialisation and continue to exert influences throughout the life span (Berk, 2012).

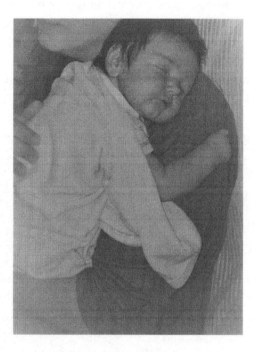

Physical attachment to a carer

The ethological theory, developed by Bowlby (1988), is a widely an accepted view of attachment today (Barnes, 1995). Belsky et al. (2007) developed understandings of attachment and argued it was not simply about a static, single or stable relationship. Rather it was the context-dependent changes that occurred as relationships evolved over time. Similarly, Dunn (1994) argued that mothers display different levels of bonding depending on the age of their infant, and as the infant's independence develops in the first two years the intensity of the attachment lessens. However, although attachment is conceived as being fluid, particularly after the first year, primary attachments remain advantageous in emotional development (Barnes, 1995). The infant develops more complex understanding of the carers who look after them and they begin to make assessments about the environmental situation including their own role and the carer's role within it (Cooper and Roth, 2003).

Bowlby (1969) described the internal images or maps that are built up because of these exchanges as internal working models (IWMs). These internal working models

127

enable the child to anticipate and interpret the behaviour of other people and plan a response. Where the caregiver is experienced as a source of security and support, the infant develops internal working models in which they have a positive self-image and in which other people are depicted as being trustworthy and responsive. Infants with non-attuned or abusive caregivers internalise a less positive self-image as being unworthy of love and without agency; they also represent others as unpredictable, unresponsive and untrustworthy. These infants build up very negative internal working models in relation to attachment.

Trevarthen (2001) agrees emotions are a central ingredient of early relationships, continually reacting and adjusting to each other at an emotional level. Vorria et al. (2003) also examined the quality of attachment in Greek residential care and showed how the children's capacity for attachment was related to the responses of their caregivers.

Practitioner's perspective

Communicating with emotions

In a study a practitioner used infant signing (symbolic gesturing) to enhance their emotional relationships with the infants in their care. They reflected on how gesturing with the infants developed their own thinking about connectivity and tuning in:

> I think particularly when children show negative emotions I am much in tune now than before because before it was 'oh are you sad?' You've now got a gesture for sad I think it's much more personal and you're really, really tuned in and I think that supports the children as well because they are much more responsive because they are using signs as well.

Reflecting on the value

> Yes, I mean I think there is because of your awareness within the group . . . and I think because even in a group you are focusing with every child . . . because it's so easy just to go sort of over them, without intending to, for example, you're singing it to the group.

Reflections of the emotional challenges by key person 3 – manager

> With newer, less experienced staff coming out of college they find showing their emotions really difficult, especially in front of people they are working with. I'm not sure why, but they seem inhibited by their own demonstration of emotion and their reactions to the children. It becomes almost like rehearsed statements. So, for example, they tend to say things like 'oh you're fine, you're fine' as a way of trying to suppress any emotions, or emotional behaviour, both in themselves and from the child. I think the child doesn't need you to say that they're fine they actually need a little bit more touching, smiling, or maybe just a different tone in your voice to show it is ok to be emotional.
>
> (Norman, 2011)

The close relationships and how the relationships evolve are central to the infant's mental health. And the tie that binds them together in space endure over time.

Creating a cherished space for emotional relationships to develop

Holding refers initially to the physical holding of an infant and relating to the infant, so she feels safely held. Davis and Wallbridge advise that 'Holding is the basis for what gradually becomes a self-experiencing being' (Davis and Wallbridge, 2012: 97). The feeling of being held is gradually internalised by the infant as emotionally holding. Winnicott also talks about the 'holding environment' as a safe environment that holds individuals and includes their pain and uncertainty and Winnicott's concept of 'holding' complements the notion of 'containment' proposed by Bion, and the term is used interchangeably in care contexts. This concept has been widened to include the 'holding in mind' of others. The concept of 'containment' (Bion, 1962) describes the process in which parent/carer is attuned to her infant's state of mind and can hold the infant's uncomfortable feelings in her own mind that would otherwise threaten to overwhelm the infant. A factor, therefore, in supporting a carer's capacity for containment is sufficient external support from others that perform similar containing and caring functions. However, the concept of containment should also include the carer processing their feelings and thereby transforming them and making them manageable for the infant. This also means taking risks when reflecting on personal experiences that may be challenging, authentically analysing observations and evaluating practice. For practitioners it can also be about changing established views in the light of new theoretical information or observational evidence. In making practice changes from emotional perspectives, practitioners are able to develop emotionally (Dowling, 2014). One way of developing this is connecting emotions with observations.

Observing using a Tavistock approach. A care-ful way of observing

The Tavistock approach as a care-ful way of observing enables the observer to immerse themselves in the interactions that take place between the infant and others present. The observer remains non-interventionist and as unobtrusive as possible, thus in theory experiencing the everyday interactions. Rustin (2009) defined the intention as 'being present in the moment as fully as possible, open to perceiving as much as possible' (p. 30) A clear characteristic of the observation method is that no notes, photos or videos are taken by the observer, but instead a report or transcript of the observation is written up as soon as possible afterwards for discussion. The transcript aims to encapsulate not only what was seen, but significantly what was felt by the observer; the emotions, thoughts and feelings that were evoked during the process, rather than on a focused end-point of what was observed. The central aspect of the method relies on seeking to understand internal emotional states rather than external factors. It can lead to a greater insight into infants' anxieties and feelings of safety in the context observed (Elfer, 2006).

Approaches to supporting attachments in practice

Zeedyk (2017) captured two key, *sabre tooth tigers and teddy bear*, insights that the science of attachment has discovered over the past several decades. The first is the frequency of infants' and young children's anxieties. They can fear many things unknown to their carer, such as being afraid of being left alone or when an unfamiliar adult leans in too close, even if they are smiling. Zeedyk uses the evolutionary illustration of 'Sabre Tooth Tigers', the past predator, who approaches infants when they cannot yet run away. The symbolisation illustrates how infants rely on carers and need to be able to call on someone to come and help. The Sabre Tooth Tiger aids as a reminder to carers of infant's anxieties and reliance on them to feel safe as a

Teddy bear love

survival mode. The second insight from the science of attachment is the importance of comfort and this was captured by the symbol 'Teddy Bears' in providing reassurance. Responsive attention from parents and practitioners helps an infant to grow an 'internal teddy bear'. It helps infants and young children to develop a self-regulatory system that will last throughout life, and will be positive in retaining calmness, even in moments when strong emotions are occurring. This capacity for infants and young children to develop in their capacity for emotionally self-awareness and calmness will be valuable in guarding against later mental and physical health problems and preventing relationship difficulties later in life.

An emotionally caring relationship

The Pikler approach is based on a respectful relationship between carer and infant, through tender care moments – naturally paced motor development, free movement and uninterrupted play. The close relationship between carer and infant, experiencing the world in physical and emotional safety, is known as intersubjectivity. Intersubjectivity was first described as the meshing that occurs between caregiver and infant, with the caregiver allowing an infant to be introduced into their understandings

131

of the society and culture they exist in (Anning and Edwards, 2006). It is considered as a meeting of minds when one person brings another into their culture. It demands considerable attention to the emotional state of the infant, and the carer needs to gradually tune into the infant's way of experiencing the world (Hopkins, 1988). Trevarthan (2001) believed that infants are born with the readiness to know another human and engage with them. He illustrated that interactions between carers can be mutual, with infants taking the lead within the interaction and not simply responding to their carer's behaviour.

The work of Gerber has been used an example and then developed in relation to forming attachments and its significance for brain development and intersubjectivity:

Principle 1: *Full attention – especially when involved in the caring activity times.* Undivided attention by carers is interpreted by the infant as the embodiment of Love. It brings stillness and quality to the carer

Principle 2: *Slowing down.* Creating calm around infants is relaxing, as well as peaceful, and allows them to be in an environment where their sacred 'unfolding' can take place respectfully.

Principle 3: *Build trust, and your relationship, during the caring activity times.* Pikler believed that parents and caregivers need to take the time to make routines nappy changing, feeding, bathing and dressing, an unhurried and pleasant quality time – with the infant being an active partner.

Principle 4: *'With' – and not 'To'. Building a cooperative relationship.* Pikler viewed infants as active participants rather than passive recipients in their care, requiring further communication and time to respond.

Practitioner's perspective

Sue was childminding twenty months' old Pete. His Mum said to Sue – 'He has a runny nose and hates having it wiped.' Sue noticed that Mum would (gently) hold his head and hand whilst she wiped his nose. Pete struggled and wiggled to escape. Later when Sue noticed that his nose was running again, she held out a tissue in her open hand. She showed it to Pete and quietly said, 'Your nose was running let's wipe it together.' She waited whilst Pete looked at the tissue, then at Sue. He looked at the tissues again and there was a space to pause. He then took the tissue and wiped it independently, holding his head up for it be checked at the end.

Principle 5: *Infants are never put into a position which they cannot get into by themselves.* The reason for this is that they become trapped – and no longer free in their movement. In essence: an infant becomes a prisoner of his/her own body.

Principle 6: *Allow infants uninterrupted time for play.* Gerber firmly believes that parents don't need to entertain their infants because given a nurturing environment and freedom to explore; infants are quite capable of entertaining themselves. The unfolding of who they truly are meant to be. As they play uninterrupted by our interaction, they are experiencing independence, and mastery of their world. Self-esteem and confidence building is taking place during this time.

Principle 7: *Infants send us cues all the time. Tune in respectfully.* Responding to the infant with respect and observe the behaviour. If an infant is quite clearly wanting to do something else do we allow this, or do we take an authoritative position in the relationship?

(www.parentingworx.co.nz/fantastic-reading/emmi-piklers-8-guiding-principles).

Family practitioner summary

Care is about being friendly, kind and loving. It is about developing a shared relationship and listening. As a practitioner we have responsibilities to support parents and share their anxieties and concerns about their infants. The one message I talk through with parents is spoiling their infant or the concern they are too dependent. I explain that by being there for them and understanding them will create independent thinkers and confident children! Caring for them doesn't end at a certain stage, it is life long and is personal.

Focused points

- Neuro science contributes to the understanding of development and the value of emotional relationships

- Brain development and biology link in the emotionally care connections we make

- Attachments has many facets although close supportive relationships is at the core of emotional care connections

- Practical approaches are ways that practitioners can reflect on their own practice and develop thinking about how they enhance the emotional relationships with infants in their care

Concluding thoughts

This chapter explored attachment and how close relationships could be enhanced from conception to infancy – amongst carers, both parents and those close to the infant, and practitioners. Practical examples were included to enable practitioners to apply thinking around attachment and professional relationships in their caring profession.

Bibliography

Abbott, R. and Burkitt, A. (2015) *Child Development and the Brain*. London: Policy Press.

Ainsworth, M. and Bell, S. (1970/8) 'Attachment, exploration, and separation: Illustrated by the behaviour of one-year-olds in a strange situation'. *Child Development* 41(49–67).

Anning, A. and Edwards, A. (2006) *Promoting Children's Learning from Birth to Five: Developing the New Early Years Professional*. London: McGrawHill.

Barnes, P. (1995) *Personal, Social and Emotional Development of Children*. Milton Keynes: Blackwell Publishing.

Belsky, J., Burchinal, M., McCartney, V., Vandell, D., Clarke-Stewart, K. and Owen, M. (2007) 'Are there long-term effects of early childcare'. *Child Development* 78(2): 681–701.

Berk, L. (2012) *Child Development*. London: Allyn and Bacon.

Bion, R. (1962) *Learning from Experience*. London: Heinemann.

Blaiklock, K. (2013) 'Talking with Children When Using Prams While Shopping'. *Early Childhood Education Journal* 16(15–28), available online at www.childforum.com/images/stories/2013_Blaiklock_published.pdf

Blakemore, S. and Frith, U. (2005) *The Learning Brain*. Oxford: Blackwell Publishing.

Bowlby, J. (1969) *Attachment and Loss, Vol. I: Attachment*. New York: Basic Books.

Bowlby, J. (1988) *A Secure Base* (2nd ed.). New York: Basic Books.

Bowlby, J. (1997) *Attachment and Loss, Vol. I: Attachment*. London: Pimlico.

Braidley, B. (1989) *Visions of Infancy*. Cambridge: Polity Press.

Campos, J., Frankel, C. and Camras, L. (2004) 'On the Nature of Emotion Regulation'. *Child Development* 75(2): 377–394.

Conkbayir, M. (2017) *Early Childhood and Neuroscience*. London: Bloomsbury Publishing.

Cooper, T. and Roth, I. (2003) *Challenging Psychological Issues*. Milton Keynes: OUP.

Davis, M. and Wallbridge, D. (2012) *Boundary and Space: An Introduction to the Work of D. W. Winnicott*. New York: Brunner/Mazel.

Department of Health (DoH) (2009) *Healthy Child Programme*. London: DoH.

Dollard, J. and Miller, N. (1950) *Personality and Psychotherapy*. New York: McGraw-Hill.

Dowling, M. (2014) *Young Children's Personal, Social and Emotional Development* (4th edtion). London: Sage.

Dunn, J. (1994) Stepfamilies: who benefits? who does not? Hillsdale. Available online at https://adc.bmj.com/content/archdischild/73/6/487.full.pdf

Eliot, L. (2001) *Early Intelligence: How the Brain and Mind Develop in the First Five Years of Life*. London: Penguin.

Elfer, P. (2006) 'Exploring children's expressions of attachment in nursery'. *European Early Childhood Education Research Journal* 14(2): 81–95. DOI:10.1080/13502930285209931.

Gerber, M. (2001) *Respecting Infants: A New Look at Magda Gerber's RIE Approach. Zero to three.* UK: National Centre for Infants.

Gerber, M (2003) *Dear Parent: Caring for Infants with Respect Resources for Infant Edu-carers.* UK: Resources for Infant Educarers.

Gerhardt, S. (2014) *Why Love Matters. How Affection Shapes an Infant's Brain.* London: Routledge.

Healthy Child Programme Service. Available online at www.gov.uk/govement/publications/healthy-child-programme-0-to-19-health-visitor-and-school-nurse-commissioning

Hopkins, J. (1988) 'Facilitating the development of intimacy between nurses and infants in day nurseries'. *Early Child Development and Care* 33: 99–111.

Johnson, M. (1999) 'Into the minds of babes'. *Science.* DOI:10.1126/science.286.5438.247

Johnson, M. (2001) 'Functional brain development in humans'. *Neuroscience* 2: 475–483. Available online at www.nature.com/articles/35081509

Kisilevsky, B., Hains, S., Brown, C., Lee, C., Cowperthwaite, B., Stutman, S., Swansburg, M., Lee. K, Xie, X., Huang, H., Ye, H., Zhang, K. and Wang, Z. (2009) 'Foetal sensitivity to properties of maternal speech and language'. *Infant Behaviour Development* 32(1): 59–71.

Murray, L. and Andrews L. (2005) *The Social Infant.* Richmond: CP Publishing.

Music, G. (2016) *Nurturing Natures: Attachment and Children's Emotional, Sociocultural and Brain Development.* Hove and New York: Psychology Press.

Norman, A. (2011) 'The professional role of key persons using symbolic gesturing and their perspectives on its value in supporting the emotional relationship with infants in day nursery'. University of Southampton, School of Education, Unpublished Doctoral Thesis.

Nutbrown, C. and Page, J. (2013) *Working with Infants and Children from Birth to Three.* London: Sage.

Porges, S., Doussard-Roosevelt, J. A. and Maiti, A. (1994) 'Vagal tone and the physiological regulation of emotion. Monographs of the Society for Research'. *Child Development* 59: 167–186.

Rosenzweig, M., Bennet, E. and Diamond, M. (1972) 'Brain changes in response to experience'. *Scientific American* 226: 22–29.

Rustin (2009) 'Work Discussion: some historical and theoretical observations'. Available online at www.bera.ac.uk/blog/observing-to-understand-using-the-tavistock-method-of-observation-to-support-reflective-practice

Rutter, M. (2002) 'Nature, Nurture and Development: From Evangelism, through Science towards Policy and Practice'. *Child Development* 73(1): 1–21.

Schore, A. (1994) *Affect Regulation and the Origin of the Self: The Neurobiology of Emotional Development.* Hillsdale, NJ: Erlbaum.

Stern, D. N. (1985) *The Interpersonal World of the Infant.* New York: Basic Books.

Trevarthen, C. (2001) 'Intrinsic motives for companionship in understanding; their origin development and their significance for mental health'. *Infant Mental Health Journal* 22: 95–131.

Vorria, P., Papaligoura, Z., Dunn, J., Marinus, H and van Ijzendoorn, V. (2003) 'Early experiences and attachment relationships of Greek infants raised in residential group care'. *Journal of Child Psychology and Psychiatry* 44(8): 37–52.

Winnicott, D. (1960) The Theory of the Parent–Infant Relationship. In Winnicott, D. *The Maturational Processes and the Facilitating Environment.* New York: International UP.

Winnicott D. (1971) The Use of an Object and Relating through Identifications. In Winnicott, D. *Playing and Reality.* London: Routledge.

Zeedyk, S. (2008) 'Infant buggies may undermine child development'. *Observational Study.* Scotland: University of Dundee.

Zeedyk, S. (2018) 'Sabretooth Tigers and Teddy bears. Connected care'. Available online at www.suzannezeedyk.com/

7 Professionalising care

Introduction and context

The growth in the number of infants attending Early Childhood, Education and Care (ECEC) settings in England has been relatively new compared to the long history of provision for three- and four-year olds. The widening provision to include infants under two years has enabled the greater participation of both men and women to enter the paid labour market as discussed in Chapter 2 (Brehony and Nawrotzki, 2010). Subsequently it is increasingly common for infants to be cared for outside of the home by carers in ECEC settings (Kalliala, 2014). Research has acknowledged the value of developing and maintaining emotional relationships with those infants in care, whilst stipulating it should not be a replication of the parenting relationship, rather a unique complimentary relationship alongside parenting. For practitioners working with infants in ECEC settings this may evoke aspirations and beliefs about how they consider the relationships could be enhanced and implemented into practice (Elfer and Page, 2015). However, as the demand for care places increases, these aspirations and beliefs may be disillusioned and compromised if there are too many infants to care for with inadequate support, too many infants in one designated space for long hours throughout the day or lack of understanding about development and care with those practitioners sharing the care (Datler et al., 2010). A further aspect of the 'professional' caring role is the pre-condition for emotionally responsive engaging interactions in practice and an attendance to the internal resources of the individual practitioner. Practitioners are charged with the task of establishing and maintaining an emotional intersubjectivity with several children at one time, regardless of their own inner resources or ability to do so' (Brennan 2014: 289). Whilst emotional management is accepted as part of working in the caring professions, in England early childhood practitioners have predominantly been those with the fewer qualifications, lower status and less experience. Low financial incentives, long daily hours and challenging parent partnerships all feature in the complexity of their existing position. This chapter introduces some of the complexities of the role and unpicks the challenges. It also advocates for professional recognition and the value of working with infants, including practical ways that have been implemented.

Leaving the primary carer

When a child leaves their primary carer to attend an ECEC setting for the first time it can be very distressing for both parent and infant. During the transition both infant and parent can feel unsettled and emotional. However, if a healthy attachment between infant and parent has been nurtured and established infants can be resilient in the separation, capable of building loving and trusting relationships with other carers, including practitioners when the relationship has been established (Dowling, 20012 Elfer, Goldschmeid and Sellek, 2011). Practitioners are allocated key children to look after in ECEC settings and act as their key person developing a caring relationship.

Out of sight BUT in mind: separation

Goldschmeid and Jackson (1994) influenced by the work of Bowlby, extended his attachment theory and introduced the key person concept. She defined the role in ECEC settings as a practitioner with primary responsibility of care for individual children, valuing the close early attachments in group care (Clasien, 2008; Goldschmeid and Jackson, 1994; Nutbrown, 2011). She believed it was important for families using ECEC settings to be supported by practitioners, using a key person approach, so close secondary attachments can be made between the infant and the practitioner. The secondary attachment can therefore influence how the infant deals and copes with changes in their life. As Dryden et al. (2005: 81) state 'the quality of learning depends on the quality of the relationship', emphasises the importance of sensitivity, stability and consistency of care.

The practitioner as a key person in ECEC settings

In England, ECEC settings including home-based childminders, creches, family centres, home and purpose-built day nursery settings are regulated by the education authority, following an Early Years Foundation Stage curriculum (2017). Practitioners working in these ECEC settings are expected to be appropriately qualified and deemed suitable regarding health and safety and safeguarding risks. Higher national qualifications continue to be central to advancing the practitioner role and increased recognition of knowledge and experience continues to be raised, particularly for those working with infants. Higher level qualifications have been linked to a positive attitude towards infants and young children and their learning. Additionally, increased knowledge gained from qualifications develops more inclusive pedagogical practices and understanding of their role in enhancing appropriate attachments and positive attitudes to individualised care and learning (Hestenes et al., 2007). The practitioner, as key person generally has responsibilities for a small group of infants, with a vested interest, promoting an intimate relationship in each of the individual infants within the group, supporting their development and acting as the key point of contact with the infant's parents (DfES 2012):

> The Key Person Approach is a way of working in nurseries in which the whole focus and organisation is aimed at enabling and supporting close attachments between individual children and individual nursery staff. The Key Person approach is an involvement, an individual and reciprocal commitment between a member of staff and a family. It is an approach that has clear benefits for all involved.
>
> (Elfer et al., 2003: 18)

Elfer (2003:19) makes the distinction between key worker and key person, the latter being embedded in The Early Year's Foundation Stage Curriculum (EYFS, 2017). Other care services use the term *key worker*, and this often includes a liaison role between services, but responsibility for their own 'clients'. Key worker systems in ECEC settings such as nurseries are an organisational strategy for sharing responsibility of children and for monitoring and record keeping as an 'impersonal' role. The key person may include the above but also has an emotional bond with the child in which comfort and care are administered; a 'personal' role. The key person approach is currently a requirement in early years setting within the Early Years Foundation Stage (EYFS, 2017).

Key aspects of a key person relationship: *Stop, Look and Listen*

- Be available
- Be tuned in
- Be responsive
- Be consistent.

Questions for discussion

An infant has been attending the nursery for two weeks, three days a week. Her mother is working. The infant is thirteen months. The practitioner is the key person to her child. She is qualified with a FDeg in Early Years and has been working at the nursery for just over six months. She sees the parents at the end of the day, if she is on a late shift. She works with two other colleagues.

A mother walks into the room and looks at her child who is in a high chair finishing tea.

'Why hasn't she got her own cup, you said it would help her to drink and I went to the shops and brought her one on Monday?'

The mother picks up the child out of her highchair and looks at her.

'She looks really grubby, is it normal for her to look so, so mucky?'

She wipes her infants face with her sleeve and looks at the practitioner. The practitioner looks flushed and avoids eye contact.

She then says 'I have her daily book filled in, sorry about the cup she had it earlier and it was being washed.'

They move to the table.

'Everything ok?' says the manager as she walks in.

'Yes thank you, works been hard. And how are you?' the parent responds.

What is going on here?

Are leaving transitional times as important as entering?

Why did the mother say all was good to the manager?

What is the infant's perception of the transitional time?

How could this interaction between the practitioner be more positive?

What does this say about parent partnership and the complexities behind verbal communication?

Practitioners in their role as key person in ECEC settings

Fundamental to an infant's healthy development in ECEC settings are the positive and close relationships between their practitioner as key person. Infants need to be validated to feel good about themselves with adults. If infants are not paid attention to and their needs or feelings not listened to they can feel emotionally rejected. This can potentially and unintentionally happen by practitioners who may not know how to support or meet infant's needs emotionally. Most early years practitioners, along with others in the 'helping' professions, have an image of themselves as giving, caring people with 'ambition to love and be of service to humanity' who may therefore be looking to the infants to 'fit the contours of their own ambitions' (Selleck and Griffin, 1996, cited in Forbes 2004). A practitioner may have decided to enter the profession of caring for infants because of their own childhood experiences or the way they were parented. If an infant responds according to what the practitioner is conveying, then this can in part, work successfully with the development of make emotional connections with each other. However, many infants, in ECEC settings, away from their home and parents, have other ideas about being so compliant and adjusted to the arrangement. Their behaviour can be challenging, and they can also reject practitioners' approaches to caring for them and resist the façade presented to them. Parents may too also feel anxious, challenging and criticising practices and care. Bain and Barnett (1980) suggested that, if the predominant motivation to work with infants arises from unresolved childhood experiences, practitioners may then feel angry and resentful when their own needs are not being met within the infant–practitioner relationship. This can lead practitioners to blame infant's behaviours, parents, managers or co-workers in complicated processes of transference and projection. It is essential, therefore, that practitioners are able gain the maturity and a sense of self-awareness to fulfil their role as key person. They should be able to have the training and opportunities to look and reflect at their own motivations and understand where they come from and through the knowledge they gain about themselves to better understand and adjust their responses to the infants in their care (Goleman, 1996; Manning-Morton and Thorp, 2003). Vorria et al. (2003, cited in Nutbrown and Page, 2008) examined the quality of attachment and showed how the capacity for attachment was related to an infant's cognitive and psychosocial development, their behaviour, temperament and the sensitive responses of their caregivers. Those infants who were securely attached to carers outside of the family home showed more frequent positive affect and social behaviour. They also initiated more frequent interactions with their caregivers, with the relationship being close and emotionally connected (Nutbrown and Page, 2013). However, this was only comparable to the primary care giver (parent) when the quality of care was consistent and there were available opportunities for with one-to-one time, a potential challenge in ECEC group care, such as day nurseries, when the ratio is 1:3 (Davis and Wallbridge, 1991).

Professionalising work with infants: a key person approach

In ECEC nursery settings, Powell and Goouch concluded there was a highly committed group of predominantly young female practitioners who felt they were unsupported and overlooked in relation to their professional development. They were unaware of the professional information they could access and few opportunities to share their experiences and communication was minimal, often working in isolation, within the designated room. However, when the opportunity did arise the practitioners wanted to learn more about aspects of their work, share experiences, and reflect on their practice.

McDowell and Clark (2011) concluded two key factors undervalued professional care work with infants:

- The persistent dominance of the maternal discourse (Ailwood, 2008, cited in McDowall Clark and Bayliss, 2012) which characterises skill and proficiency as 'natural' and 'innate' attributes
- The emotional connection to young children that is such a key aspect of the role (Elfer et al., 2011). The maternal discourse stems from a view of childcare as providing a substitute mother role, a gendered image that assumes research and education is unnecessary to undertake the role and it either comes 'naturally' and if not experience will prevail (Moss, 2006).

Taggart (2011) challenged the outdated equation between caring and the female discourse and anti-intellectualism, arguing that there is 'seriousness' to the professional work. In professionalising the work of care with infants, graduate level qualifications promote the reflection of meaningful involvement with infants linking theory and practice and addressing assumptions which are then challenged by the practitioner, in their own experience. A new respect is gained for the specific skills and aptitudes of those working with infants, recognising the professionalism and need for deeper thinking, inherent in the role. This is imperative for practitioners working with the younger infants, because the support of their colleagues working with other age ranges can help them to maintain confidence in their own professionalism and value the complex role of infant room care (Osgood, 2010).

Professionalising a caring approach

Practitioner's perspective

I don't get paid much but I love my job

I have had to clean sick up today, the poor infant, we stroked his head until his mum came

I spent most of the day changing nappies as we were short staffed and they had curry for lunch!! I had to laugh!

I spent lunch time rocking an infant to sleep to music he was so anxious

We were playing with dough and an almost two-year-old girl came over to me and gave me a big hug, she sat with me and chatted . . . it was quite a moment as English was her second language and she had really struggled at settling

Csikszentmihalyi (1997) considered the autotelic personality as one in which a person performs acts because they are intrinsically rewarding, rather than a bid to achieve external goals. Csikszentmihalyi describes the autotelic personality as a trait possessed by individuals who can learn to enjoy situations that most other people would find challenging and unrewarding. Research has shown that aspects associated with the autotelic personality include curiosity, persistence, and humility. Considering the daily challenges and rewards of caring for infants, the practitioner has an intrinsic desire to work and support the wellbeing of infants and a relational approach. It is a caring engagement and interaction between carer and infant (Noddings, 2015).

Noddings (2015) considered caring processes can be unpredictable and the reciprocity in these relationships challenged as a result in the uncertainty of such interactions between children and adults. This can be difficult for practitioners who may fall back toward more dominant power relationships, taking charge in perhaps a mother hen way and being more directive in creating certainty in their practice, rather than unknown territory of what the interaction may prevail if it was more equally balanced. The anxiety and ambivalence many practitioners working with infants appear to feel could be a significant factor in the extent to which stated beliefs and aspirations translate into practice. This anxiety includes apprehension about parents' resentment if infants become too attached to a specific staff member (Hopkins 1988) and about infants' dependency and the distress this may cause if attachments become too strong (Hochschild, 2003). There is also a perceived unease about behaving inappropriately from a child protection point of view (Piper and Smith 2003). Staff working with infants bring to their work a depth of personal feeling and involvement, alongside professional beliefs values (Manning-Morton 2006; Osgood 2004). This may be a mechanism that as some key person practitioners employ to separate their professional and personal self to protect them self emotionally from becoming too involved in the emotional attachment (Hochschild, 2003). In addition, when there is a high turnover of underpaid practitioners and no systems of support, they are more likely to be unwilling to become emotionally involved with infants, and at worst avoid any emotional investment thus resulting in little or no eye contact, little holding, and little comforting – the very things infants are seeking and need most (Belsky and Rovine, 1988). Subsequently they may unsuccessfully recognise and interpret what the infant is trying to express through body language or otherwise (Dryden et al., 2005; Elfer et al., 2011). Gerber (1988, cited in Mooney, 2010) observed practitioners in ECEC and nursery settings and found at times emotional investment was lacking when they carried out care routines. The infants she observed were at times viewed as inanimate objects by staff looking after them without emotional responses and there was minimal quality time spent individually. This was an area also reflected on in Gerhardt's studies (2014) and both concluded it was better to provide good quality one-to-one care some of the time, than half of the attention all of the time, because then the infants would have some opportunity to be active participants in the relationship with their carer (Gerber, 1988 cited in Mooney, 2010).

Goldstein pointed out that caring encounters are also learning experiences for the very young, and that 'it is by being the cared-for that he or she will learn how to be the one-caring' (1998, cited in Schore, 2016: 3). For the practitioner learning, care and upbringing are not distinct fields that must somehow be joined up but interconnected facets of life that cannot be envisaged separately. Dalli (2006) argued that a theorised discourse about professional practice regarding care would allow an unacknowledged part of practitioners' lives to be heard. She proposed the notion of love and care to be reflected on as a pedagogical tool. Dalli endorsed Goldstein's (1998) contention that the image of a caring practitioners as smiling and offering warm hugs obscured the complexity and intellectual challenges for teachers.

The ethics of care

Taggart (2011) presented an argument for recognising the moral aspect of care as a practitioner, especially those working with infants in ECEC day nursery contexts. Care is conceived as being guided by the practitioners own guiding principles (Noddings, 2003) and for Taggart greater recognition and discourses needs to be shared and challenged as part of professionalism. When the ethics of care is considered as framing the practitioner's professional role then discourse about compassion, love and connectivity come to the fore professionally as opposed to a role which is often viewed as domestic and personal. This chapter does not specifically draw on a singular viewpoint of ethics but rather introduces the concepts and complexity associated with care. In training programmes Taggart argues many programmes would question whether personal qualities should be nurtured and whether they were necessary. I firmly believe in supporting infants holistically – training courses should be including discourses about the ethics of care and ways to enhance personal qualities. Taggart (2016) argues training programmes should be including the ways compassion is visible and conceptualised in developing thinking about ethical care rather than focusing on instrumental, outcomes based and patriarchal view of female suitability that currently exist. Ethics of care certainly raises questions about the emotional involvement in paid employment as well as the complexities of care giving in forming close emotional relationships. How do we nurture emotional relationships, whilst retaining a professional identity in a compassionate and loving way with the infants we care?

Questions for discussion

Why are baby rooms upstairs?

A senior practitioner works in a nursery chain that has three settings. One setting was the owner's previous home and the two other settings were purpose built and occupied the baby rooms upstairs, with one having windows at adult height. Due to the large group of infants attending the session the practitioners organised the time so they would take smaller groups of infants throughout the day to the garden rather than a whole group together. This seemed to work satisfactory. However, an infant, one years old, had begun attending the setting where the baby room was situated upstairs. The infant had been going to the setting three days a week for

---

several weeks but despite the various methods supporting the infant she continued to scream and cry throughout the days and when she was not screaming seemed unsettled and anxious. The parent and the practitioners were unsure about how to resolve the anxiety although it was agreed the infant was becoming overwhelmingly stressed. Through careful consideration and discussion, the parent made the decision to move the infant to the smaller home setting within the chain to see if the number of infants in the room was impacting on her stress. The setting the infant moved to also had the baby room on the ground floor. After a couple of weeks, the infant seemed more settled and happier in general. The senior practitioner held meetings with the staff from both settings and discussed ways of improving practice. During the meetings she spoke positively with the staff about the connection between transitional theory, practice and infant's emotions so they could actively reflect on why the infant had not settled. The senior practitioner and the practitioners in the settings concluded that the constant transition between going upstairs and downstairs throughout the day was contributing to a high level of anxiety and this infant had verbalised it more openly. Due to the larger number of infants attending the practitioners in their role as key person also reflected on ways they could create opportunities for focused time to enhance relationships. They also agreed they needed to verbalise to each other if they themselves were becoming stressed and anxious with the infants crying. More regular supervision was arranged on a rolling four-week schedule. As a result of the supervision practices were modified. Staff re-arranged the outdoor time to begin the session outside and then slowly transition inside during the session, so it was less disjointed. Certainly, the free movement of the indoor and outdoor to the baby room on the ground floor provided a gentler way of transitioning between areas than being picked up and taken up and down stairs throughout the day.

The senior practitioner fed back her observations to the senior management team and it was noted that if the chain was to expand the design of the building needed to reflect a baby room that supported varying needs, remain homely, not exceed nine infants at any one time and be on the ground floor to promote opportunities of free flow.

Do you agree with the practitioner's conclusions?

What are your thoughts about the physical space and baby rooms upstairs?

Do you think quality can be maintained in baby rooms occupying large numbers of infant?

How would you have supported the parent during this transition?

Recognising professional love

The word love has recently gained attention in the way practitioners reflect on their experiences with the infants they care for (Page, 2017). However, as a term used professionally, love is often replaced with terms such as early childhood care, affection, empathy, understanding in articulating the feelings towards an infant (Cousins, 2017).

> Defining love in professional roles is problematic because there is no skill set that can be applied, taught or measured. Nevertheless, to deny the existence of love, particularly when research has already confirmed that love matters, is unhelpful. It is the debate and theorisation of love and care that is important.
>
> (Page, 2011)

- Define professional love
- How do you construct areas of intimacy?
- What concerns may there be?
- How do we define care and is there a difference?

Professional love beyond gender stereotypes

Familiarity, pattern and predictability of carer responses give infants a sense of self. Continuity of attention from key people who know children well, who are interpreting and responding to their gestures and cues, enable children to attend to their inclinations and to play freely is known as 'tuning in' (Elfer et al., 2011). Tuning in to infants can be helpful in unexpected ways, because they often express emotions that are challenging to manage and with the support of the key person they can share their feelings. Tuning in can also be advantageous as a reflection tool for key persons to acknowledge infants who are less expressive and more insular in conveying their emotions (Mooney, 2010) Vallotton (2009) studied whether infants can influence their quality of care and concluded that infant communicative gestures predicted caregiver responsiveness. In this way infants influenced, through their own actions, the behaviour of the caregivers. Infants' behaviours on caregivers' responses is critical in helping caregivers appreciate their own behaviour toward the infants they look after.

> It is astonishing to me that the words 'loving and secure' have been eroded from the recent iterations of the EYFS (2012, 2014) in relation to 'how children learn to be strong and independent', as if love no longer has a rightful place in early years practice. Respondents have told us of their 'utter relief' that research on love and intimacy is 'at last' being conducted.
>
> (Page, 2015)

'Professional Love' in Early Years Settings (PLEYS) used a range of methods to reveal the conceptions and practices of love, intimacy and care in early years settings. The project findings produced an 'Attachment Toolkit' and is intended to complement the safeguarding policies and procedures of any early years setting which are designed to protect infants from abuse or harm in all its forms. It included videos and examples that addressed practitioners' own feelings as an integral part of 'Professional Love'. The materials were designed and to be used as a way for practitioners to gain confidence about their professional decisions in relation to love, care and intimacy and how to determine the appropriateness of 'Professional Love' in the context of their attachment relationships with infants and young children in their own early years setting (www.professionallove.group.shef.ac.uk).

More recently, infant-toddler professional's narratives were evaluated in relation to their professional love, attachment theory and relational ethics. Their responses revealed continuing concern about where love and intimacy should be placed alongside safeguarding protocol in non-familial pedagogical relationships. The study concluded training and guidance on care, love and intimacy was a continuing necessity on how to safely interpret these theories in their everyday practice (Page, 2017).

Without knowledge and support practitioners continue to grapple with their own emotions in their complex professional role, therefore uncertain about how to connect lovingly with the infants in their care.

Practitioner's perspective

A member of staff was on her honeymoon and on extended leave – for the infant she cared for full time it was like he had to be resettled with the parent . . . it was really upsetting.

Some parents don't like you to have a too close a relationship and it is awkward at the end of the day as if they are saying it is their infant . . . love seems a strong word. Love is quite personal, and I am not sure I am comfortable with it . . . should I say love or care? I sometimes question my actions – should I hug and tell them I love them and how much cuddling is allowed – is it more appropriate at certain times of the day – it then feels a bit unnatural.

Emotional management: practitioners in their role as key person

Emotional management is the ability to create a publicly observable facial and bodily display. It requires emotional work, because learning how to do it takes effort (Taggart, 2011). This is learning the difference between public expression and private feelings (Goffman, 1959). In the caring profession the public persona is an important aspect of the job although still requires emotional investment to do the job successfully. Emotional labour being the 'work' therefore required of a person in maintaining their perception of a professional role, whilst at times in the day to day of work, feeling something different is not unusual within the caring profession (Theodosius, 2008). Employment of this nature can cause stress and feelings of inadequacy, with feelings inwardly different to the outward visible appearance. Reliance on the goodwill and emotions of the practitioner to successfully do their job can be assumed without consideration to how they are feeling and personally managing their role by those who employ them (Taggart, 2011; Theodosius, 2008). The way the practitioner acts in their role as key person may be in contradiction to how they feel in private and how they present themselves publicly in the workplace. Their public persona could be smiling to the parents and infants in their care role whilst feeling nervous and unsure internally. However, they may be unable to express their true feelings for fear of appearing inadequate or incompetent as a professional practitioner. Feeling and expressing different emotions can lead to caring for infants in a rather mechanical and superficial way which undoubtedly the infant will sense (Barnes, 1995). Emotional management therefore describes the kind of caring which stems from conscious effort of investing in the emotional relationship and reflecting on one's own emotions for self-management to be successful (Theodosius, 2008). Currently, there is little training for practitioners in their role as key persons in this respect. Cheerful, amateurish enthusiasm is seen to be all that is necessary, particularly in the infant room whist in reality stress levels can be consistently high and complex relationships created and developed with the infants and their families (Clasian, 2008). This in turn has led to both surface and deep acting within their role (Taggart, 2016). Practitioners may initially feel disingenuous, particularly when conveying an emotional message. Hochschild (2003) suggested that this was commonplace, and individuals managed their emotions through a process known as surface and deep acting. In surface acting, the individual used their bodies to portray feelings that they do not really have, such as smiling, shrugging and laughing. There is a disconnection between this outward display and genuine feelings. In deep acting, however, practitioners eventually learn to really believe and feel the emotions they are expressing through conscious mental work (Hochschild, 2003). Eventually, in learning to deep act so well, practitioners could authentically feel what the deep acting produced, unaware they had worked on it. Subsequently, this created the required feelings and expressions,

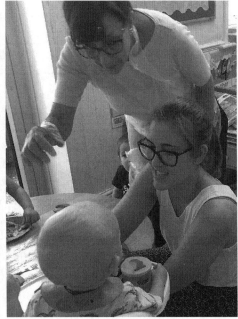

provoking long-lasting and genuine emotional relationships between themselves, parents and infants in their care (Berk, 1989). A practitioner working in a group care situation creating an emotional an emotional holding environment needs to be emotionally in tune and contain the emotions positively with the individual infant within the group and they may have to consciously use effort to ensure this occurs (Winnicott, 1965; Bion, 1962; Holmes, 1993).

Creating communities of learning: supporting practitioners

Communities of learning potentially offer the opportunities to make learning happen, by creating enhanced learning environments for students in education (Wenger, 1998). Communities of learning have taken a variety of forms in further and higher education, including cohort groups, seminar dialogue groups, and extra curricula activities and mentoring schemes.

Practitioners peer observing and listening to each other

Individuals learn by knowledge of construction process rather than assimilating what they are told. To learn how to construct knowledge it is necessary they believed the process is modelled and supported in the surrounding community.

To create the community of learning, three dimensions of a group need to occur;

151

- What the group is about: what is being planned and discussed?
- How does it function: does everyone have a voice and how are roles distributed?
- What capability it has produced (Wenger, 2008): following through with activities and practices and then reflecting on its successes and challenges.

The collaborative relationship of learning together also has benefits in terms of creating social support and reducing stress. If less experienced staff feel supported, feelings of attachment and higher self-esteem is evident. Clough and Corbett (2001) suggest learning is linked to experiences – analytical thinking to experience of practice – through different modes such as listening to each other.

Developing a community of practice is not without anxiety and tension and it is one where there is inevitably going to be issues to resolve for harmony to occur (Garvey, 2009). Wenger believed tensions exist in order to hide personal thinking when an individual is unsure or lacks confidence. When open discussions about constraints and possible issues are revealed, a sense of community is created (Seifert and Mandzuk, 2006). Boundaries and tensions are openly discussed and worked through with the coming together and reflecting on experiences. Through reflective practice and a community practitioner a sense of identity and their engagement in certain projects can be achieved (Schön, 1983).

Wenger (2008) recognised that knowledge was a key asset to building a community of learning and practice. He believed knowledge fulfilled a number of functions, including nodes for exchange for communities to become successful and develop. He drew on the following themes where knowledge can enhance a sense of community:

- Self-reflecting
- Retaining knowledge in living ways: being aware and making sense of each other as a collective group
- Homes for identities: recognising and celebrating individual differences.

Supervision: home for identities

Supervision support normally occurs every four to six weeks and is carried out by the supervisor and practitioner for an ideal duration of approximately one to two hours.

The appraisal tends to be target focused and performance discussed with some emotional input. Supervision can be helpful in sharing the ethical principles of care and the practitioners own care pedagogies. In sharing opportunities to talk and discuss the challenges and successes of their role discourses are shared and communities of practice developed.

Practitioner's perspective

Supervision

As a supervisor it is my role to carry out regular appraisals and supervisions. Positively I have found this to be a steep learning curve and a way of understanding the people I work with. However, it does come with its own challenges. I have to be very clear of the differences and tend to focus the appraisals around targets and measurable outcomes. The supervision tends to include the individual progress and the issues about the role. I try to make these frequent because I think communication is the key to working relationships. The supervision is also a mentoring session in a way as it is about sharing and sometimes guiding, a process of moving forward together and developing practice and reflecting on past events.

An aspect I think challenging is the role of supervisor comes with experience and I used to use the time initially as a way of appraising them. Supervision takes effort, frequent meetings and time for the relationship to flourish. Practitioners

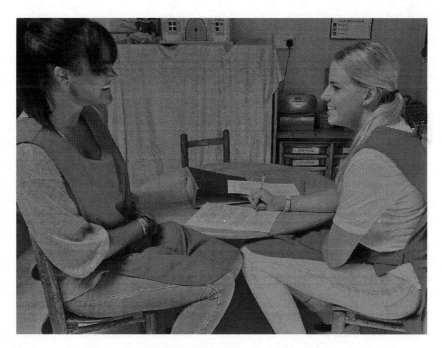

Supervision: professional relationships can still be warm, open and congruent promoting a community of practice

will then reflect honestly and compassionately about their role, sharing their feelings constructively as a way of moving forward in their role. We have found training programmes around mind mindedness, therapeutic approaches to play and learning together has also enhanced and complimented the supervision meetings. This has created and developed a community of practice (Taggart, 2016).

Therefore, although ratios of 1:3 in ECEC nursery settings are deemed sufficient in caring for infants adequately, they are not sufficient on their own to guarantee good outcomes. Higher levels of staff satisfaction, and qualified staff with up-to-date understandings of infants also have positive effects, creating a case for both pre-service and further in-service training (Munton et al., 2002). The content of the training must be relevant to the age group and reflect current knowledge about infant learning and development, including an understanding of neuroscience and pedagogical work (Elfer and Dearnley, 2007). Specifically, it should include time for supervision as a support mechanism alongside critical reflection, focusing on understanding the diversity of infants within families' contemporary lives, with a research and evaluation focus of their context (Nimmo and Park, 2009). Opportunities for home visits, meeting the parents during their prenatal and perinatal period can be advantageous and contribute to the settings aim of creating a practice of community.

Family practitioner summary

With safeguarding and culture today kissing and hugging infants and children in our care is still frowned upon. We have to carefully manoeuvre the child to sit next to us. The professional love research I studied, and hearing mums view made me aware they did want us to 'love' their children. We have now changed our policy at my setting and it includes touch, picking up and holding as part of practice. Kissing is still a contentious issue though. . . . This has really brought home to me the complexities of my role and how I act with other people's children as a paid professional. I am also acutely aware of how I present myself to others and when I have a 'bad' day. Having meetings with colleagues and support them.

As a key person I am meeting my senior management team regularly about my role. Since completing my degree, I have vocalised some issues that have been concerning me. As a leader in the infant room I have more and more key children to support and over a week much more than advocated by the curriculum we follow. Rather than being negative I have suggested we arrange more meetings and give the less experienced staff some infants to be second key person's so they can share in the responsibilities. I have then developed supervision time for each of them. I have to have support from my senior management through otherwise this will not work.

Concluding thoughts

This chapter examined the professional perspective of working with infants and parents from conception to infancy. It included the trajectories of linking maternal instinct characteristics to caring in a professional discourse. It also introduced some key concepts of professional love and communities of care with the hope practitioners will be encouraged to explore concepts further.

Bibliography

Ahnert, L. and Lamb, M. (2003) 'Shared care: Establishing a balance between home and child-care setting'. *Child Development* 74(4): 1044–1049.

Bain, A. and Barnett, L. (1986) *The Design of a Day Care System in a Nursery Setting for Children Under Five.* London: Tavistock Institute of Human Relations Document number 2T347.

Barnes, P. (1995) *Personal, Social and Emotional Development of Children.* Milton Keynes: Blackwell Publishing.

Bayley, R. and Featherstone, S. (2003) *Smooth Transitions. Ensuring continuity from the Foundation Stage.* Lutterworth: Featherstone Education Ltd.

Belsky, J. and Rovine, M. (1988) 'Nonmaternal care in the first year of life and the security of infant attachment'. *Child Development* 59: 157–167.

Belsky, J. Burchinal, M., McCartney, K., Vandell, D., Clarke-Stewart, K. and Owen, M. (2007) 'Are there long-term effects of early child care?' *Child Development* 78(2): 681–701.

Berk, L. (1989) *Child Development.* Boston: Allyn and Bacon.

Bomber, L. (2007) *Inside I'm Hurting.* London: Worth Publishing.

Bowlby, J. (2005) *The Making and Breaking of Affectionate Bonds.* London: Routledge;

Bowlby, J. (1988) *A Secure Base: Clinical Applications of Attachment Theory.* London: Routledge.

Brehony, K. J. and Nawrotzki, K. D. (2010) From Weak Social Democracy to Hybridized Neo-liberalism: Early Childhood Education in Britain since 1945. In Hagemann, K., Jarausch, K.

and Allemann-Ghionda, C. (eds) *Children, Families, and States: Time Policies of Childcare, Preschool, and Primary Education in Europe.* New York, Oxford: Berghahn Books.

Brennan, M. (2014) 'Perezhivanie: what have we missed about infant care?' *Contemporary Issues in Early Childhood* 15(3): 284–292.

Brooker, L. (2010) 'Constructing the triangle of care: power and professionalism in staff/parent relationships'. *British Journal of Educational Studies* 58(2): 181–196.

Brownlee, J., Berthelsen, D. and Segaran, N. (2009) 'Childcare workers' and centre directors' beliefs about infant childcare quality and professional training'. *Early Childhood Development and Care* 179(4): 453–475.

Clasien, J. (2008) *Children's' Attachment Relationships with Day Care Caregivers: Associations with Positive Caregiving and the Child's Temperament.* Oxford: Blackwell Publishing.

Clough, P. and Corbett, J. (2001) *Theories of Inclusive Practice.* London: Sage.

Colley, H. (2006) 'Learning to Labour with Feeling: class, gender and emotion in childcare education and training'. *Contemporary Issues in Early Childhood* 7(1): 15–29.

Cousins, S. (2017) 'Practitioners' constructions of love in early childhood education and care'. *International Journal of Early Years Education* 25(1): 16–29. DOI:10.1080/09669760.2016. 1263939

Csikszentmihalyi, M. (1997) *The Masterminds Series. Finding Flow: The Psychology of Engagement with Everyday Life.* New York: Basic Books.

Dahlberg, G., Moss, P. and Pence, A. (2013) *Beyond Quality in Early Childhood Education and Care. Postmodern Perspectives.* London: Falmer Press.

Dalli. C. (2006) 'Re-visioning love and care in early childhood Constructing the future of our profession'. *New Zealand Journal of Infant and Toddler Education* 8(1): 5–11.

Dalli, C., White, J., Rochel, J. and Duhn, I. (2011) 'Quality early childhood education for under-two-year-olds: What should it look like? A Literature Review'. Ministry of Education, New Zealand.

Datler, W., Datler, M. and Funder, A. (2010) 'Struggling against a feeling of becoming lost: a young boy's painful transition to day care'. *International Journal of Infant Observation* 13(1): 65–87.

Davis, M. and Wallbridge, D. (1991) *Boundary and Space. An Introduction to the Work of D. Winnicott.* US: Brunner.

Degotardi, S. and Pearson, E. (2009) 'Relationship theory in the nursery: attachment and beyond'. *Contemporary Issues in Early Childhood* 10(2): 144–155.

Department for Education (2014) *The Revised Early Years Foundation Stage.* London: DfE.

Drugli, M. and Undheim, A. (2012) 'Partnership between parents and caregivers of young children in full-time daycare'. *Child Care in Practice* 18(1): 51–65.

Dryden, L., Forbes, R., Mukherji, P. and Pound, L. (2005) *Essential Early Years.* London: Hodder Arnold.

Elfer, P. (2006) 'Exploring children's expressions of attachment in nursery'. *European Early Childhood Education Research Journal* 14(2): 81–95.

Elfer, P. (2007) 'Infants and young children in nurseries: using psychoanalytic ideas to explore tasks and interactions'. *Children and Society* 21: 111–122.

Elfer, P. and Dearnley, D. (2007) 'Nurseries and emotional well-being: evaluating an emotionally containing model of professional development'. *Early Years. An International Journal of Research and Development* 27(3) 267–279.

Elfer, P. and Page, J (2015) 'Pedagogy with babies: perspectives of eight nursery managers'. *Early Child Development and Care* 185(11012).

Elfer, P., Goldschmied, E. and Selleck, D. (2011) *Key Persons in the Nursery*. London: Fulton.

Fabian, H. and Dunlop, A. (2006) *Transitions in the Early Years*. Maidenhead: OUP.

Forbes, R. (2004*) Beginning to Play: Young Children from Birth to Three*. Milton Keynes: Open University Press.

Garvey, R. (2009) *Coaching and Mentoring*. London: Sage.

Geddes, H. (2006) *Attachment in the Classroom*. London: Worth.

Gerber, M. (2001) *Respecting Babies: A New Look at Magda Gerber's RIE Approach. Zero to Three*. UK: National Centre for Infants, Toddlers and Families.

Gerber, M (2003) *Dear Parent: Caring for Infants with Respect*. UK: Resources for Infant Educarers.

Gerhardt, S. (2014) *Why Love Matters. How Affection Shapes an Infant's Brain*. London: Routledge.

Goldschmied, E. and Jackson, S. (2004) *People Under Three, Young Children in Day Care* (2nd edition). London: Routledge.

Goleman, D. (1995) *Emotional Intelligence, Working with Emotional Intelligence*. London: Bloomsbury.

Goouch, K. and Powell, S. (2010) *The Baby Room Project*. UK: Esmée Fairbairn Foundation.

Gopnik, A., Meltzoff, A. and Kuhl, P. (2001) *How Infants Think: The Science of Childhood*. London: Weidenfeld and Nicolson.

Hestenes, L., Cassidy, D., Hegde, A. and Lower, J. (2007) 'Quality in inclusive and non-inclusive infant and toddler classrooms'. *Journal of Research in Childhood Education* 22(1): 69–84.

Hochschild, A. (2003) *The Managed Heart*. Los Angeles: University of California Press.

Holmes, J. (1993) *John Bowlby and Attachment Theory*. London: Routledge.

Holmes, K. and Holmes, D. (1980) 'Signed and spoken language development in a hearing child of hearing parents'. *Sign Language Studies* 28: 239–254.

Hopkins, J. (1988) 'Facilitating the development of intimacy between nurses and infants in day nurseries'. *Early Child Development and Care* 33: 99–111.

House, R (2011) *Too Much Too Soon: Early Learning and the Erosion of Childhood*. Gloucestershire: Hawthorne Press.

Jackson, S. and Forbes, R. (2014) (2nd ed) *People Under Three, Young Children in Day Care*. London: Routledge.

Kalliala, M. (2011) 'Look at me! Does the adult truly see and respond to the child in Finnish day-care centres?' *European Early Childhood Education Research Journal* 19(2): 237–253.

Kalliala, M. (2014) 'Toddlers as both more and less competent social actors in Finnish day care centres'. *Early Years* 34(1): 4–17.

Karen, R. (1994) *Becoming Attached*. New York: Warner.

Leach, P. (2009) *Childcare Today; What We Know and What We Need to Know*. Cambridge: Polity Press.

Leach, P., Barnes, J., Nichols, M., Goldin, J., Stein, A., Sylva, K., Malmberg, L. and the FCCC team (2006) 'Child Care Before 6 Months of Age: A Qualitative Study of Mothers' Decisions and Feelings About Employment and Non-maternal Care'. *Infant and Child Development. An International Journal of Research* 15(5): 471–502.

Manning-Morton, J. and Thorp, M. (2003) *Key Times for Play: The First Three Years*. Maidenhead: Open University Press.

Manning-Morton, J. (2006) 'The personal is professional: professionalism and the birth to threes staff'. *Contemporary Issues in Early Childhood* 7: 42–52.

Mayeroff, M. (1971) *On Caring.* New York: HarperCollins Publishers.

McDowall Clark, R. and Bayliss, S. (2012) '"Wasted down there": policy and practice with the under-threes'. *Early Years. An International Journal of Research and Development* 32(2): 229–242.

Miller, L. (2010) *Supporting Children in the Early Years.* London: David Fulton.

Mooney, C. (2010) *Theories of Attachment.* St Paul: Redleaf Press.

Moss, P. (2006) 'Structures, Understandings and Discourses: Possibilities for re-visioning the Early Childhood Worker'. *Contemporary Issues in Childhood* 7(1): 30–41.

Munton, A., Mooney, A., and Rowland, L. (1995) 'Deconstructing quality: A conceptual framework for the new paradigm in day care provision for the under eights'. *Early Child Development and Care* 114(1): 11–23.

Music, G. (2011) *Nurturing natures: Attachment and Children's Emotional, Sociocultural and Brain Development.* Hove and New York: Psychology Press.

Nimmo, J. and Park, S. (2009) 'Engaging Early Childhood Teachers in the Thinking and Practice of Inquiry: Collaborative Research Mentorship as a Tool for shifting Teacher Identity'. *Journal of Teacher Education* 30(2): 93–104.

Nodding, N. (2002) *Starting at Home: Caring and Social Policy.* Berkeley and Los Angeles, CA: University of California Press.

Noddings, N. (2003) 'Is Teaching a Practice?' *Journal of Philosophy of Education* 37(2): 53–58.

Noddings, N. (2013) *Caring: A Feminine Approach to Ethics and Moral Education.* US: University of California Press.

Noddings, N. (2015) *Philosophy of Education.* US: Westview Press.

Nutbrown, C. (2011) *A Student's Guide in Methodology.* London: Sage.

Nutbrown, C. and Page, J. (2010) *Working with Babies and Children.* London: Sage.

Nutbrown, C. and Page, J (2013) *Working with Babies and Children: From Birth to Three.* London: Sage.

Osgood, J. (2004) 'Time to get down to business? The response of early years practitioners to entrepreneurial approaches to professionalism'. *Journal of Early Childhood Research* 2(1): 5–24.

Osgood, J. (2006) 'Professionalism and performativity: the feminist challenge facing early years practitioners'. *Early Years* 26(2): 187–200.

Osgood, J. (2010) 'Reconstructing Professionalism in ECEC: The Case for the "Critically Reflective Emotional Professional"'. *Early Years* 30(2): 119–133. DOI:10.1080/09575146.2010.490905

Page, J. (2011) 'Do Mothers Want Professional Carers to Love Their Babies?' *Journal of Early Childhood Research* 114:1–14. DOI:10.1177/1476718X11407980

Page, J. (2013) 'Will the "Good" [Working] Mother Please Stand Up? Professional and Maternal Concerns about Education, Care and Love.' *Gender and Education.* DOI:10.1080/0954025 3.2013.797069

Page, J. (2015) 'Love, Love, Love'. *Nursery World* 28(6). Available online at www.nursery world.co.uk/nursery-world/opinion/1152266/love-love-love

Page, J. (2017) 'Reframing infant-toddler pedagogy through a lens of professional love: Exploring narratives of professional practice in early childhood settings in England'. *Contemporary Issues in Early Childhood* 18(4): 387–399. Available online at http://journals.sagepub.com/doi/abs/10.1177/1463949117742780

Page, J., and Elfer, P (2013) 'The Emotional Complexity of Attachment Interactions in Nursery'. *European Early Childhood Education Research Journal.* DOI:10.1080/1350293X.2013.766032

Piper, H. and Smith, H. (2003) 'Touch in Educational and Child Care Settings: Dilemmas and Responses'. *British Educational Research Journal* 29(6): 879–894.

Powell, S. and Goouch, K. (2012) 'Whose hand rocks the cradle? Parallel discourse in the infant room'. *Early Years. An International Journal of Research and Development* 32(2): 113–127.

Prior, V. and Glaser, D. (2006) *Understanding Attachment and Attachment Disorders: Theory Evidence and Practice.* London: Jessica Kingsley.

Read, V. (2010) *Developing Attachment in Early Years Settings.* Oxon: Routledge.

Rodd, J. (2005) *Leadership in Early Childhood.* London: OUP.

Rogoff, B. (2003) *The Cultural Nature of Human Development.* Oxford and New York: Oxford University Press.

Rutter, M. (2002) 'Nature, Nurture and Development: From Evangelism, through Science towards Policy and Practice'. *Child Development* 73(1): 1–21.

Schön, D. (1983) *The Reflective Practitioner.* USA: Basic Books.

Schore, A. (2016) *Affect Regulation and the Origin of the Self.* New York: Routledge.

Sears, S. and Sears, M. (2003) *Baby Book.* Harper Collins: London.

Seifert, K. and Mandzuk, D. (2006) 'Student cohorts in teacher education: Support groups or intellectual communities?' *Teachers College Record* 108(7): 1296–1320.

Siren Films Ltd (2007) Life at Two DVD "Attachments, Key People & Development" Siren Film & Video Ltd. Available online at www.sirenfilms.co.uk

Taggart, G. (2011) 'Don't we care? the ethics and emotional labour of early years professional-ism'. *Early Years. An International Journal of Research and Development* 31(1): 85–95.

Taggart, G. (2016) 'Compassionate pedagogy: the ethics of care in early childhood profes-sionalism'. *European Early Childhood Education Research Journal* 24(2): 173–185. DOI: 10.1080/1350293X.2014.970847

Theodosius, C. (2008) *Emotional Labour in Healthcare, the Unmanaged Heart of Nursing.* London: Routledge.

Vallotton, C. (2009) 'Do infants influence their quality of care? Infants' communicative gestures predict caregivers' responsiveness'. *Infant Behavior and Development* 32: 351–365.

Wenger, E. (1998) *Communities of Practice: Learning, Meaning and Identity.* Cambridge: Cambridge University Press.

Wenger, E., McDermott, R. and Snyder, W. (2002) *Cultivating Communities of Practice: A Guide to Managing Knowledge.* Cambridge, MA: Harvard Business School Press.

Winnicott, D. (1958) 'The Capacity to be Alone'. *International Journal of Psychoanalysis* 39: 416–420.

Wood, E. and Bennett, N. (1999) 'Progression and Continuity in Early Childhood Education: Tensions and Contradictions'. *International Journal of Early Years Education* 7(1): 19.

Xu, Y. (2006) '"Toddler" emotional reactions to separation from their primary caregiver: suc-cessful home-school transition'. *Early Child Development and Care* 176(6): 661–674.

8   Connecting with care

Introduction and context

This chapter reflects on how emotional relationships in relation to care and attachment can be applied in practice within and beyond the home. What type of care giving and taking do we observe in practice? Caring practice with infants is the provision of supporting health, welfare and protection with professional concern and interest. As care givers, whether parents or practitioners, we are continually observing and interpret the behaviour of the infant in seeking how best to care for them, engaging with their feelings and responding to cues. Right from the start it is the carer's role in a nurturing, caring environment to provide attachment scaffolding opportunities, so the infant increasingly recognises themselves as 'other', developing independent control of their actions and movements. The two-way attachment process goes beyond meeting care needs in promoting health and physical protection. Rather a dance of interactions occurs between carer and infant within the care routines and it is the dance of communication that will be explored in this chapter. Whilst discussions will be focused around infants from conception to two, the chronological age has not mapped the chapter. There are many texts that map the chronological age to capabilities and mapping routines accordingly. This chapter will instead introduce and discuss some everyday practices within care routines and how attachment led practice can support infants holistically within these routines

The emotional age of the infant: attachment led care

Attachment led practice informs us that infants have a biological need to be close to their parents. The infant is totally dependent on the carer for survival, protection and comfort. In having sensitive, responsive parents, the infant begins to make sense of their own thoughts and feelings. Through emotional and social experiences, between parents and infants a dance occurs, and the parents can reflect on not only what they feel but also the infants they care for. This stimulates the secure attachment, further enhancing close and nourishing relationships. The physical and mental health needs of the infant are met. In responding to the emotional stages of the infant too rather than relying on the chronological age the care can be supported further. For parents and practitioners there has been an abundance of what an infant should be expected to do and what age they should be achieving. Many parenting books have advocated restricted care routines as a way for parents to regain a sense of the life they had before birth. They also offer regimes on how best to cope with the transition to parenthood, to reduce sleep deprivation, convenient feeding options and domestic care approaches such as nappy changing. Unfortunately, because many parenting books are aiming to attract a wide audience they will endorse regimes irrespective of individual contexts. Subsequently,

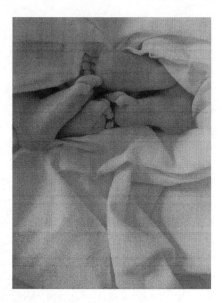

Close connections

parents following these regimes will approach care in a rather mechanical way. Alternatively, infant led parenting information advocates respond to infant desires with practices including prolonged breast feeding, co-sleeping with minimal direction initiated by the parents. As a practitioner, and supporting attachment led practice, I believe a balance can occur and certainly working towards the emotional age of the infant is an appropriate place to begin. Infants are individuals, socially and emotionally influenced by their parents and environment. Therefore, each infant will from conception develop sleep wake patterns, temperaments, genetically influenced and developed within the environment. It is worth pausing for a second and reflecting that within the 1000 first days of life, approximately:

- 300 days are spent in the pre-pregnancy and pregnancy stage
- 700 days living postnatally experiencing the world.

This reminds us that infancy is a small yet valuable opportunity of time in creating a nurturing here and now perspective, enjoying the moment rather than anticipating the next stage and focusing on what has been less successful. In considering care routine practices, reflecting on their emotional age carers can then scaffold infant development, support their emotional regulation and capacity for securing attachments, enhancing long term fruitful relationships and self-assured adults.

Attachment and care: linking theory to everyday care practices

Bowlby (1969) considered infants have an innate and evolutionary need to be close to an adult carer, predominantly the parent, seeking care and comfort. The way infants develop emotionally is determined predominantly by the sensitivity and characteristics of their parents. The more sensitive and reliable, the more secure attachment flourishes. Tuning into infant's behaviour and feelings enables the infant to regulate their own emotions and begin to make sense of how they feel themselves. There is also recognition that attachment is not 'fixed' and Dozier et al. (2006) study of adopted children draws attention to 'attachment biobehavioural catch up' (ABC) educating the parents about the behaviour they observe in infants. They evaluated that the effects of disrupted attachments can be reduced and how negative experiences in early life do not necessary determine a life's emotional trajectory. Parents were taught to observe and read infants rejecting and ambivalent behaviour as an expected response to their nurturing and provision of positive care. Parents were supported in offering care and bonds when it is not physically sought by the children as a way of re-regulating their emotional and social capacities.

By reflecting on practice, parents reviewed and moved forward through effective interactions during everyday care routines supporting the emotional wellbeing of young infants in their care.

Understanding attachment: past to present

Attachment theory and its subject matter was re-emphasised from the mid-twentieth century to mirror the economic and political climate of the period in England. In contemporary society we continue to share a discourse about the value of attachment in light of the availability of neuroscience and the understanding brain processes. However, attachment has also been argued to be a theory supporting and maintaining maternal relationships, potentially excluding other relationships. I have not attempted to include a critique of attachment theory but rather map the historical theoretical and practice influences that culminated in contemporary thinking about attachment within the ECEC context.

Questions for discussion

John Bowlby and attachment

Bowlby (1907–1990)

John was the fourth child of six in an upper middle-class family. Like most middle/upper class families, the children were cared for by 'nanny' and 'nurse maids'. Children lived in the nursery on the top floor of house (fresh air good for them). Parents did not come to the nursery – children were taken to their parents. John was cared for by a nurse maid called 'Minnie' who left when he was four years old. This was as tragic as the loss of a mother.

Consider the effect this would have on John and his subsequent theory of attachment.

He trained as a doctor and then as a psychoanalyst. From 1936 to 1939 he worked in Child Guidance with young offenders. What distinguished these young offenders from others attending the Child Guidance Clinic was their family history – broken families, no continuing relationship, no love.

Bowlby worked with Harry Harlow (an ethologist). The behaviour of monkeys when anxious/stressed convinced him that attachments, even in the animal world, were not primarily about food/protection.

> He published *Child Care and the Growth of Love* (1953) and, in 1969, a trilogy of books entitled respectively *Attachment, Separation* and *Loss*.
>
> Summarising human attachment behaviour:
>
> Do you consider the historical period significant to attachment?

In taking a critical lens observational behaviour evaluates the emotions of infants resulting in practitioners making assumptions about what their internal feelings are. Behaviourist perspective of attachment (Dollard and Miller, 1950) suggested that attachment is a set of learned behaviours. The basis for the learning of attachments was the provision of food and an infant will initially form an attachment to whoever feeds them. They learn to associate the feeder (usually the mother) with the comfort of being fed and, through the process of classical conditioning, come to find contact with the mother comforting. They also found certain behaviours such as crying and smiling conveys desirable responses such as attention and comfort from others and through the process of operant conditioning learn to repeat these behaviours to get the things they want.

Schaffer and Emerson (1964) also identified how attachment could be framed into a sequential mode through their observations in young infants. They studied sixty infants at monthly intervals for the first 18 months of life. The children were all studied in their own home, and a regular pattern was identified in the development of attachment. There have since been studies to dispute the areas within this frame, such as a preference to the mother to that of another from a very early age. However, Schaffer and Emerson continue to be drawn on in critically reflecting on the BROAD sequential progression of attachment proposed. The infants were visited monthly for approximately one year, their interactions with their parents were observed, and parents were interviewed. A diary was kept by the parent, in this study predominately the mother, to examine the evidence for the development of attachment. Three measures were recorded:

- Stranger anxiety – response to the arrival of a stranger
- Separation anxiety – distress level when separated from a parent, the degree of comfort needed on return
- Social referencing – the degree a child looks at their carer to check how they should respond to something new (secure base).

They discovered that infant's attachments develop in the following sequence:

> Asocial (0–6 weeks): They considered young infants as being asocial in that many kinds of stimuli, both social and non-social, produce a favourable reaction,

such as a smile. In a sense they have not discriminated but beginning to learn about their environment.

Indiscriminate attachments (six weeks to seven months): Arguably, infants indiscriminately enjoy human company, and most infants respond equally to any caregiver. They get upset when an individual cease to interact with them. From three months infants smile more at familiar faces and can be easily comfortable by a regular caregiver.

Specific Attachment (7–9 months): Special preference for a single attachment figure. The infant looks to familiar carers for security, comfort, and protection. It showed fear of strangers (stranger fear) and unhappiness when separated from a special person (separation anxiety).

Multiple Attachment (ten months and onwards): The infant becomes increasingly independent and forms several attachments. By eighteen months many infants have formed multiple attachments.

The results of the study indicated that attachments were most likely to form with those who responded accurately to the infant's signals and not necessarily the person they spent more time with. Schaffer and Emerson called this sensitive responsiveness. Intensely attached infants had mothers who responded quickly to their demands and interacted with their child. Infants who were weakly attached had mothers who failed to interact. Many of the infants had several attachments by ten months old, including attachments to mothers, fathers, grandparents, siblings and neighbours. For the majority, however, the mother was the main attachment figure at eighteen months old and the father for most of the others. The ethological theory of attachment (e.g. Bowlby, Harlow, Lorenz), as discussed in a previous chapter, suggested that infants are biologically pre-programmed to form attachments with others, and the infant produces innate 'social releaser' behaviours such as crying and smiling that stimulate innate caregiving responses from adults. The most important fact in forming attachments was not therefore who feeds and changes the child but who plays and communicates with him or her most. Therefore, responsiveness appeared to be the key to attachment and one referred to in contemporary contexts.

Testing attachment theory: Harlow and his monkeys

In Harlow's study of attachment, he evaluated that it does not always have to be reciprocal and one person may have an initial attachment to an individual which is not shared. We now know emotional relationships are complex and require the active ongoing intersubjectivity and tuning in of both carer's and infant's attachment to be successful. Therefore, on a simplistic level, attachment in this context is the initial biological drive to *seek* attachment, even if it is not responsive and reciprocal but simply physically present. Attachment was characterised by specific behaviours in infants, such as seeking proximity to the attachment figure when upset or threatened (Bowlby, 1969). Harlow's explanation was that attachment develops as a result of the carer providing 'tactile comfort', suggesting that infants have an innate (biological) need to touch and cling to something for emotional comfort. Harlow carried out a number of studies on attachment in rhesus monkeys during the 1950s and 1960s. His experiments on rearing took several forms and he concluded that infants reared without a 'real' mother were:

- More timid.
- They didn't know how to act with other monkeys.
- They were easily bullied and wouldn't stand up for themselves.
- They had difficulty with mating when they were older
- The female monkeys became inadequate mothers when they reached adulthood.
                                                              (Harlow and Zimmerman, 1959)

Other physically observed behaviours were that when the monkeys were exposed to prolonged stress their stools were softer and they had digestive problems. These behaviours were observed only in the monkeys who were left with the surrogate mothers for more than ninety days. For those left less than ninety days the effects could be reversed if placed in a normal environment where they could form attachments. He concluded early positive parenting was vital in an infant's life for healthy development although negative exposure could be reversed in monkeys if an attachment was made before the end of the critical period (Berk, 2010).

A note of hope

- Deficits that occur in the early years may be overcome with later enrichment, though the process will likely be more difficult
- the brain has plasticity and can recover over time with positive support and consistent emotional relationships.

Rutter (1984) considered the importance to emotional development and maternal deprivation as a "vulnerability factor" rather than a causative agent, with several varied influences determining which life path a child will take. In 1989, Rutter led the English and Romanian Adoptees Study Team, following many of the orphans who had been exposed to extreme neglect and deprivation in their earliest years through to their adoption into Western families. They were observed and studied during their latter childhood into their teens in a series of substantial studies, focusing on the effects of early privation and deprivation. They concluded that attachment and the development of new relationships were successful, yielding some reason for optimism that if an infant is removed from the emotionally deprived environment and placed in a positive and warm environment emotional growth could occur. However, it was agreed that the earlier they were removed from the emotionally deprived context, replaced with warm, physical and mental care, the greater the recovery and ability to thrive emotionally. Therefore, sensitive periods were described as key periods of emotional growth rather than critical periods suggesting healthy emotions are fluid and not sequentially determined.

Emotional security and associated behaviours can be observed

So, what does secure attachment look like and do all children experience the same type of attachment at a given age or is it a result of their experiences in early life? Rather than waiting until the infant is an adult and asking retrospectively, Ainsworth (1913–1999) drew on what she termed the Strange Situation in understanding the importance of close relationships and emotional attachments. Ainsworth's Strange Situation (1979) used structured observational research to assess & measure the quality of attachment. It has eight pre-determined stages, including the mother leaving the child, for a short while, to play with available toys in the presence of a stranger and alone and the mother returning to the child.

Stage 1 – Mother and child enter the playroom

Stage 2 – The child is encouraged to explore

Stage 3 – Stranger enters and attempts to interact

Stage 4 – Mothers leaves while the stranger is present

Stage 5 – Mother enters and the stranger leaves

Stage 6 – Mothers leaves

Stage 7 – Stranger returns

Stage 8 – Mother returns and interacts with child.

The results highlight the role of the mother's/significant and consistent carer behaviour in determining the quality of attachment (Cohen and Waite-Shipansky, 2017). This led to the conceptualisation of the Caregiver Sensitivity Hypothesis, which suggests that a mother's behaviour towards their infant predicts their attachment type (Ainsworth, 1979).

Transitions in practice: responding to the Strange Situation

Whilst there has been criticism to this experiment and the limitations to being able to connect with the internal feelings of the infant it does provide some thinking to behaviours that perhaps we assume and interpret as something else. In reflecting on behaviours and scenarios we move closer to thinking about how we support those infants during transitional periods (Degotardi, 2014).

Transitional periods form part of everyday routines

Questions for discussion

Reflecting on the infant's perspective and how they perceive their own transitions, consider the following transitional moments:

Some days I am left with different carers, sometimes in a different place and sometimes in my home. Sometimes I know them, sometimes I don't

Everyday my mother, or sometimes dad comes back to take me home after I have eaten

> Every day I move from the room I know into the garden, to another to eat, for a walk. I can sometimes crawl on my own to a space but sometimes I am taken
>
> I am lifted, and my bottom is changed a lot and then I am placed in a bed to rest
>
> I am used to drinking a bottle but sometimes I am given a cu, I am never sure when though
>
> I was on my own but now I have a new infant in my family
>
> These are all daily transitions that we cope with as practitioners but as infants we are sometimes not talked to about.
>
> What are your thoughts about transitions?

Typically, a child's response to the Strange Situation follows one of four patterns.

Securely-attached children: Free exploration and happiness displayed upon the mother's return. If he cries, he approaches his mother and holds her tightly and is comforted by being held. Once comforted, is keen to resume his independent exploration.

Avoidant-insecure children: Little exploration, and little emotional response to the mother. Little emotion observed when his mother leaves and tends to avoid or ignore her when she returns (Ainsworth, 1979).

Resistant-insecure (also called 'anxious' or 'ambivalent') children: Little exploration is carried out in the room and there is greater separation anxiety. There is an ambivalent response to the mother upon her return (Ainsworth, 1979).

Disorganised-insecure children: Little exploration, and a confused response to the mother. The disorganised child may exhibit a mix of avoidant and resistant behaviours. The main theme here is one of confusion and anxiety (Main and Solomon 1986).

Care as a pedagogy: practitioner and infant

Caregiving routines make up a large part of an infant's day and provide practitioners with many opportunities to involve them in caregiving experiences through respectful, reciprocal and responsive interactions. The daily routine should include time for interactions to be nurtured, introduced established and maintained, an opportunity for the infant's development. Learning and wellbeing should be conveyed in a way that responds to infant's individuality, deepening their relationship with their carer (Tankersley et al., 2015). The pedagogy of care breaks down the false dichotomy that there is a difference between early education and care. In the past, caring tasks may have been viewed as safekeeping based on meeting hygiene needs. In the emerging future, care is viewed as requiring specialised knowledge about learning and early development. Caring routines involve engagement around bodily functions (elimination, cleaning, eating, sleeping) and therefore they hold the most intimate importance. Respectful caring is the key to growing trusting relationships and intellectually stimulating education, we find ourselves doing it 'with' children instead of doing it 'to' children (Pikler, 1970).

Variations in pedagogic practice with infants

Questions for discussion

Comments made by both practitioners and parents during everyday care routines:

> 'He's showing favouritism to one adult; that is not right.'

No an attachment has been formed that is good!! Support with a secondary attachment but do not undermine the special relationship

> 'He hates his nappy changed so I do it as quickly as possible and it is always a battle.'

Think how you carry it out what messages are you conveying. Do you speak? Do you pull a face? Could you do it on the floor and how are you handling the infant. If they can sit up can they get their own nappy . . .

> 'I can't sing so I always pop on a cd when we eat.'

Communication comes in many forms singing and signing shows you are interested and listening. Turn the cd down and sing with it!

> 'He always cries when we move rooms.'

Value and be sensitive to transitional periods it is a new space and full of potential fear

> 'They all need to sleep now otherwise I do not get a break and its tricky as Harry takes ages.'

Reflect on the individual infant, caring is unique and should of quality share the group practices with colleagues and consider alternatives. Ultimately, if you're anxious so are they.

> 'I can't rock them all day, why do they need rocking, what is it about rocking that calms them?'

Reflect on how they feel, are they new, does their parent rock them. Can a transitional object help?

> 'Mum wants to breastfeed at lunch. It is really difficult to accommodate.'

Why?!

> 'I spilt some of the breast milk on the floor – what do I do?'

Reflect on the amount of storage/accessibility to mum.

> 'It is easier to feed in a bouncy chair or highchair as I then have a free pair of hands.'

A concern of caring for multiple infants – both for parents and practitioners – balance the bouncer!

> 'He needs to learn to quieten.'

By not attending he learns no one is coming.

> 'He loves being on his own.'

How do you observe this and as a social being why is this so?

Are these familiar comments shared by colleagues and how would you respond if these comments were made?

As researcher and practitioner, I have been very fortunate for the opportunities to reflect and observe the way pedagogy has been approached with infants through an educare approach. Pedagogy is not only about the how and why of what early year's educators do in their professional roles, but also extends to the way educators engage with the expectations presented to them in their work setting. Infants learn best in atmospheres that provide a stimulating and prepared environment where children learn from their own perspectives (Lilley, 1967). In the setting, time to plan areas for children to engage with their emotions and be cared for by a listening and observant practitioner is essential for development and wellbeing to occur.

Gerber (1978, cited in Gerber 2001) considered respect as the basis of an educaring approach, demonstrating respect every time we interact with them. Respecting a child means treating even the youngest infant as a unique individual.

> *An authentic child*: An authentic child is one who feels secure, autonomous, competent, and connected.
> *Trust in the infant's competence*: We have basic trust in the infant to be an initiator, to be an explorer eager to learn what he is ready for.
> *Sensitive observation*: To observe carefully to understand the infant's communications and his needs.

The more we observe, the more we understand and appreciate the enormous amount and speed of learning that happens during the first two or three years of life. We become humbler, we teach less, and we provide an environment for learning instead.

Caregiving times: involving the child

During care activities such as nappy changing, feeding, bathing and dressing we encourage even the tiniest infant to become an active participant rather than a passive recipient of the activities. Parents create opportunities for interaction, cooperation, intimacy and mutual enjoyment by being wholeheartedly with the infant during the time they spend together anyway.

In care giving I have selected some routine practices to illustrate how as practitioners we can connect with care, building on contemporary attachment theory, using a key person approach.

Transitions from home to care settings: transitional objects

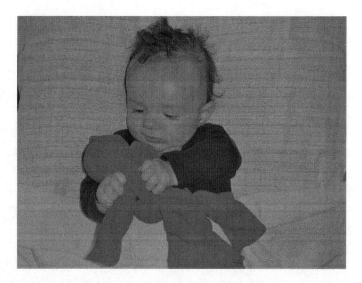

Comforted by a transitional object

During infant development there is a tendency to use objects as an inanimate comforter, a little like Harlow's monkeys but in this case alongside practitioner's physical care. For some infants a thumb is sucked, and the fingers caress their hair with their fingers or stroke the upper lip. An external object may also be sought such as a soft sheet or blanket to stroke and suck. These items become vitally important when infants settle themselves to sleep or as a defence against anxiety. Within this transitional phenomenon of experience, beginning to show at four, six and twelve months, the items are known as transitional objects. Parents appreciate their value and allow it to be taken to bed and on travels. The smell and grubbiness of the cloth is part of the appeal and parents may refrain from washing it, knowing this could destroy the value and meaning of the object to the infant.

Winnicott (1950, cited in Davis and Wallbridge, 1991) focused on the special qualities observed in the relationship of the infant to the transitional object

- The infant assumes rights of the object
- The object may be cuddled, excitedly loved and mutilated
- It remains the same unless altered by the infant themselves

- Emotions are expressed onto the object and remain constant

- Tends to have texture, move or give warmth as a separate object with a sense of reality

- Its fate is that it gradually loses its significance, so it is not forgotten or mourned, rather its meaning diminished with time during the course of years.

Winnicott (Davis and Wallbridge, 1991) believed the connection to the transitional object was in bridging the inner world of the infant to the outer world. He saw the transitional object as initiating a sense of imaginative play and infants gaining a sense of their separateness to the environment they are in and a relationship to the outside world had begun. He also considered the use of them positively and negatively and did not propose mothers initiate their use and extend the duration of transitional objects in the popular assumption they are desirable and necessary for sound emotional development. For him it was the spontaneous attachment of use and the inner creativity of the infant in processing their inner and outer reality.

Nevertheless, transitional objects have been considered valuable for those infants settling into new environments and connecting the sense of the family home to a new external environment. The emphasis, therefore, would be directed towards reducing anxiety and the permanence of the object during times when external things and familiar people (parents) are 'hiding' or 'gone'. Winnicott makes a clear rationale for reflecting on the individual infant and allowing them to take the lead in what sooths them through this process rather than forcing an object upon them (Davis and Wallbridge, 2012).

Practitioner's perspective

At lunch time Sue, a mother who works down the road, comes and attends to her infant at lunch, three times a week. Occasionally, dad comes too and will help change the nappy or chat to his partner. When this was first discussed at the induction I was quite anxious how it was going to work with the other infants in the setting and quite frankly was a little put off with the inconvenience!! The infant was eleven months and I wasn't sure how long she was going to continue breastfeeding her, changing her nappy and sharing the care. Initially I had assumed it would be for a few weeks but soon realised she wanted to continue indefinitely.

We created a space for her in the nursery and as the weeks followed a pattern soon emerged when she left he would snuggle into his smelly silk scarf and fall

---

asleep content. He didn't carry the scarf all day but when he became tired or tearful he would call for it and snuggle and chew it, twisting it around his finger. I felt the silk scarf reduced some of his anxiety and he became aware of the lunch time pattern too. It worked really well but made me acutely aware of the other infants I cared for (we had five others in the room) and their observations. In a way I felt really protective of them . . . and was really pleased in the way the parent had wanted to retain regular contact beyond the morning and evening of the day . . . it was quite an unusual arrangement but generally worked well for everyone, especially the infant who seemed to settle and view us as an extension to his home. Practices were discussed and we both voiced our thoughts over the details of his care.

A professional dummy: tensions of practices between practitioners and parents

Comforters in a variety of forms have been used for many years and, specifically, pacifiers or dummies as they are commercially known, remain less researched as a

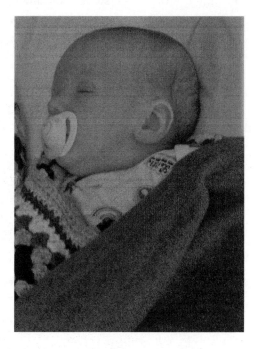

How pacifiers are perceived

care practice. These are sucking tools bidding to calm and self-comfort. As a soothing intervention, comforters have predominantly been used in early years settings, with guidance from the parents who in turn have tended to rely on generational advice. Comforters are generally used to settle an infant to sleep or to reduce crying. Medically, the sucking of pacifiers has been associated with creating an emotional calm. More recently, the use of pacifiers, regulating a sucking rhythm to calm and relax the infant, has been considered one approach in potentially reducing sudden infant death syndrome (SIDS). Language development has also been associated with the amount of time spent using a pacifier. Whitmarsh (2008) evaluated the use of pacifiers in ECEC a nursery setting and offered a valuable example to the discourses associated with certain practices and how parental rights and practitioners own ambivalent views can contradict authoritative knowledge and how this was managed. She concluded practitioners considered pacifiers to be unhygienic in group care and possibly inhibited communication. This was supported by the speech and language therapists they had spoken to. However, the practitioners continued to follow parent requests and regarded parents as the leaders of care opposed to other professionals they had spoken to alongside their own care pedagogues. One practitioner voiced the contradictory advice of her own existing perceptions to the negative impact and media attention to using pacifiers but continued to give the infant a pacifier, albeit with a sense of reluctance. The study for me, although a small scale study, highlighted not just the use of pacifiers but, more importantly, the everyday complexities of parental choice, group care and tensions between practitioners and care practices.

Questions for discussion

When are pacifiers offered to infants in care contexts?

Do you consider soothers such as cloths different to pacifiers that an infant sucks?

Does the use of pacifiers contradict practitioners own care pedagogies?

What are your thoughts about them as reducing stress and anxiety?

Do parents request the use of pacifiers during specific times of the day, such as rest time?

Caring for sleep: night and day

Ways of supporting infant sleep have predominantly been anecdotal from family members and friends, alongside the professional guidance, imparting appropriate ways to encourage sleep. The infant sleep information forum online provides unbiased, evidence-based information on safe sleep patterns and health associated issues. The forum aims to enable parents to understand and cope with their infant's sleep patterns.

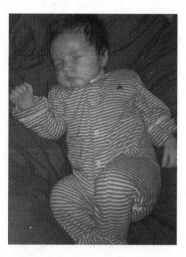

The forum is embedded within the Durham University's sleep laboratory which has been operational for several years. Risks associated with sudden infant death syndrome (SIDS) have also been studied, providing studies around minimising the risks.

The overall message is infants should be sleeping in the presence of a significant adult in the first six months. In day-care, infants should be checked regularly and available practitioners present in settling routines. This perhaps reinforces the value of treating sleep time in the same way as play time. Sleep should be met as part of the routine rather than a period of reduced care. In ECEC contexts sleep patterns may be established and supported with transitional objects and personalised care extending parent's care at home. Familiarity of using the same cot and establishing quiet time prior to sleep is helpful in creating a calm and relaxing environment. Many group care settings have recently updated their sleep rooms, describing them as nesting rooms, including soft furnishings and neutral colours to create a restful ambience (Gallagher and Arnold, 2018). Cots have been replaced with floor baskets to enable the infant to be able to crawl in and out and reduce the separation of wake and sleep time. The infant is able to enter into the basket themselves and wake at a level they can again move from. This potentially reduces the anxiety revolved around forcing sleep times with little autonomy from the infant themselves (www.naturesleep.co.uk).

Feeding

Feeding as a care routine is as much about communicating as the food itself. It is an opportunity to connect with an infant emotionally and provide one-to-one opportunities to connect.

Exploring food

Whilst parents are encouraged to take the lead in weaning with the support of the health visitor many have turned to their ECEC for advice. The nutrient value of food and the amount given after six months is guided by the Healthy Child Programme (2017). Infant led weaning has been recently promoted as an alternative way to encourage weaning from the traditional approach of giving smooth transitioning to lumpy food offered on a spoon from six months. Infant led weaning emerged partly in response to changes in weaning guidelines and enables infants to experiment with different food combinations, tastes, textures and methods of encouragement. In allowing the infant to feed themselves with their own fingers rather than spoon fed it directs the parent/practitioner to how much they want to eat. It also enables infants to familiarise themselves with various types of food rather than an undistinguishable processed (mixed) substance. It also promotes choices and makes eating more fun experiential time. Regardless of the weaning approach used many infants are offered finger foods and these are foods that can be cut up into pieces big enough for an infant to hold in their fist and pieces about the size of an adult's finger (Brown, 2018). Finger foods can be given alongside traditional approaches and a gentle transition to more lumpy textures. As a practitioner, giving finger foods at an appropriate age, generally around one year, I considered it a balance between the traditional and baby led approaches.

The NHS guidelines of readiness for solid foods

- They can stay in a sitting position and hold their head steady
- They can co-ordinate their eyes, hands and mouth so that they can look at the food, pick it up and put it in their mouth, all by themselves
- They can swallow food.

(www.nhs.uk/conditions/pregnancy-and-baby/solid-foods-weaning)

Questions for discussion

Feeding is viewed as a social event and infants in ECEC settings or indeed any form of group care are encouraged to sit together and communicate while they eat. It is an opportunity for carers to tune into their requests and listening and responding to their needs. In a study on symbolic gesturing the practitioners observed how these could enhance meal times. The participants used some gestures during mealtimes to aid expected behaviour and this was also discussed by key person two when considering her own use of language during the day: There was almost too much language in my key group and I have noticed I have better relationships since signing. I have been more responsive, and I think that having the space to use signing has helped. Similarly, when key person one discussed mealtimes she concurred she used specific signs to aid conformity:

> I used more subtle signs – sit down, drink – all the vital actions for 'doing' words during the day and at meal times. I do vary them slightly and have used them in conjunction with my body language if a child is getting anxious and when I need the infants to do something for example, sit for lunch.
>
> (Norman, 2011)

What do you do during meal times that supports eating alongside opportunities for communication and care connections?

The art of nappy changing

I have often thought about the experiences infants encounter during a typical day and nappy changing is certainly one that is frequented numerous times during a typical day. In practice I have encountered nappies being changed on mass – the group being taken to have their nappy changed at scheduled times alongside the continual nappy changer, a designated person to carry it out. The key concerns around routine nappy changing have been:

- The invention of nappies that are super absorbent therefore not needing to be changed as frequent and promoting a hands-off approach
- The concern for safe guarding leading to two adults being present while an infant is being changed
- The avoidance of cleaning the genitals and concern of exposure
- The response to a soiled nappy, verbally and facially
- Whether on the floor changing or on a high table is preferable
- Changing an infant with protective clothing: use of gloves aprons and masks to avoid cross infection
- Ways of distraction if an infant wriggles.

Whilst each of the above has a sensible and authentic rationale to be included there is little consideration of the infant's perspective in the processes. Yet, in the first year, there can range from five to approximately ten changes per day each lasting approximately five minutes. Therefore, the emotional experiences the practitioners give infants while changing their nappies is being built in the brain. Zeedyks (2017) concluded nappy changing is similar to a dance whereby connections can occur and emotional responses are observed by the infant to the mother's movements and facial expressions. This care routine resonates with myself in terms of the emotional experiences and the ways modern society encourages us to look at nappy changing.

Questions for discussion

What do we think about the following?

- cloth/fabric nappies
- Do we find soiled nappies disgusting, smelly, challenging, a chore?

- Do we make nappy time fun or do we address nappy changing with humour with colleagues?

- Do parents make comments about bodily fluids and soil and how do we share information about them? Are we comfortable in the conversation?

The infant's perspective of the nappy being changed:

- Scared

- Frustrated

- Ashamed

- Embarrassed when looking at adult faces.

Infants are attuned and reading other emotions facial expressions and behaviour. They learn about themselves by how they are treated.

Some nappies state they last twelve hours. More and more devices are reducing infant's opportunities for touch. Touch is the most important for infants, the first sense to be developed in the womb and the most developed at birth. The sensations of the skin can send pain relief. The value of touch is that it can regulate emotions. Maybe nappies should not be so efficient and infants' emotional health considered of primary importance.

As a practitioner how are nappies managed in group care?

Have you considered the eco value?

Have you considered the rationale as to why they are so efficient from a marketing perspective?

Massage and kinaesthetic storytelling

Leading on from nappy changing and the physical handling of infants for health purposes is a consideration of the appropriateness of touch in ECEC settings. In a culture of safeguarding concern, massage of the hands or feet is an area that could be carried out regularly in a healthy and positive nurturing environment. It is an extension of touch discussed in Chapter 4 and can be shared with parents in ways that may support the care and relaxation of infants in times of stress, a need to relax and calm. The popularity of infant massage in Western countries is a relatively recent phenomenon; the trend has probably developed due to the perceived health benefits. Massage therapy has led to weight gain in preterm infants when moderate pressure massage was provided. In studies on passive movement of the limbs, preterm infants also gained significantly more weight, and their bone density also increased. Further studies have explored the father's role in massage in forming a close attachment with their infants in the early postpartum period, which, in turn, decreases their parent-related stress.

We can draw a lot from the therapeutic arts in supporting emotional development and connecting with the infant. One such approach I consider relevant is the art of touch in communicating. It is a combination of massage and storytelling. Through gentle touch, images are drawn on the infant's back whilst vocalising guided imagery. For those that are concerned with safeguarding issues, the promotion of developing a caring attachment through touch is essential for those to heal and move forward. In this context the support in sharing with parents is beneficial. The parent initiates the contact and though the touch of gently touch and massage the during the telling of a story also involves listening to the infant and responding back to their vocalisations and body movements. It is a positive way of promoting attachment, whether enhancing primary or secondary attachments (Courtney and Nolan, 2017).

McGlone et al. (2012) also specifically looked at the power of touch and the consequences of touch. They argued through a nurturing touch the social brain is developed, and this can happen in utero as well as after birth, as described previously in kangaroo care. The skin itself responds to touch and sends messages to the brain. He found pleasure parts of the brain were triggered when a slow stroke was administered, specifically the length of 3–5cm per second. He found this corresponded to the way a mother cuddles and strokes her infant. He also found that certain body parts were less attuned to touch, such as the palms and soles of the feet, finding the most pleasurable areas to stroke to be the forearms and the thighs. The systems of touch have two parts: we are familiar with our response to temperature and pain but there is further, less known system, linked to C-fibres. These are the pleasure fibres and different types of touch are essential for bonding and social development, providing a neurobiological basis to his theory. This is a relatively new finding; C-fibres are also known as C-tactile fibres, associated with pleasant touch and able to convey the emotional quality of touch. It also works with the brain in interpreting the feelings and context of when the stroke is given. It therefore helps the body translate the sensation of touch into an emotional experience of the world. What we can learn from his work as practitioners is that with infant relationships that touch matters, not just in early life but as a continual basis to physical health and physical communication throughout the lifespan (McAndrew 2012).

Communicating in daily routines

There are many forms of communication that infants may use (Gopnik et al., 2001). These include facial expressions, body language, gestures, and speech. Malaguzzi referred to these forms as the 'hundred languages' of children (Edwards, 1999). An understanding of the many languages young children use enables the practitioner to listen to and communicate with infants in order to gain an appreciation and better understanding of their emotions when interacting. Listening and recognising infants' emotions therefore becomes more than a simple interactional engagement (Rinaldi and Samson, 2008). It requires reflections on the part of the practitioner about their own emotional state and the communicative approaches they use.

Interpreting language and language as part of complex chain of utterances emphasising the unique meanings an infant may bring to the understanding. Through parental sharing. an understanding of language beyond the immediate context is also made and understood (White, 2015).

Sometimes we need a reminder that humour and fun can influence a caring and compassionate practitioner

Communicating humour during daily routines

Loizou's (2005) study illustrated how humour with infants can become part of the care routine, evaluating how six infants in a group child care setting produced and appreciated humour. As more infants are being cared for in educational settings, it is important to consider every aspect that can enhance, add and improve the quality of care provided for them. The aim of this study was to focus on the ways that six infants produced and appreciated humour in their infant group setting (three boys and three girls), between the ages of fifteen and twenty-two months. The caregivers who participated in the study were two full-time staff caregivers and five part-time student caregivers who were working with the children during the period of the study. These events were defined as 'humorous events' because the only indicator of humour considered was smiles and/or laughter. The findings of this study found caregivers in the infant room suggest that 'some [children] use physical ways to express humour, some are much more expressive, and animated with their bodies' and that 'infants produce and appreciate humour through actions, noises and facial expressions' (Loizou, 2005: 52). For example, children enjoyed bending their knees, lifting their bottom up and looking through their legs. This was one of the favourite activities that brought smiles or laughter to the producer of the activity as well as to the partner of the activity. Also, there were events where the children would make different facial expressions or gestures, look at the caregiver, and smile or laugh. Usually the caregiver or a peer would repeat the child's action and that would make the child smile or laugh more.

For me humour summarises how connected care is serious and should be sensitively supported but at the same time recognise the value of enjoyment, fun and humour in caring for infants in ECEC settings. The act of humour is considered a social relationship between at least two people and has been viewed 'as a component of social competence' (McGhee, 1989: 119). Two social indicators of humour are smiling and laughter. Smiling is 'a gesture of invitation to bond' whereas laughter is seen 'as a gesture of communion through shared freedom from constraint' (Pollio, 1983: 221–222). In observing smiles and laughter, we share a bonding experience and a meeting of minds in an open and honest way, reminiscent to that of a person-centred approach (Rogers, 1969).

Family practitioner summary

I think it is important for practitioners to understand the theory of attachment especially during transitional times with infants and children. Understanding the theory and then being able to put it in practice helps us to think reflectively, critically and with empathy. As experienced staff we can then model this to less experienced practitioners.

Focused points

- Care should be authentic
- Care should be reflective
- Care should include understanding of the infant
- Caring for infants is as much as the 'care task' as the process of caring between the infant and carer.

Concluding thoughts

Caring authentically is much more than autopiloting through the day with a mind elsewhere, projecting future tasks or thinking about something else in the present. A historical map of attachment provided an insight to the developing thinking of connecting with care today. The chapter then used specific care practice examples regularly carried out in ECEC settings to highlight the way practitioners could enable infants to confidently reveal their true self and have fun, communicating and sharing.

Bibliography

Ainsworth, M. (1979) 'Infant–mother attachment'. *American Psychologist* 34(10): 932–937. DOI:10.1037/0003–066X.34.10.932

Berk, L. (1989) *Child Development*. Boston: Allyn and Bacon.

Bowlby, J. (1953) *Childcare and the Growth of Love*. Harmondsworth: Penguin.

Bowlby J. (1969) *Attachment and Loss: Vol. 1. Loss*. New York: Basic Books.

Brown, A. (2018) 'Feeding Approaches'. Available online at www.youtube.com/playlist?list=PL ofLgxNjBdyr7i2Zx-ArwTEU2PwXWgf4

Cohen, L. and Waite-Shipansky, S. (2017) *Theories of Early Childhood and Education*. London: Routledge.

Courtney, J. and Nolan, R. (2017) *Touch in Child Counselling and Play Therapy in Ethical and Clinical Guide*. New York: Routledge.

Davis, M. and Wallbridge, D. (2012) *Boundary and Space: An Introduction to the Work of Dr Winnicott*. London: Karnac Books.

Degotardi, S and Pearson, E. (2014) *The Relationship Worlds of Infants and Toddlers*. Berkshire: OUP.

Department for Education (DFE) (2011) *Supporting Families in the Foundation Years*. Available online at www.education.gov.uk/childrenandyoungpeople/earlylearningandchildcare/early/ _a00192398/supporting-families-in-the-foundation-years

Department for Education, Skills (DfES) (2006) *The Childcare Act 2006*. London: HMSO.

Department of Health (DoH) (2009) *Healthy Child Programme*. London: DoH.

Department of Health (2015) *Healthy Child Programme, Pregnancy and the First Five Years of Life*. London: DoH.

Dollard, J. and Miller, N. (1950) *Personality and Psychotherapy*. New York: McGraw-Hill.

Dozier, M., Roben, C., Caron, E., Hoye, J. and Bernard, B. (2018) 'Attachment and Biobehavioral Catch-up: An evidence-based intervention for vulnerable infants and their families'. *Psychotherapy Research* 28(1): 18.

Dozier, M., Pelos, E., Lindhiem, O., Gordon, K. and Manni, M. (2006) 'Developing Evidence-Based Interventions for Foster Children: An Example of a Randomized Clinical Trial with Infants and Toddlers'. *Journal of Social Issues* 62(4): 767–785. DOI:10.1111/j.1540–4560.2006.00486.x

Edwards, A. (1999) Research and practice: Is there a dialogue? In Penn, H. (2014) (ed.) *Early Childhood Services: Theory, Policy and Practice*. Buckingham: Open University Press.

Elfer, P., Goldschmied, E. and Selleck, D. (2011) *Key Persons in the Nursery. Building Relationships for Quality Provision.* London: David Fulton Books.

Essick, G. and McGhee, P. (1989) The contribution of humour to children's social development. In McGhee, P. (1989) (ed.) *Humour and Children's Development. A Guide to Practical Applications.* New York: Haworth Press.

Gallagher, T. and Arnold, C. (2018) *Working with Children Aged 0–3 and their Families. A Pen Green Approach.* London: Routledge.

Gerber, M. (2001) *Respecting Infants: A New Look at Magda Gerber's RIE Approach. Zero to Three.* UK: National Centre for Infants.

Gopnik, A., Melzoff, A. and Kuhl P. (2001) *How Babies Think: The Science of Childhood.* London: Weidenfeld/Nicholson.

Harlow, H. and Zimmermann, R. (1958) 'The development of affective responsiveness in infant monkeys'. *Proceedings of the American Philosophical Society* 102: 501–509.

Lilley I. (1967) *Friedrich Froebel, a Selection from his Writings.* Cambridge: Cambridge University Press.

Loizou, E. (2005) 'Infant humour: the theory of the absurd and the empowerment theory'. *International Journal Early Years Education* 13(1): 43–53. DOI:10.1080/09669760500048329

Mohr, M., Kirsch, L. and Fotopoulou, A. (2017) 'The soothing function of touch: affective touch reduces feelings of social exclusion'. *Scientific Reports.* DOI:10.1038/s41598-017-13355-7, 7.1.

McAndrew, S. (2012) 'Self-agency in psychotherapy: Attachment, autonomy and intimacy'. *Counselling and Psychotherapy Research* 12(2): 162–163. DOI:10.1080/14733145.2011.624839

McGlone, F., Cerritelli, F., Walker, S. and Esteves, J. (2017) 'The role of gentle touch in perinatal osteopathic manual therapy'. *Neuroscience & Biobehavioural Reviews* 72(1).

McGlone, F., Olausson, H., Boyle, J., Jones-Gotman, M., Dancer, C. and Guest, S. (2012) 'Touching and feeling: differences in pleasant touch processing between globous and hairy skin in humans'. *European Journal of Neuroscience* 35(11): 1782–1788.

Meier, R. and Newport, E. (1990) 'Out of the Hands of Babes: On a Possible Sign Advantage'. *Language Acquisition. Language* 66(1): 1–23. DOI:10.2307/415277.

Norman, A. (2011) 'The professional role of key persons using symbolic gesturing and their perspectives on its value in supporting the emotional relationship with infants in day nursery'. University of Southampton, School of Education. Unpublished Doctoral Thesis.

Pikler, E. (1970) 'The Competence of the Infant'. *Acta Pediatric Academiae Scientiarum Hungaricae* 20(2): 2–3.

Piper, H. and Smith, H. (2003) 'Touch'. *British Educational Research Journal* 29(6): 879–894.

Pollio, H. (1983) Notes toward a field theory of humour. In McGhee, P. and Goldstein, G. *Handbook of Humour Research* (vol. 1). New York: Springer.

Prior, V. and Glaser, D. (2006) *Understanding Attachment and Attachment Disorders: Theory, Evidence and Practice.* London: Jessica Kingsley Publishers.

Rogers, C. (1980) *A Way of Being.* London: Routledge.

Rinaldi, C. and Samson, J. (2008) 'Teaching exceptional children. English Language Learners and Response to Intervention Referral Considerations'. *English Journal* 40(5): 6–14. DOI:10.1177/004005990804000501

Rutter, M. (1984) 'Psychopathology and Development'. *Australian and New Zealand Journal of Psychiatry* 1893: 225–234.

Schaffer, H. and Emerson, P. (1964) 'The development of social attachments in infancy'. Monographs. *Society for Research in Child Development* 1–77.

Tankersley, D., Vonta, T. and Ionescu, M. (2015) 'Quality in early childhood settings: Universal values and cultural flexibility'. *Early Childhood Matters* 124: 78–81.

Walker, S. C., Trotter, P., Woods, A. and McGlone, F. (2017) 'Vicarious ratings of social touch reflect the anatomical distribution & velocity tuning of C-tactile afferents: A hedonic homunculus?' *Behavioural Brain Research* 91: 96. DOI:10.1016/j.bbr.2016.11.046, 320

White, J. (2015) *Introducing Dialogic Pedagogy: Provocations for the Early Years.* London: Routledge.

Whitmarsh, J. (2008) 'The good, the bad and the pacifier unsettling accounts of early years practice'. *Journal of Early Childhood Research* 6(2): 145–162.

Zeedyk, S. (2018) Available online at www.suzannezeedyk.com

9 | Playful care

Introduction and context

This chapter provides playful activities within care pedagogies, supporting the relationship between the practitioner and the infant. The choice of activity inclusions has been initiated by asking students on degree programmes over several years. I considered treasure basket play to be an area well documented although interestingly student feedback demonstrated variable knowledge of the way Goldschmied proposed how the basket could support development. I therefore felt this remained an important play opportunity, not only supporting infant holistic development but also enabling practitioners to observe the way infants play through non-participatory, active observations. As an educator reflecting on Froebelian philosophy, I have also included the value of mother's songs and experiential play. It was not my intention to dominate this chapter with the different ways music could be used. However, through research on playful care with infants I reflected music to be at the forefront of emotional engagement, highlighting the way it engulfs holistic development and should form a large part of the young infant's external experience. Developing a pedagogy according to Froebel culminates in practitioners understanding the present moment of child's play and their associated emotions, using music as examples. Finally, I have also included an example from the therapeutic arts, play therapy. I am not advocating practitioners practice play therapy but rather focus attention on the way therapeutic approaches in play could be delivered. In appreciating a therapeutic approach there is an appreciation of the emotional connections between practitioner and infant, through music.

Questions for discussion

Creating open dialogue through a photovoice approach: Reflecting on an issue through images and how it could be addressed.

I am often asked about where to go to find the best toys for infants. There are some well-known brands that do cloth toys and rattles etc. However, they can be expensive and restrictive in their use. In our setting we have been thinking about the issue of accessing, using and appeal of toys in and outside of our environment for the infants we care. During our observations we decided to take photographs as a photovoice approach to observation and below are a couple of examples.

We then explored questions such as:

    Too much colour
    Too many toys
    Storage – putting away and placing out
    What we could include or replace in the use of resources and toys.

As an exercise take some photographs of what 'depicts' infant resources, infant care... and use the images as way to reflect and provoke discussion. If possible support the images with observations carried out.

Share with colleagues and reflect on what was revealed in terms of a playful care lens and what each practitioner's value, prioritise regarding infant care.

Playful experience 1: treasure basket play

Playing with everyday objects is often replaced with manufactured, commercially appealing toys for specific purposes. However, in recent years there has been a movement in early childhood education and care settings (ECEC) and home contexts toward reflecting on the impact of plastic and waste in our environment. Practitioners are promoting eco-friendly environments infants and children can engage in. Open-ended resources such as Loose Parts have re-emerged in settings with revitalised interest and a developing understanding of how they could be used (Nicholson, 1974). For many practitioners this is a novel approach to play and one less familiar to their own family or educational pedagogy. Goldschmied developed *the treasure basket* experience, a popular and valuable way of allowing a young infant, generally from six months, to engage with everyday open-ended items. Her approach, using a treasure basket, placed infants at the centre of the experience, with a focus on developing the importance of a genuine personal relationship with individual children and their carers (Goldschmied and Hughes, 1992).

A basket of treasures: this is a modified approach as there is a plastic chain and cup which would not be included in a treasure basket as advocated within heuristic play model

Defining a treasure basket

Essentially a treasure basket is what it states: a circular basket made of wood with a depth that a sitting infant can lean over and pick out objects independently. The basket is then filled with a selection of objects from around a home. It can include metal, natural mediums, open ended resources such as items that on their own could be interpreted as anything the imagination allows, for example a stick (Hughes, 2015). Plastic items should be generally avoided and Goldschmeid reminded carers that play equipment can be found around the home rather than toys made with specific and often limiting functions. The key concept to treasure basket play is that it allows the infant a satisfying sensory play experience without interference from an adult. However, the presence of the carer remains part of the process and the items should be selected with a consideration of their appropriateness to safety and health precautions. Smaller items should be avoided as the need to mouth everything is often met with refusal to allow this sensory experience and therefore reduces the potential of the basket play experience. Goldschmeid believed infants should be able to have access to any type of natural material, using their mouth and tongue as a sensory detector. Exploration of items such as a whisk, not often associated as a toy can be included in the basket. I have used different types of spoons and pots before and this has allowed the infant to put things in their mouth safely whilst continuing to explore items (Goldschmeid and Jackson, 2004; Jackson and Forbes, 2014).

A treasure basket would contain household and natural mediums

- Observe the infant rather than intervening – although I would say responding is appropriate too just be mindful of directing and allow the space for the infant to explore

- Offer the basket for a defined time frame – this is negotiable, and the items changed to attract renewed interest

- There is no right or wrong

- It should be inclusive and therapeutic

- Natural items from everyday life rather than manufactured toys.

Encouragement of two infants to sit side by side with other infants and observe their peer relationships has also highlighted interactional relationships between peers rather than parallel play. Infants are born 'sociable,' and as they develop this can extend to peer relationships. Bradley et al. (2002, cited in Selby and Bradley 2003) recorded how artful infants were from six months in their interactions and the value of providing opportunities for infants to play together with peers at an early age (Selby and Bradley, 2003). Treasure basket is one way this could be supported and observed.

Treasure basket and observing schemas

In my experience teaching students and practitioners, observational skills can be one of the most rewarding and yet challenging aspect of their roles. Recording observations can be time consuming in the organisation process of deciding when to do them, how they are going to be done and what purpose they have. We observe holistic and discrete areas of development to enable us the knowledge to plan for their future interests and development. Different observation techniques are taught, including the Tavistock approach described in Chapter 6, alongside learning journeys to the pre-coded charts and apps we download. However, even with all the equipment and understanding about how to observe infants, the everyday practicalities of it can still be challenging. When I have observed infants, I have found on occasion that I was standing back – both physically and metaphorically – so much that sometimes I lost sight of what I was observing. When I re-read what I had written later I had found it challenging to make an objective evaluation of it. I would then end up making bullet points and map them quickly to the curriculum rather than reflecting on meaningful observations relevant to the infant behaviour. Observing treasure basket play has enabled practitioners to evaluate repeatable behaviour patterns infants engage in. This ranges from the rolling of objects or the lining up of materials. We may also see infants putting objects into one another and encasing objects in the corner of the basket. This

Containment and enclosure of the whole body

behaviour, known as schemas has been extensively written about by Piaget, extended and made accessible through the works of Athey in the 1980s. More recently Arnold (2014) has explored emotions and schemas in developing our understanding about development through observations. Essentially schemas are mental frameworks that develop to help organise knowledge They are 'a pattern of action as well as pattern for action' (Athey, 1991: 35) 'An infant may perform one schema on a range of objects or a wide variety of schemas on one object' (Piaget, 1956 in Athey, 1991). Repeatable patterns of behaviour or action could include

- Orientation
- Vertical and horizontal
- Containment and enclosure
- Circles and lines
- Rotation
- Connection
- Ordering

And many more!!

Schemas and emotion

Observing connections, placing the baskets together, enclosure, containment and rotation

Understanding schemas and emotion makes explicit the connections between young children's spontaneous repeated actions and representations of their emotional worlds. Drawing on the literature on schemas, attachment theory and family contexts, Arnold (2014) placed schema theory into an emotional context, making it relevant to the social and emotional development strand in early childhood. Based on research carried out with a small number of individual children, Arnold developed new links between cognition and affect. She inferred meaning by combining the current observation with knowledge of the family context she had previously gained. In this approach, further understanding about specific events enabled meanings to be interpreted. In Arnold's study, the repeatable actions provided a sense of comfort for infants and developed internal thinking about events beyond their play, as they became more sophisticated in their emotional thinking and learned different ways to communicate in a playful way.

Practitioner's perspective

In a setting I visited the practitioners created a book sharing project whereby the infants selected a book and took it home or brought a book in from home. It worked on a library principle. They concluded the parents really liked this project but were unsure of what books to use in the first two years, especially those under one. The practitioners said parents, and even some of themselves, had associated books with older children. The sharing of books has therefore helped in creating an intimate space between the infants and their carers and the infants have physically engaged with the books through actions, sharing their emotional schema patterns. In developing this further, poems and nursery rhyme books were made and given to each family. These were copies of well-known nursery rhymes and finger songs. The idea behind the books and nursery rhyme leaflet was to encourage daily bed time readings with the infants in our care. After two months they have already noticed differences of:

Recognition of songs

Singing and babbling

Signs attempted with finger rhymes

Schemas observed and emotional connections

Parental enjoyment of the process

Practitioners engagement with the parents in a shared, playful and non-threatening way

Hypothesis maker within a dancing dialogue

Bruner described the infant as an early hypothesis maker and evaluated that observed random and hard to read behaviour was in many cases predominately due to the infant tiring or losing concentration. He believed when an infant is given a sense of agency frustration and boredom lessens. An infant who has a sense of control over what is happening develops a communicative framework combined of words, gestures, facial expressions, body language and signals. Infants are therefore social, and their learning and understanding is developed primarily throughout interactions with others, alongside a growing awareness of understanding of the feelings and motivations of others in understanding their own (Smidt, 2011).

Observing the interaction between an infant and carer (practitioner or parent) has often been referred to as sharing a moment and responding to each other verbally and physically, as explored in care practices such as nappy changing illustrated in Chapter 8. They respond to each other and take it in turns to initiate the conversation and mutually engage. The proto conversation Trevarthen (2000) refers to is a dialogue that does not always include words but a turn taking of responses with the infant, showing respect and intunement with the infant (Bruce, 2012; Read, 2010). Musicality in its various forms offers a way of exploring and supporting the infant's social and emotional world, as a communicative medium.

Questions for Discussion

In ECEC settings how often are infants taken outside and allowed the pleasure of listening to nature, the birds, the wind against the trees and the rustle of the bushes and flowers as they are felt?

For many infants the allowance to wallow in the pleasure of nature provides opportunities for experiential discovery, connectedness and being at one with themselves and others. As a sensory experience the musicality of the outdoors connecting to the sounds can be shared between the adult and the infant, with songs shared as a reminder of those open-ended experiences (Froebel, 1920; Davies, 2003).

Playful experience 2: the power of music

Singing is conveyed by many parents to their infants in societies around the world. Lullabies have, across many cultures, had the dual aims of passing on cultural traditions and helping mothers to express their own feelings. However, evolutionary theories have also suggested that singing to infants has potentially evolved from motherese, the language parents (although literature highlights the mothers voice I have included both parents) use when they talk with their infants, involving exaggerated speech melodies and frequent repetition. as a mechanism of reassuring infants and promoting parent–infant bonding (Trevarthen, 2000). Powell et al.'s (2015) study of Froebel's (1920) Mother Songs within contemporary care contexts beyond the home concluded that practitioners felt initially inhibited in singing to the infants in their care and it felt a less natural part of their caring practice. However, when encouraged to regularly sing lullabies to infants they concluded connections were made of a caring and intimate nature, whilst simultaneously learning songs and social relationships.

Finger rhymes and Mother Songs

Friedrich Froebel's theory of education was unique in that he advocated mutual respect and holistic learning. He promoted learning through experience and considered Mother Songs to be the initial stage in developing early physical skills of the body and senses. In Froebel's book, titled Mother Songs (1844), the contents referred primarily to the mother and infant relationship, and then later to both parents' involvement. It develops the relationship between parent and infant within the family context, with a reciprocal communication gaining a sense of belonging to their family, community and culture. He considered mother songs as a way in forming close supporting emotional relationship through actively engaging and gain a sense of rewarding responsibility in supporting the development of the infant in their care.

> Indeed, mans whole development requires that his surroundings speak to him clearly. . . . So in words and songs the mother tries to express this and bring the life of his environment closer to him.
>
> (Froebel cited in Lilley, 1967: 105)

International musical instruments made from wood

Musical awareness develops communication and expresses emotions. Using finger rhymes involving musical voice and finger manipulation development occurs in unique ways.

> Music is especially important, since the sounds which a child produces in singing . . . serve to give creative expression to feelings and ideas.
>
> (Froebel cited in Lilley, 1967: 113)

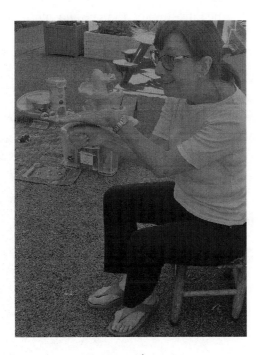

Signing with music

Actively engaging in a close relationship and using the same finger rhymes stimulates connections between brain neurons therefore developing the capacity to increase brain development (Clifford, 1982). Froebel believed that, through repetition, the use of finger rhymes, using finger manipulation and forming close bonds all contributed to the journey of more complex thinking and learning about literacy such as story making. He established the value of musical finger rhymes as being not only beneficial in developing a bond between carer and infant but also as an educational tool involving the infant as part of the educational process. It is not just a mere cosy time, keeping an infant happy for a few minutes. Listening to the actual voice in songs and rhymes, rather than recorded music, can therefore result in the carer taking more responsibility for what they are conveying, leading to increased responses from the infant and reciprocal communication being developed.

Practitioner's perspective

Inclusive finger rhyme play

Music is sometimes associated with those who can hear it and I often share an experience with a hearing-impaired infant and music as an example of inclusion.

The infant had a significant hearing loss so with the use of a hearing aid we encouraged finger rhymes and lip reading of the songs. We also provided instruments with vibrations that could be felt to enhance the beat of the songs. He used to get really excited about using the instruments and could convey finger rhymes to his parents at home. We also included pictures and props in sharing the content of the rhymes and all the infants benefitted from this.

Some popular finger rhymes today

- Tommy Thumb
- Incy Wincy Spider
- Five little ducks
- Twinkle Twinkle
- Old McDonald
- Here's the Steeple
- Pat a cake

Playful experience 3: playful classical music

Listening to music and singing to infants daily is associated with lower symptoms of postnatal depression and enhanced wellbeing, self-esteem and self-reported mother-infant bond. In the setting I support music has always featured in some form throughout the day. We have also used it to support settling times and quiet times, particularly classical music.

Siblings sharing finger rhyme songs

Classical music is defined as being serious music following long-established principles rather than a folk, jazz, or popular tradition. Specifically, classical music is: Music written in the European tradition during a period lasting approximately from 1750 to 1830, when forms such as the symphony, concerto, and sonata were standardized.

(Wikipedia, 2015; Pound and Harrison, 2003)

Why classical music?

The music most people call 'classical' music is from the works by composers such as Bach, Beethoven, or Mozart. It is believed classical music is perceived to have a more complex musical structure than more contemporary music such as rock or pop. Infants have been observed in recognising classical music selections they have heard and listened to in the womb. This has been recorded through their behaviour change and their facial expressions. Taking these suggestions further, the complexity of classical music is what primes the brain in solving spatial problems. Known by some researchers as the 'Mozart effect', the phenomenon was first suggested by a scientific study published in 1993 evidencing the learning impact on those exposed to music prior to a test, highlighting the influence of classical music. Although the Mozart effect has been criticised in terms of its impact in developing spatial and specifically improved brain function, I think using classical musical as a medium has been anecdotally shared as a positive experience. Csíkszentmihályi (2009) argues people are happiest when they are in a state of *flow*, a state of concentration or complete absorption with the activity at hand and the situation. Listening to music, in this case classical music, could be considered an experience whereby the flow state is an optimal state of *intrinsic motivation*, with the practitioner fully immersed in what they are doing with the infants in their care. This could also be dancing, listening, connecting socially and emotionally to music and the variable hearing of instruments in an orchestral form.

From a therapeutic perspective, music has been a central aspect to supporting the wellbeing of infants' relationships with both parents and practitioners in developing emotional connectivity. In using a person-centred approach, a practitioner can respond and allow the infant to take the lead, using music and song as a means of communication in creating the present moment, in tune and listening.

Practitioner's perspective

Therapeutic support music projects using music

Antenatal Rockabye is a small six-week group which gives mothers the chance to reflect on their issues about becoming a parent. During the sessions they can take time to enjoy their pregnancy and connect with their infant through relaxation exercises and creative activities. Founded by the late Lucy Livingstone, a dance-movement therapist, it offers a safe and supportive space for mothers struggling with a variety of issues (post-natal depression, anxiety, other mental health difficulties, domestic abuse, substance abuse and parenting generally) to share their experiences and explore the complexities of modern-day parenting.

This is one of many programmes supporting parents through music and dance. A further workshop is:

> Breathe Arts Health Research runs singing workshops in partnership with Guy's and St Thomas' NHS Foundation Trust for women with post-natal depression across the south London boroughs of Lambeth and Southwark.

Below are some current groups either privately run or funded by local Health Authorities.

Explore some other groups that support connectivity with parents and enhance emotional communication and tuning into infants (Celebi, 2017).

Infant sensory groups
Infant signing groups
Infant massage groups
Antenatal and postnatal yoga classes
Jo Jingles group

How can classical music be included in a relational care pedagogy in ECEC settings?

Relational pedagogy works at the level of one to one interactions, requiring sensitive responsive caregiving that relies on attunement and intersubjectivity. It recognises that while pedagogy is played out in the here and now, it also stretches out to the in-between spaces that connect to the past as well as to the future. A key implication of this pedagogy is therefore the necessity that practitioners remain reflective and critically engaged with their pedagogy and its potential for long-lasting impact (Papatheodorou and Moyles, 2009). Throughout the day, music is a communicative tool for infants to become aware of the time of day, transitional times and to support both the infant and practitioner in creating or maintaining a routine. Selected classical music pieces played at a low level at appropriate learning times enable infants to respond in a calm and productive manner. Some infants find it difficult to relax and sleep, becoming quite stressful so the inclusion of music in the room can create a calm and relaxing ambience. Lullabies, for example Brahms's Lullaby, could be played to lull infants to sleep or slow things down a little. Classical music is therefore beneficial for infants in self-regulating their behaviour and their bodies (American Music Therapy Association, 2016). In practice, this enables an infant to take the lead in how they feel and act appropriately at different times of day, such as quiet times. Listening to music is also a positive infant calming technique, whether rocking an infant in a practitioner's arms or swaying to the rhythm. It is soothing and an opportunity to bond and interact on a one to one level.

Classical music provides a wide range of colourful auditory experiences

The American Music Therapy Association compiled a list of attributes that classical songs for children should possess. These characteristics include:

- A steady beat
- A steady and regular rhythm. Music without a steady rhythm can stimulate infants, but it will not relax them, nor will it potentially encourage the development of memory skills
- The song should be simple and easy to understand. Orchestral works and operas are often simply too complex for young infants to grasp, rather use music with no vocals that utilize only one or two instruments.

Family practitioner summary

Play is essential; it is an opportunity for uninterrupted engagement, either in solitude or with others self-selecting toys, activities and open-ended objects. As a practitioner linking theory to practice is helpful and knowing about schemas has enabled me to talk confidently about their infants in a professional, educational and still fun (!) way.

Music for me is a way to engage infants in fun and shared experiences. As a practitioner music is used in many forms and enjoyed by all.

Focused points

- Learning is intertwined with emotional understanding as highlighted in schemas and treasure basket play
- Communication can be playful and musical
- Musical communication can be used educationally, supporting practice, and therapeutic.

Concluding thoughts

This chapter focused on playful opportunities that also included a caring aspect. In this context, music has been used widely and was the focus of the chapter. From Froebel's Mother Songs to the use of dance with parents/carers, the chapter highlighted the ways in which care can be intimate, physical and interactional.

Bibliography

American Music Therapy Association (2016) Available online at www.musictherapy.org

Arnold, C. (2014) 'Schemas: a way into a child's world'. *Early Child Development and Care* 185(5): 727–741. DOI:10.1080/03004430.2014.952634

Athey, C. (1991) *Extending Thought in Young Children: A Parent-Teacher Partnership*. London: Sage.

Bamberger, J. (1991) *The Mind Behind the Musical Ear: How Children Develop Musical Intelligence*. Cambridge, MA: Harvard University Press.

Breather Arts (2018) *Health Wellbeing Newsletter*, 3. Available online at www.bbc.co.uk/news/health-42607141

Bruce, T. (2012) *Early Childhood Practice: Froebel Today*. London: Sage.

Celebi, M. (2017) *Weaving the Cradle*. London: Kingsley.

Clifford, D. (1982) 'Froebelian Implications in Texts of Early Childhood Songs Published near the Turn of the Century'. *Journal of Research in Music Education* 30(1): 49–60.

Csikszentmihalyi, M. (2009) *Creativity: Flow and the Psychology of Discovery*. London: HarperCollins.

Davies, M. (2003) *Movement and Dance in Early Childhood*. London: Sage.

Froebel, F. (1888/1920) *Mothers, Songs, Games and Stories*. US: General Books.

Goldschmied, E. and Hughes, A. (1992) *Heuristic Play with Objects* (video). London: National Children's Bureau.

Goldschmied, E. and Jackson, S. (2004) *People under Three. Young Children in Day Care*. London: Routledge.

Gopnik, A., Melzoff, A. and Kuhl, P. (2001) *How Infants Think: The Science of Childhood*. London: Weidenfeld/Nicholson.

Gully, T. (2014) *The Critical Years: Early Development from Conception to Five*. Northwich: Critical Publishing.

Heller, L. (2004) *Sign Language for Kids: A Fun & Easy Guide to American Sign Language*. London: Sterling.

Hughes, A. (2015) *Developing Play for the Under 3s*. London: Routledge.

Jackson, S. and Forbes, R. (2014) *People under Three. Young Children in Day Care*. London: Routledge.

Lilley, I. (1967) *Friedrich Froebel, a Selection from his Writings*. Cambridge: Cambridge University Press.

Murray, L. and Andrews L. (2000) *The Social Infant*. Richmond: CP Publishing.

Nicholson, S. (1974) *The Theory of Loose Parts*. New York: Plenum.

Nutbrown, C and Page, J. (2013) *Working with Infants and Children*. London: Sage.

Papatheodorou, T. and Moyles, J. (2009) *Learning Together in the Early Years*. London: Routledge.

Pound, L. and Harrison, C. (2003) *Supporting Musical Development in the Early Years*. Maidenhead: Open University Press.

Powell, S., Werth, L. and Goouch, K. (2013) *Mothers Songs in Day Care for Infants*. London: Froebel Trust and Canterbury Christchurch University.

Smidt, S. (2011) *Introducing Bruner: A Guide for Practitioners and Students in Early Years Education*. London: Routledge.

Selby, J. and Bradley, B (2003) 'Interpreting infants in groups: The ethical imperative'. *Human Development* 46: 197–221.

Tovey, H. (2012) *Bringing the Frobel Approach to Your Early Years Setting*. London: Routledge.

Trevarthen, C. (2000) 'Musicality and the intrinsic motive pulse: evidence from human psychobiology and infant communication'. *Musicale Scientia*: 155–215.

Trevarthen, C. (2012) 'Finding a place with meaning in a busy human world: how does the story begin, and who helps?' *European Early Childhood Education Research Journal* 20(3): 303–312.

Trevarthen, C. and Aitken, K. (2001) 'Infant intersubjectivity: research, theory, and clinical applications'. *Journal of Child Psychology and Psychiatry* 42(1): 3–48.

10 Conclusion – moving forward

The main purpose of the book was to give practitioners, or those on higher education courses intending to be practitioners, further knowledge and understanding regarding conception to infancy. The central themes were to explore reflective practice – the first chapter was dedicated to thinking about reflection and this then continued in subsequent chapters. In each chapter I wanted to retain the practitioner's voice, and these examples have predominantly been from my experience or from practitioners I have conversed with over the years of teaching and practice. The specific practice I wanted to focus on was the complexity of the caring approach. This involves caring for the infants, the parents and the practitioners within a community of practice, situated in ECEC settings where infants attend for many hours and the parents are seen regularly at designated times. This was important to me as the area of infant care has often been viewed as passive or as requiring a less active involvement than 'educating' older children under five. I hope therefore the book has continued to raise awareness about the value of care. I anticipate the book has also provided insights which give confidence and ideas about pedagogies of care and how these can be perceived and fostered in supporting relationships, attachments and further development areas.

The key aspect of the book is the thinking about infants 'from conception'. Many practitioner colleagues in early years talk about caring from birth and I firmly believe we should expand this in the rhetoric to include 'from conception'. I often encounter parents during pregnancy and this has been the beginning of the relationship. I also believe we should be supporting the roles of the health specialists in their role of caring for parents and infants from the time of conception. Although we primarily care for infants after birth, this should not mean we consider the time before as less relevant or outside of what we are informed about.

There is a growing acknowledgement that those first early years of a child's life are absolutely crucial. Getting it right as parents with professional help and public resource to support where needed has the potential to make a huge difference to how that child will grow into an adult contributing to society.

(Loughton, 2015)

In promoting a parent relationship and caring for their infants, surely we would be supporting the infant and families during the totality of time we are involved in their care, asking questions and listening to parent stories, alongside connecting with other early years services.

Family practitioner

I have consistently used the term 'family practitioner' in the text to highlight the importance of family when thinking about infants. Many other names have been used such as professional, educator, carer and key person, family worker, nursery nurse. Personally, practitioner for me covers the broad range of roles but also implies an active professional, carrying out a significant role. As a family practitioner, I felt this has worked positively as a key term for those identifying themselves as working with infants and parents, within ECEC settings, particularly those childminding, in receiving greater recognition for their role and identified as such.

Theory

Following on from family practitioner and caring from conception to infancy the continuous thread weaving through each chapter has been attachment and the value of close relationships. Whilst close relationships were supported through a person-centred approach and a Froebelian philosophy underpinning a playful care, the underlining theory was to encourage and support close attachments. Through close, personal and intimate, homely environments, attachment can be fostered in a flexible and individual way, with the parents involved in the process and the care. Whilst this book does not intend to devalue ECEC settings, which accommodate large number of infants whose parents require long hours of daily care, it aimed to celebrate and include smaller nursery settings and childminders who offer intimate and person-alised care. These types of settings can potentially support the close relationships with vulnerable families who may also find the transition to parenthood physically and mentally challenging. In providing a home/ly environment with few infants and fewer primary carers (within ratio) the relationships have the potential to be more personalised and transparent with opportunities for frequent communication. This creates occasions for both practitioners and parents, contributing to the relationship and working successfully. Personalised care also potentially enables individual care to be implemented with greater flexibility than the regimes needed to support infants in larger group care, with many practitioners having differing roles during the day. A value-based early years philosophy is therefore advocated in the book that celebrates the competence of infants in the present context rather than what they may become in the future. It requires practitioners who are fully 'tuned in' to infants and allow them to teach us to listen, communicate and interact in different, more inclusive ways (James, 2014).

Recommendations

The rationale of this book, therefore, is to view development and growth as inevitable transitions, rather than focusing on forced regimes. Having strict regimes places external pressures on both the infant and the carer and can arguably de-sensitise the carers to the infant's individual needs and prevent them from tuning into what they are trying to convey through their cries. This is not arguing for a complete lack of routine, as infants thrive on familiarity and expectations of what is happening next in fostering their security. Rather, it is about creating a flexible frame for the day, with the infant leading the way, particularly in the first few months. In balancing spontaneous and unforeseen events in a flexible and adaptable way, a routine will naturally occur and establish the rhythm of the day. In approaching connected care this way, authenticity with the practitioners increases, as they recognise and communicate their own emotional management of their role within the community of practice in which they work.

Some key points for further recommendations

- Continue to raise concerns and lobby for extended paid maternity and paternity leave. Berger and Waldfogel (2004) found that it is only paid leave which is associated with better maternal and child health, lower maternal depression, lower infant mortality, more breastfeeding and general positive wellbeing

- Connect local services' prenatal pathways to support and make connections with early years settings from education, social and health sectors (www.1001criticaldays.co.uk/)

- Learn knowledge from established programmes with existing research on theory around neuroscience and attachment rather than create new research work

- Communicate the value of attachment and neuroscience to practitioners, parents and families through training and multiple supportive, cohesive and compassionate ways. Prevention rather than intervention is the key (www.whataboutthechildren.org.uk/)

- Reflect on development from differing viewpoints and the link to practice in making positive connections to enhancing emotional relationships

- Celebrate services such as childminders who could potentially lead the focus on pedagogies of care and education for under twos

- Encourage playful care so as to value the seriousness of the role whilst simultaneously enjoying quality time and seeking enjoyment and rewarding relationships with both parents and infants during a precious and wonderful, small window of time that can have a lasting impact.

Bibliography

Allen, G. (2011) *Early Intervention: The Next Steps*. London: Cabinet Office.

Berger, L. and Waldfogel, (2004) 'Maternity leave and the employment of new mothers in the United States'. *Journal of Popular Economics* 17(2): 331. DOI:10.1007/s00148-003-0159-9

James, A. (2014) *Constructing and Reconstructing Childhood: Contemporary Issues in the Sociological Study of Childhood*. London: Routledge.

Loughton, T. (2015) Available online at www.1001criticaldays.co.uk

Final comments

A personal journey

My interest in writing this book came from personal experiences as a practitioner working in a variety of Early Childhood Education and Care (ECEC) settings. I then taught students, who were gaining higher level qualifications about the importance and value of the earliest years, specifically focusing on the period from conception to two years. Reading related books about infants, I unearthed a plethora of information around development from conception. However, I was finding the readings I was drawn to were predominantly from health, psychology or social work professional areas. Many books and studies, particularly from conception, supported midwifery practice and health visiting professional roles, whilst safeguarding and supporting vulnerable families from conception, birth and infancy were directed to social work practice or psychologists. Within the early years day care context, many books explored these aspects of care but tended to do so from birth and from an educational perspective rather than from prenatal period. This was assumed to be because it is from birth that practitioners, working in ECEC settings, would meet the family and care for the infant, regulated by a national early year's curriculum However, I regularly met parents during the mother's pregnancy who were seeking advice about out of home care and what would suit their family in terms of support. In meeting these prospective parents, I was also finding that they were seeking advice about out of home care for reasons beyond employment issues. At one time, this was the usual reason for organising childcare because maternity leave in England was restricted to a few weeks, and status in employment and salaries were affected if more leave was taken. However, with the introduction of financial support and maternity options, the landscape of choices and rationales for choosing childcare beyond the home has shifted. In a day nursery where I worked, many parents chose

211

childcare for reasons beyond returning to employment. Parents were opting to go back to study to further their career choices and need childcare. For some parents whose English was not their first language and living in the UK during term time, short term childcare was also sought as a way of meeting people in the local community and allowing parents opportunities to train or work part-time. Many families I worked with who had a child attending the setting stayed on when the mother became pregnant again. I found many parents were seeking practical and emotional support beyond the health visitors and other professionals to whom they were assigned. As an early year practitioner, I was regularly meeting parents to talk about development and play opportunities, becoming the bridge to other professionals responding to questions about care needs including diet and sleep patterns. In addition, sensitive and complex issues such as bereavement, pre-natal depression, medical conditions or attachment, would also be addressed as part of my role. In becoming a parent myself, this became even more prominent as I, too, relied on those early years practitioners for support when my children were attending nursery, particularly when I was expecting twins. Having four young children close in age was challenging and to convey this to those who were supporting me in the care of my children was something I found invaluable. Similarly, further meetings with practitioners who worked at ECEC family centres, developing programmes to support parents from pregnancy to two years, was also helpful in seeking out practical issues and ways to connect to my new-born infant that I hadn't previously appreciated. I realised how much I had relied on quite old information or generational anecdotal advice, some things working well, whilst other areas needing updating and contradicted advice received from other professionals. This developed my reflective thinking about the ethics of care and how I approached the care role I was placed in as both practitioner and parent. In returning to work as an early year's lecturer, with the opportunity to teach modules specialising in the period of conception to infancy. The teaching and learning experiences shaped my theoretical thinking further. It was during this time that I appreciated objectively how much information was received about this period of development and care by differing services. However, as a practitioner working with under twos and their families it remained a somewhat less revered place to be in, particularly within ECEC settings. For many practitioners, aspirations to be in the pre-school room in a traditional teacher role seemed to be culturally accepted, particularly after undertaking higher education. For those wanting to remain working with infants, they would often move into specialist roles such health visiting assistant roles, childminders, nannies, maternity nursery nurses or family support workers roles, in developing their own care pedagogies. This was where the initial idea of a book began to take shape. In parallel with this, and in support of my own thoughts, were the practitioners I met and students I taught in universities who were studying infancy and practice. These were predominantly experienced and senior practitioners working in ECEC nursery or childminding settings, who were passionate about their role in working with infants, wanting to understand, reflect and improve their practices. My aim for the book was, therefore, to bridge the gap in creating and complementing existing literature for those practitioners seeking to explore development and care from conception to infancy, adding a further contribution about care within and beyond the home context. The focus was on understanding and supporting the practitioner's role in caring for families and infants from conception. This is where I found the greatest gap between the literatures and what I believe needs further discussion and examination. Parenting books provide another practical and helpful source of information, as they include creative tips and practical suggestions from conception. However, these were aimed mainly at parents and unless a practitioner took a keen interest in these books the contents were not quite there in helping develop and appreciate practice and care from a practitioner's perspective.

My core audience for this book is the practitioner working closely and regularly with parents and infants in a variety of day to day ECEC settings. I would like to think parents and other professionals would take an interest in the book and use it where they deem appropriate. However, for me it is those key practitioners caring for infants from before birth through to two years, linking theory and research to contemporary and everyday practice, who remain at the heart of this book. I hope the chapters within the book will arouse reflective thinking in my readers about development and their own roles as professional practitioners and ignite further interest to read beyond this book in areas of specific interest.

Index